PASTORAL
COUNSELING

PASTORAL COUNSELING

By
Seward Hiltner

ABINGDON
Nashville

PASTORAL COUNSELING

MANUFACTURED BY THE PARTHENON PRESS AT
NASHVILLE, TENNESSEE, UNITED STATES OF AMERICA

To

MY TEACHERS OF PASTORAL COUNSELING

Donald C. Beatty
Anton T. Boisen
Charles T. Holman
Carroll A. Wise

Foreword

THIS BOOK IS INTENDED AS AN INTRODUCTORY SURVEY of pastoral counseling. It is built upon the conviction that an introduction ought to present concrete, practical facts and fundamental theory together and show the relationship between them rather than follow some median or "easy reading" course which is neither practical nor theoretical. I have included a good deal of the most concrete material in pastoral counseling—interview reports—and no small amount of discussion of fundamental issues. A practice without a theory is noncorrectable. A theory without a practice is irrelevant.

The accounts of interviews have come from many sources: reports of pastors and theological students in seminary classes and courses of clinical pastoral training; reports passed on to me by pastors in various parts of the country; my own experiences; and representative fictitious situations. All reports which come from real experience, and most of them do, have had considerable amounts of information changed so that in no case could identification be possible. And permission has been secured on those situations in which there might be any reasonable doubt.

The fictitious interviews have been introduced because there does not yet exist, at least in my report file, sufficient material to cover all the points I wanted to make. I hope that writing in this field will increasingly set forth specific case histories. But this study is an introductory discussion of basic principles rather than a research report. We do need research reports, though, so that the next book in this field, and the next, for educational purposes may be based on fewer hypotheses—however persuasive—and on more tested reports of actual experience. Only in exchanging concrete experience and studying it by the best methods we know or shall discover can we amplify, correct, and confirm the approach to and methods of pastoral counseling.

Since the focus of this study is pastoral counseling, pastoral work is treated in its relationship to counseling. The work of the pastor

7

apart from counseling is valuable in its own right, but will be considered only as it is connected with the present study.

In presenting my constructive view of pastoral counseling I have had in mind those readers who, while interested in this view, may be only slightly concerned either with its origin or with the way in which it seems to me to be related to the views of other workers. The reader who is interested in the origin of my view and its comparison with the views of others may use the notes supplementing the text, which are intended as such a guide rather than as a comprehensive bibliography.

For hospitality which helped greatly in the writing of this book I am especially indebted to Crozer Theological Seminary, the Chicago Theological Seminary, and the Yale University Divinity School. I want to express special appreciation to my four formal teachers of pastoral counseling, to whom this book is dedicated: Donald C. Beatty, Anton T. Boisen, Charles T. Holman, and Carroll A. Wise. There are a host of other less formal teachers to whom my indebtedness is large, each of whom has made some particular contribution to my understanding of pastoral counseling although many of them are not pastors. Harold Leonard Bowman of Chicago and J. Russell Chandler of New York have each welcomed me on the staff of their churches. Harrison S. Elliott and Harry Bone have taken me on as a counseling colleague at Union Theological Seminary. From years of collaboration with Russell L. Dicks, Rollin J. Fairbanks, and Otis R. Rice I have learned more than I can say.

Harry Bone, Maria Brick, Erich Fromm, Lewis B. Hill, and Carl R. Rogers have been especially helpful in the development of my psychological thinking. Edwin E. Aubrey, Cushman McGiffert, Albert C. Outler, David E. Roberts, and Paul Tillich have performed a similar service for my theological thinking in relation to counseling. For valuable comments on this book I am grateful to Maria Brick, Lennart Cedarleaf, Paul B. Maves, Thompson L. Shannon, and Thornton W. Merriam. I am indebted to the Earl Lectureship Foundation of the Pacific School of Religion, under the auspices of which several chapters of this volume were presented in 1948.

The real heroes of this volume are the students, pastors, parishioners, and friends who have helped to provide the report material so important in this book. Though they remain anonymous, I am grateful to them, and hope they will agree that my use of their material sets our mutual cause ahead.

To my colleagues in the Federal Council of Churches, and especially Roswell P. Barnes, I owe a debt for day-by-day encouragement to keep out of the rut of administration and try my hand at such things as writing books. I am grateful to Helen G. Yergin for help on reading proofs.

James Seward Hiltner and Anne Porter Hiltner, my children, have been deprived of a few weeks and week ends of my presence, in the interest of this book. My wife, Helen Johansen Hiltner, had to put up with the children, with my absence, and, when I was home, with a sometimes preoccupied husband. Without the family-induced perspiration I should probably have finished the book sooner. But without a family-induced inspiration, I should likely never have written it at all.

—SEWARD HILTNER

Contents

PART I: *Principles of Pastoral Counseling*

Aims and Assumptions of Pastoral Counseling

Chapter One IN ONE CONGREGATION OF A LITTLE LESS THAN ONE HUN-dred people there was a boy on parole from the state penitentiary who was trying to "go straight," another on probation by the local police, a third who was known to be flirting with a type of life that was bound to bring unhappiness and ruin, a young woman confused with intellectual doubts, a girl despondent over a broken love affair, a young couple who had just buried a child, a family where the mother had just died, a woman struggling with a morbid fear, a man who was desperately try-ing to overcome drink, a middle-aged couple whose home was going on the rocks, another couple who were worried over the conduct of their child, a young man who faced a serious operation within a month. If the minister had known his people better he would have undoubtedly been aware of other problems—these had all consulted him.[1]

Is any argument needed that the pastor has a function and a re-sponsibility to such people as are described in the above statement? The twofold command of Christ was to preach the gospel and heal the sick.[2] The number of those who are temporarily or permanently sick in our society—ranging all the way from broken arms to de-feated creativity—is large.

Consider a few figures. Nearly a fourth of all the men examined for military service during the war were rejected as unfit, and almost half of these because of emotional difficulties. On any one day dur-ing the winter at least seven million people in the United States are unable to work, attend school, or pursue their usual activities be-cause of obvious illness, injury, or physical impairments.[3] There is a suicide on the average of every twenty-seven minutes.[4] More than a half million people are in mental hospitals at any one time, and more would be there if therapeutic services were better.[5] There are about three quarters of a million alcohol addicts or chronic alcoholics in the United States, to say nothing of another two million persons who drink so much that scientists class them as excessive drinkers.[6] About 30,000 accidents occur daily.[7] These result in over 100,000 deaths and more than 350,000 permanent disabilities a year.[8]

As medicine gains increasing control over infectious and other germ diseases, the number and proportion of people with degenerative types of illness increases. Especially has there been an increase in diseases of the heart. Despite the medical knowledge of early detection and treatment, cancer and tuberculosis still take a huge toll.[9] There are a hundred thousand mentally deficient persons in institutions, and at least another half million without sufficient capacity to be wholly self-dependent in a complex industrial society.[10] And who can estimate the number of persons whose neurotic patterns are a serious handicap to achievement and fulfillment in life? The number must run into millions.

Of course, the average span of life has lengthened in recent years, and we have made progress against the ravages and sufferings of illness and accident and disease and social wastage in many forms. But if one reviews all the types of figures, through some such means as the excellent *Human Conservation,* by Lawrence K. Frank, he cannot but be deeply impressed with the volume of human loss and wastage and disease which still exists.[11] By bringing together available figures and making estimates on others, I once calculated very roughly that perhaps a fifth of the population of the United States is enduring, at any one time, some kind of obvious wastage through handicap, accident, sickness, imprisonment, severe neurosis, and the like.[12]

These sample figures from many which might be given are not put forth to suggest that our country has a poorer health record than others. Conditions in many other countries are far worse. The point of the statistics is to suggest instead that any time we pastors get the temptation to lump all people together as if we had nothing to do for them except a normative job, we are neglecting half our task. We are to preach the gospel, but also to heal the sick. That must mean the mental patient as well as the surgical patient, the mentally deficient boy as well as the sufferer from chronic arthritis, the man in prison as well as the youngster who is slowly starving, the girl who is depressed because a love affair has broken up as well as the potential divorcee, the couples frustrated by sterility as well as the mothers who must bring babies into the world without sterilized medical equipment.

Whatever their specific nature, all these troubles concern people. We pastors may or may not be able to deal with the technical aspects of the particular situations, but we need always to deal with the people. And dealing with the people often means dealing with the difficulty itself, indirectly or directly.

We are properly concerned with social prevention of these ills, with the establishment of such an order of society that many of them will grow smaller or even disappear. More power to that task! But at our peril do we allow our interest in social prevention to over-shadow our obligation to give help to the people in difficulty now.

THE PASTOR'S RESPONSIBILITY

THE pastor's task of helping is not, fortunately, something which can be carried out in splendid isolation. He is not the only healer concerned with aiding alcoholics, or tuberculosis patients, or psychoneurotics, or persons with emotional growing pains. Later on we shall discuss those aspects of the pastor's work which are distinctive to him as a representative of the Christian fellowship. At this point we shall suggest the reasons why all these problems have some relevance—though in varying degree—to the pastor as a helper.

In the first place, all these "sicknesses," temporary or permanent, have psychological or spiritual aspects.[13] Indeed, modern medical science has discovered that, directly or indirectly, even many physical disorders are caused at least in part by sick attitudes and sick emotions. If people are sick not only because of germs and falls but also because of short circuits in the emotional hookup, then the pastor, as representative of an army of salvation in the realm of the spirit, has to become interested. Besides, there is increasing evidence that some sickness or destructive attitudes involved in sickness can be properly understood only in a broad time perspective.[14] To put it more simply, people may get sick emotionally not only because of immediate frustrations but also because they are troubled about their own meaning and destiny. If this fact does not bring their problems within the pastor's range of interest and potential capacity to help, then the pastor is no helper at all.

These problems are also relevant to the pastor, paradoxically enough, because in part they represent the fruits of sin and because in part the individual is a victim and not merely willful. "As a man thinketh in his heart . . ." The pastor is concerned with motives and purposes.[15] As the doctor is not content to know merely that there is a fever, so the pastor is not content to know only that there is sin or alienation from God. He wants to know what concretely produced the alienation. He is not satisfied, for example, to know merely that a person is irritable and that this quality tends to cut the man off from other people and from God. He wants to know what lies back of that particular irritability, for he assumes that

God's Holy Spirit and God's promise of salvation are potentially there, waiting to break through if the bonds can be cut.[16]

Conversely, the pastor is interested in people as victims and in their troubles as signs of disorder and sin in their culture and society. The juvenile delinquent is rarely the youngster who has had genuine love in his family, a decent neighborhood in which to grow up, a good school in which to learn, and a church to help his family mold his religious and ethical education.[17] Delinquency is directly proportional to degradation, though be it noted that emotional degradation is at least as bad as physical, and a boy who comes from a "good home" may still be lacking in that which he needs most. The usual word of the church for persons in this victim situation is "compassion." [18] When the man is lying by the side of the road, we help him or see that he gets the help he needs.[19] We do not stop to moralize.

In other words, we combine a compassion for people with a sense of their responsibility for bringing on their own special predicament. But if we are thinking in terms of the individual, our concern to help the sinner needs to be greater than our desire to blast the sin. The sin of society, that of permitting neighborhoods and cities and even countries to become breeding grounds of delinquency and prejudice and defeatism, needs condemnation. But the condemnation which counts is that which helps to change the very patterns which have been chiefly responsible for the misuse of the individual's freedom.

In the third place, these difficulties are relevant to the pastor because he is, after all, a shepherd. The shepherd of the parable went after the one sheep that was in trouble, allowing the ninety and nine to get along temporarily by themselves. Of course one may retort that after all this hundredth sheep was a part of this shepherd's flock, and the shepherd might not have been so solicitous of a stray sheep or one from the flock of another shepherd. There is relevance in this remark. No pastor can serve everyone, even in his own locality, and certainly he cannot serve those who will not be served. But pastors of churches which are moving mightily in an ecumenical direction, and which have never swerved from their conviction that all men need Christ, cannot be content to serve only those already enrolled. They are evangelists in the deeper sense of that word—bringers of the good news of salvation to all who need to be saved from whatever particular things have made them be lost.[20]

Finally, these difficulties are relevant to the pastor because people have looked to him for help throughout Christian history.[21] It may be true that people now are more confused and uncertain about this than they have been at some quieter times in the past. Protestants do not use compulsion to get the sheep to submit to a periodic inventory by the shepherds, and most sheep forget that the Reformation did not abolish the inventory but merely took the compulsion out of it.[22]

It is also true that the rise of specialism in the modern world has tended to make people think that only a specialist can help them. Thus they attempt to be their own diagnosticians—with the unfortunate results that usually come from such attempts.[23] The pastor is a kind of general practitioner. It is true that he has his special field, but he cannot imply, as many experts necessarily and properly do, "You are now outside my field." If many people are confused about the helping role of the pastor, and if some are antagonistic to it, that does not gainsay the fact that the pastor can, if he will, utilize the role of helping or standing by in difficulty of all kinds as his predecessors have done all through the Christian ages. Today, as these pages will suggest, we know more about the "how" of such help than did the past ages.[24]

BASIC ASSUMPTIONS OF PASTORAL COUNSELING

THERE is a sense in which the aims of pastoral counseling are the same as those of the Church itself—bringing people to Christ and the Christian fellowship, aiding them to acknowledge and repent of sin and to accept God's freely offered salvation, helping them to live with themselves and their fellow men in brotherhood and love, enabling them to act with faith and confidence instead of the previous doubt and anxiety, bringing peace where discord reigned before. Where each, or all, of these general aims of Christianity is relevant—and my purpose is not to present an exhaustive list, but only to suggest—the pastoral counseling situation should bring them out.

In another sense, however, pastoral counseling has special purposes. It consists, so to speak, of certain rungs in a long ladder which leads toward the general aims of the church and the pastor. As such, it can appropriately have certain special purposes of its own. Broadly speaking, the special aim of pastoral counseling may be stated as the attempt by a pastor to help people help themselves through the process of gaining understanding of their inner conflicts. Counseling is sometimes referred to as emotional re-education, for in addition to its attempt to help people with a problem immediately confronting them, it should teach people how to help themselves with other problems. Indeed, there is a sense in which the counselor needs to guard against being blinded by the immediate situation; for if a method of problem solving is used which will not at the same time better prepare the person to face the next problem, a shove backwards may unwittingly have been given despite the apparent solution of the present problem.

In some situations the pastor "does" more than in others. By and large, however, it seems true that the aims of pastoral counseling are sound only when the following assumptions are revealed in the counseling situation.[25]

1. *The parishioner senses that something is wrong, and at least in a measure that the difficulty may be seen within himself.*[26] If there is nothing at all except an attempt to get the pastor to move against someone else, then the pastor faces an administrative situation without an opportunity for the time being to help the person to help himself. The willingness to face the fact that something is wrong and to believe that one may have something to do with it does not have to be at the forefront of consciousness. For instance:

A WIFE: I was afraid it would happen, and it has. My husband got drunk again last night.
PASTOR: You didn't think he would stay on the wagon.
WIFE: Not really, though I hoped so. But last night at dinner we had one of our fights, and then he started drinking afterwards.

This, it may be noted, is quite different from what it would have been if she had said: "No, he's just no good, that's all." For, however dimly, the wife is suggesting that there may be something in her own feelings and behavior which has something to do with the drinking. The literal words do not always tell us whether a person senses this. But if the counseling process is to go on, this needs to be present in some degree.

2. *Counseling proceeds by understanding, and not by agreement or disagreement.* For example:

MRS. THORN: I really think I'd be justified in getting a divorce, don't you?
PASTOR: You think it's right, but you still have some doubts.
MRS. THORN: Well, yes, I do. I think I'd be justified, and yet a divorce isn't what I really want.

That shows understanding, not agreement or disagreement. It might have gone this way:

PASTOR: Of course you've been badly treated, but divorce, Mrs. Thorn, is a very serious matter.

MRS. THORN: I know you ministers are against it; but if you'd had to put up with what I have, you'd think you were justified too.

The pastor thought a point had come where his moral convictions had to be asserted. Yet without realizing he was doing so, he was aiding in crystallizing Mrs. Thorn's decision around a divorce.

Or again:

PASTOR: I certainly think he's been a brute to you; and if the children didn't suffer too much, you could have a clear conscience in going ahead.

MRS. THORN: Yes, I suppose so, but (pause).

He has not understood or helped her to understand. He has agreed, judged, and the result is to move her further from understanding what is really the best thing under the circumstances.

3. *Counseling is usually helping another person to help himself, not doing something for him.*[27] For example, here is a man in his thirties, married about two years, who has found everything going wrong with his marriage. As he has talked of his background, it is apparent that he has had a very strong dependence on his mother. He has told of going to another minister soon after the marital difficulties began, and we may put into dialogue form a bit of what happened there:

MR. HAY: Yes, it usually starts at the breakfast table. We'll be talking along about plans for the day, and then she'll suddenly burst out and say she wants to eat out tonight and that she's too tired to cook after working all day. And then I'll say it seems to me she could at least cook dinner once in a while, when after all I'm willing to help. And then we'll both get mad.

PASTOR: Now I'll tell you. You just make it a rule to decide the night before what your plans are going to be the next day, and don't discuss this kind of thing at all at breakfast.

MR. HAY: Why, that's a wonderful idea. I think she'll be willing to try it too. You've helped me a lot, and I certainly do thank you.

But as Mr. Hay tells his story, it is clear that it did not help, and that he had not gone back to this pastor. He asked to be told what to do, and he got what he asked for. It failed to work, not because the suggestion was not ingenious enough, but because it was given and was not Mr. Hay's own. Let us see how another pastor handled this:

MR. HAY: And of course it's gotten worse. Sometimes we hardly speak to each other at breakfast. She doesn't really seem like a wife any more somehow.

PASTOR: A wife ought to act differently?

MR. HAY: Yes, she should. I know she works and all that, but she ought to be getting ready for when she quits work and we start a family.

PASTOR: Then what you're worried about is the future?

MR. HAY: Well, yes, but not altogether, I guess. She just doesn't look after me the way a wife ought to look after her husband. Isn't there a good book you could suggest that we could read together and that would explain this kind of thing to her?

PASTOR: I'm sure we could find a book, if that's what you really want.

MR. HAY: Don't you think that would help? I know some of the fault is probably mine, and wouldn't it do me good to read a book you know is good?

PASTOR: I take it you're wishing that I could suggest a book and then assure you that reading it with your wife would help your situation.

MR. HAY: Well, of course you could hardly guarantee it. But if that isn't the right thing, can't you tell me something I *can* do that will help?

PASTOR: The other pastor you mentioned didn't seem to have very good results at that.

MR. HAY: Well, no, but his idea—you know, I guess maybe I *am* trying to get you to tell me what to do.

From that point counseling could proceed. From here on both persons understood that the pastor could only help Mr. Hay to help himself.

4. *Counseling involves clarification on ethical issues, but not coercion.*[28] For example, Tom, a clean-cut college athlete, not a brilliant student but a charming fellow and actively interested in the church, has come to the pastor and told a tale of getting through a vital examination by cheating. He has said no one knows it, that he did get through due to the cheating, that he's bothered about it and wants to know whether he should go tell the dean.

TOM: I know it was wrong, and I feel worse about it because I guess I wouldn't have got through if I hadn't. But if I do go to the dean, I'll probably get thrown out. And that won't do anybody any good.

PASTOR: Tom, my boy, there are many times in life when it hurts, really hurts, to do the right thing.

TOM: I know, sir, but I can't see that it will do anybody any good if I tell them now.

PASTOR: Perhaps no one but you, Tom. But you see that you've got to do it, don't you?

TOM: Well, I guess so. But—

Tom doesn't know what else to say. How might the pastor have handled it after Tom's first statement as given above?

PASTOR: No one would gain anything if you told the dean?
TOM: I wouldn't exactly say that. I suppose I'd gain something. At least I'd be sure I'd done the right thing.
PASTOR: But you think that being thrown out of school is a pretty heavy price to pay for a clear conscience.
TOM: Well, yes, I do. I want to go to the dean and yet I don't. If I could do something else, like taking an incomplete on the course and doing it over, I'd be O.K. I mean, I'd like to correct what I really did wrong in the first place, which was failing to study on this stuff.
PASTOR: You deserve a penalty, but what you really want to do is to dig in where you made the first mistake.
TOM: Yes, that's it, if it can be done. If it can't, well, I'm going to do the right thing about this, but I'm not going to leave school without a struggle.

We judge Tom's action wrong. But does not the second approach go much further than the first? As a matter of fact, Tom decided against going to the dean, and later came to the pastor to make sure he would keep the situation in confidence. Through his use of moral coercion the first pastor unwittingly pushed Tom away from an ethical decision. We have good reason to believe that Tom, who must have had real courage to come to the pastor in the first place, would have been ready if the second approach had been used. Note that this not only moves toward a decision which the pastor thinks is right on abstract principle but also it is clearly Tom who does the moving. Tom is not forced to commit himself, and that very fact moves him closer to an ethical decision. Furthermore, Tom is gaining in problem-solving capacity. He sees that what he does is up to him, that he must look at the question himself and use his own brains on it, and that he must start with the fundamental mistake of failing to study as well as deal with the cheating. Tom, with this approach, would gain in capacity to be ethical.

5. *The counseling situation involves real respect for the parishioner, and does not proceed through use of a bag of tricks.*[29] For example, here is an instance of disrespect for a parishioner. The wife of a young veteran, whose husband has left her two months before, when she told him she had once had sex relationships while he was away, has poured out her story to the pastor with a good deal of weeping and blaming herself for having gone to a party one night, drunk a lot, and then had sexual intercourse.

MRS. GODWIN: At first I didn't think I'd tell him at all. I hadn't meant
to do it. It was just the loneliness that got me to go on the party, and
then—I knew it would be a blow to him. We were both virgins when
we were married, and I'm sure he was faithful to me while he was away.
He wrote me every day. I know I was all wrong, but I just don't think
he should have left me.
PASTOR: I agree with you. You did a wrong thing, but so far as it's human-
ly possible, you did your part to make it right. And I can see you're
truly sorry. I think I'd better go around and talk to that young man.
Don't you think I should?
MRS. GODWIN: Oh yes—well—oh, I hate to put you to that trouble.
PASTOR: No trouble at all, I assure you.

And of course it did not work. Not because the pastor's ethical
judgment in the situation was wrong, but because he had no real
faith in the young wife, no respect for her capacity to handle the
situation if given some help and understanding. The lecture to the
husband, which the pastor found the only way he could talk to him
at all, succeeded only in reinforcing the young man's legalistic
decision.

No method can work if there is not present a basic respect for
the parishioner's personality. Here is an administrative type of
counseling situation.[30] The father of a sixteen-year-old girl has come
to the pastor to complain about the Friday night parties for young
people. The previous Friday his daughter had gone out with the
crowd after leaving the church and not arrived home until after
one o'clock. He is blaming the church and the pastor for not en-
forcing the agreement which had been reached by church, parents,
and young people when the parties were started, that participants
would go directly home after the party was over at eleven thirty.[31]

FATHER: I know you'll say you can't keep your hand on them after they
leave the church. Maybe not, but if you had the right kind of atmos-
phere here at the parties, they wouldn't do this kind of thing.
YOUNG PASTOR: [who thinks the trick in counseling is to listen, be passive,
never cross anybody, never assert himself] Then you feel we ought to
have better parties.
FATHER: Better parties! I think you shouldn't have any parties at all,
that's what I think, if you can't do any better with them than this.
PASTOR: You're inclined to favor discontinuing the parties?
FATHER: I don't care whether you have them or not. But I'm not going to
allow my daughter to come to them if this is what goes on.
PASTOR: Then you feel it would be better if your daughter stayed at home?
FATHER: Stayed at home! Man, haven't you got any spine? Sitting there

and letting me talk to you like this, and looking cool as a cucumber. I know I'm letting off steam, but you just act like a sponge—taking it all in. Maybe you really don't know how to run parties for young people.

There are more ingenious tricks than the one this young man picked up, but they never work any better. By concentrating on method as if it were a series of tricks and neglecting entirely the real emotional tone of the situation, the young pastor lost the father's confidence even more thoroughly than he would have if he had become angry and thrown the visitor out of his office. In this case there was the appearance of respect for the father, but none in reality. The accusation was largely unfair, but it expressed real feeling. The pastor could have denied the breadth of the accusation and still respected the man's feeling, as for example:

PASTOR: There is certainly some point in what you say, for when these parties were started, the young people did agree to go directly home afterward. But I hardly think we can get at the cause of this merely by blaming the church.

FATHER: Well, I can't help blaming the church to some extent, but I suppose there may be some special reason why this happened last Friday.

PASTOR: As you were talking, I was trying to think of something. The only thing I can think of is that Bob Jenks wasn't there, because he was drafted last week. But I don't see—why, perhaps that's it after all. His girl friend is Joan, one of your daughter's special friends.

FATHER: I see what you mean. But for heaven's sake why didn't Sue tell me if that was the reason? (*Silence for a few seconds.*) You know, I'd like to talk to you about Sue. We've always gotten along so well until lately—

We cannot be sure the situation would have moved in this way, but there is a good chance that it might. One can show respect and at the same time properly stand up for his own rights in the counseling situation.[32]

6. *The situations that give occasion for counseling are viewed by the counselor, and eventually by the parishioner, not only as difficulties to be overcome but also as opportunities for growth and development.*[33] This is a practical translation of the theological statement that God can use suffering constructively even though he does not send it. Here is a theological student who has come to an experienced pastor several times, impelled originally by a growing inability to concentrate on his studies. He has been an oversolicitous kind of person, whose friends have said that nothing is too much

trouble for him to do for them. Through the counseling he has begun
to discover that he has some inner anger and bitterness whose existence he has not previously been able to acknowledge. He has begun
to assimilate the fact that this is part of him, but the knowledge
frightens him.

STUDENT: I can see it's a good thing for me to face up to what I really
am, but it's pretty hard to take.
PASTOR: It *is* hard, but I don't suppose you like the alternative any better.
STUDENT: Gee, no, I just can't imagine myself any longer not really knowing this about myself. It would—well, you just can't go back on a thing
like this.
PASTOR: Even if it hurts, in other words, it makes you grow.
STUDENT: That's it. I'm moving in a more honest direction than I was
before, and I guess that's growth.

HUMAN NATURE AND THE COUNSELING TASK

WHEREVER there are attempts by one person to help another
solve particular problems of living, there are bound to be assumptions about human nature. I shall not attempt a discussion of the
different current theological views on human nature and their
significance in relation to pastoral counseling.[34] But since counseling
is not a profession, but a helping activity carried on by various
professions at different levels and from somewhat different assumptions, it is essential to grasp at least the main types of assumption
with regard to basic aims which lie behind counseling as a practice in
the United States today.[35]

The social-adjustment view. Among psychiatrists, social workers,
psychologists, and most other nonpastoral counselors, some form
of the social-adjustment view of counseling is probably still dominant.[36] In its extreme form this position assumes that when something is emotionally wrong with an individual, one can explain the
trouble by saying he has failed to adapt himself properly to the
society in which he lives. If he is constantly getting into financial
difficulties, then in order to correct himself he must learn what there
is in himself and in his past experience which impels him to get
into these difficulties. The idea that part of the trouble might be
with the financial arrangements of society would be objected to, in
the extreme forms of this view, as merely an effort to cloak the real
problem. If a middle-aged captain of industry develops a crippling
essential hypertension, then the only problem before the counselor
is to help him so to adjust his inner life that he can proceed with his
work without the necessity of developing hypertension.

Ordinarily this view is seen in less extreme and more attenuated form. And in such form, and so far as it goes, it is true and important. The positive point could be stated in this way: The individual must develop an adequate capacity to change those patterns of life which have become unsatisfactory. There can be no substitute for such change. When a doctor is dealing with gastric ulcer, which Walter C. Alvarez has called the "wound stripe of civilization," there can be no other permanent way of aiding the patient than helping him to make alterations in his way of approaching life.

The difficulty with the social-adjustment approach is not that it is untrue or invalid, but that it so often gives rise, uncritically, to a superficial view of human nature, and that this in turn affects the counseling itself. If the physician is dealing with stomach ulcer, it may well make little practical difference whether the patient is a stockbroker, a junior executive, a labor leader, a minister, or a truck driver. The patient's views on religion, ethics, politics, economics, and race relations may be ignored by the doctor, or considered merely as aspects of the patient's personality structure. For it is probably true that the ulcer patient, whatever his job or his convictions, is consumed with an ambition he fears himself unable to consummate, and possesses a restless craving for an unconditional love or acceptance which cannot be given. Hence it is this inner syndrome of need which must be altered if the patient is to be prevented from returning for repeated surgical operations for ulcer. The pragmatic level really is the immediately important level. After all, society has put the treatment of ulcers in the hands of doctors and not theologians—for which even the theologians ought to be glad.

How easy it is, though, for the doctor to conclude from repeated experience with ulcers, or for other counselors to conclude from experience with similar problems, that the only important assumption they need to make about human nature is that individual circumstances tend to put it out of adjustment with its society, and that counseling can help in the readaptation process. Before they realize it, then, such counselors have become mere tools of the culture in which they happen to live. If this conclusion seems farfetched or theoretical, think of its significance in relation to Nazi Germany or Communist Russia or a primitive African tribe. If individual difficulties are always and only symptoms that something is wrong in the individual, if nothing but the mores of a particular society are available to suggest what the proper adaptation should be, then the counseling enterprise—wittingly or not—becomes if not a tool of the state at least a mere reinforcer of the lowest common denominator of the cultural patterns of a society.[37]

In the United States there seems to be a growing awareness of this danger. As a matter of fact, this idea has not been consciously accepted as a view of human nature, but it has been a more or less unconscious assumption. The questions that would lead to a deeper insight have not been asked. Better questions, however, are now being asked in many quarters.

The inner-release view. The second approach to human nature which is gaining in strength among the various kinds of counselors is what we may call the "inner-release view." Freud's theory is, in an older and less sophisticated form, the first important modern exposition of this view. Man begins, said Freud, with certain biological needs. Either man must find expression of his biological desires, directly or indirectly, or he will unconsciously repress them, and then they will sneak out by themselves and cause him difficulty.[38]

Later workers have reached a similar conclusion, though from somewhat different premises. Seeing the fallacies in the uncorrected social-adjustment view, they have asked themselves if the only thing which can be said of human nature relates to its malleability, and their answer has been in the negative.[39] Clinical and experimental studies, even of children, have suggested that there are distinct limits to human malleability.[40]

There is no inherent reason why the inner needs, the beyond-which-as-a-human-being-I-cannot-adjust view, must be conceived of mainly in biological terms. Undoubtedly the needs have biological aspects, but we are on sounder ground to conceive of them in terms of the whole personality, or in social terms in the sense that we know personality to be a social product.[41] The essential point is that we know there are within the individual, despite his enormous capacities for malleability, limits beyond which change is ruinous, needs which must somehow be met regardless of what any particular society may say about their legitimacy. The careful observer could eliminate such things as sex from these inner needs only at the peril of clinical contradiction. At the same time, the center, or focus, of the inner needs, whose frustration causes so much difficulty, can usually be understood only in a broader context centering around positive self-respect and productive creativity.[42] Thus Jung, for example, believes that neurosis is essentially a lack of balance, a person's being out of relation to important aspects of his own self, an overdevelopment of some aspects of the self at the expense of others.[43] Denial of these aspects of the self does not, however, render them powerless;

they struggle in one way or another to express themselves. Counseling or psychotherapy might then be seen as the effort to introduce a person to the neglected aspects of himself.

This view has been still further refined in the United States, for it is in fact highly consistent with democratic assumptions about human nature. Impetus to the American development was given by Otto Rank, who criticized the dropping of the whole idea of "will" because the old "will power" concept of will was no longer tenable.[44] Even though will could no longer be considered as a faculty, there was something conative, something driving for expression and release, in human personality which had to be taken into account. Furthermore, this purposive striving could by no means always be equated with the individual's conscious purposes. Hence there must be some way of referring to the purposes of the whole personality as against either the mere consciously accepted purposes or the idea that there is no purpose in the personality. Rank tried to reinstate the word "will" to perform this function. The word has not proved popular, but the idea has.

From the standpoint of counseling the most important developments in this inner-release approach to human nature have been made by several of the American schools of psychotherapy, which would seem to include on this point the Karen Horney group, the Washington School of Psychiatry, the Chicago Institute for Psychoanalysis, and the "non-directive" group of therapeutic psychologists.[45] Carl Rogers has carried the point so far that he believes there are almost no limits to the capacity of distorted or conflicting personality to find and express its own inherent purposes, provided only that the counselor does not interfere by diverting through giving directions. This view is considered extreme by other groups sharing the essential theoretical assumption with Rogers. Whatever the limits of Rogers' point of view may turn out eventually to be, however, he has certainly demonstrated that most previous counseling work, even while asserting that the curative strengths as well as the distorted weaknesses can only be seen within the personality, not foreign to it, has unwittingly attempted to put something in instead of evoking or educing what is existentially there. Rogers has influenced even his critics.

I have intentionally presented the inner-release approach with a great deal of sympathy. For not only is it true in a very considerable degree, but it is true to an extent which is far from being practiced by most counselors, pastoral or otherwise. There is a sense in which we may say that our pastoral counseling during the next few years will improve in the degree to which we accept and use the practical importance of the inner-release view, properly interpreted.[46]

But theoretically, and even practically, it is not enough. If that inner something which is demanding release is considered at the deepest level, it will be found thoroughly consistent with social interest as viewed from the Christian conception of human brotherhood and mutuality.[47] But it would be utopian to think that all we had to do, even as counselors, was to help release the inner something. No counselor claims to reach every depth.

One must recognize, therefore, that the criterion of expression of even the deepest individual inner need is not sufficient, however important it is; that it should be in practice merely the basic operating center of the counselor's daily work. A further criterion is needed which, while taking into account, to put it in semitheological terms, that the brotherhood of man is less an ideal to work for than a reality which we have denied, will nevertheless bring together the conflict of interests within the individual and the conflict of interests among even the best-intentioned individuals and groups. This can not be found solely in the inner-release view, however far-reaching it may be.

The objective-ethical view. We found the social-adjustment view valid up to a point and the inner-release view valid to a more distant point. Even with the latter, however, we saw a deficiency, chiefly because it had only one focus. It was founded either on an uncritical faith that what is really good for the individual in his deepest aspects is also good for mankind or on the more pessimistic hypothesis that if this is not true, there is no hope for democracy, counseling, or even Christianity. Either of these views is deficient theoretically, for both tend to ignore a certain order of facts from which it is possible to induce more accurately the degree to which this faith may be held.

Suppose that we begin with the inner-release view in our counseling experience and see whether we can observe any similarities in the deepest level of inner need—or core of the self—in all kinds of cultures and people.[48] No one has as yet attempted to systematize our observations from this point of view, and I am not competent to do so. But I suspect many similarities can be found. To put it backhandedly, the line beyond which the malleability of human nature will not permit social adjustment seems to be concerned with degradation or lack of fellowship as essentially social beings.

If we turn then to the work of cultural anthropologists who have studied cultures other than our own, we find that they tend to confirm the conclusion that for all its malleability there seem to be certain points beyond which human nature rises up in revolt. In other cultures the content of neurosis may be quite different from what it is in ours. A neurotic in a cannibalistic society might be a humanitarian from our point of view. And a neurotic in the placid and passive culture of the Zuni Indians of the American southwest might still be considered as lacking in ambition in our own society despite his being too aggressive for his own.[49] Thus the content of the neurosis, the particular points where individual needs run counter to any society's demands, varies with the culture. But running beneath this is the *ne plus ultra* of being wholly cut off from fellowship or being completely degraded as essentially social beings.

Perhaps this generalization is sufficient for our immediate purposes. For what this kind of thinking begins to approach is ethics—*objective ethics*, I have termed it, to suggest that it can be understood only if we see certain minimum personality demands as being an objective or existential or created part of essential human nature. According to the demands of his particular culture and the conditions of his own rearing, the individual may develop one or another pattern of personality. But if in the process the most essential *human* needs of personality—distinguished from purely biological needs—are denied, the struggle for their release and expression cannot be understood merely in the terms of the individual who is struggling, but must be viewed as the inexorable revolt of human nature against that which has denied fulfillment of its most basic needs.

This would seem to have some practical as well as theoretical significance. If one stopped with the inner-release approach, even though he interpreted it in the best and most far-reaching sense, he would inevitably face one of two pitfalls. One would be that of pessimism, the fear that however effective one may be in releasing something valuable from inside, it is still uphill work. The other would be that of mechanism, the process of viewing even the depths of the human spirit on such a pragmatic level that all sense of awe or mystery or wonder has disappeared, like turning on the light switch without ever reflecting upon electricity. Ultimately, a counselor who sees his job as nothing but uphill work, or who believes he is only turning on lights, will manifest and communicate these attitudes in his counseling, despite the real interest in and understanding of parishioners which he may have.

The Christian-theological view. It is plain to the pastor that there is in Christian theology an undergirding for what has been stated above. The pastor does not believe merely that there is something of an ethical character which conditions man's life; he believes God has made this and supports it. When he sees positive potentialities emerging from a hitherto confused and divided personality, he identifies their source as the operation of the Holy Spirit or of Divine Grace. He has a metaphysic, a conception of the structure of the universe in which he can place his operational understanding of human personality.

This point of view enables the pastor to see the deficiencies in the social-adjustment view or the inner-release view if left by themselves. And yet because of this vantage point he does well to be especially careful not to deny their significance as stages in the process of reaching aims. Of course it is true that in a broader sense the question about adjustment is not whether one will adjust, but to what he will adjust. But that is not the place for a doctor to begin with an ulcer patient, nor for the pastor himself to start with a parishioner. Discussion of this sort is postgraduate work, and counseling begins on a nursery school basis. There may be truth in the aphorism about the feast of the soul being more basic than the feast of the belly, but it must have been first said after a good dinner. It is quite true, provided one is not being gnawed by hunger.

We need also to be especially careful not to minimize the relevance and significance of the inner-release view. We know there are devils as well as angels inside. If the angels are to find egress, some of the devils have to be chased out first. It is easy to become a bit afraid of this process. It is particularly easy to moralize our fear and to assume that most inner-releasing involves only devils.

We shall of course welcome what seems to be a still infrequent but gradually more sensitive awareness on the part of many kinds of counselors of what is here called the objective-ethical view. This view can be held, it seems to me, with or without theological assumptions supporting it. As a Christian I do hold such assumptions.[50] But I do not believe it a mere matter of terminology which separates my view from that of others who share my concern for an objective-ethical view, and who yet fail to see this, as I do, undergirded by the structure of the universe itself. At such points evidence of a different order becomes relevant, and that is not discussed here. I believe, however, we should welcome the trend toward the objective-ethical view, even if it is often unaccompanied by what seems to us to be an essential theological corollary.

SUMMARY

THE pastor's counseling task is part of his total task. His counseling contributes in a special way to the fulfillment of his aims. It is the shepherding aspect of his work—with the difference that people are not merely sheep to be led but are individuals to be helped to find the way to help themselves. The special aims of counseling are a development of this assumption.

The pastor carries out his counseling in a particular kind of practical setting.[51] He also carries it out, whether he realizes it or not, on the basis of some particular theoretical setting, some particular doctrine of human nature. While there are divergences in current theological convictions about human nature, these are less important than the differences between Christian views and various secular views. In so far as these views are believed to condition the practical work of counseling, they have been briefly set forth, in order to make the distinction between the essential findings of fact, which we too need to adopt, and the sometimes unnecessary philosophies of counseling which have been erected using these as a base.

Chapter Two THERE ARE TWO WAYS IN WHICH THE STUDY OF pastoral counseling may be approached, and both can be effective. We can begin with psychological dynamics and life histories, studying the factors that made this or that person what he is and then moving to a consideration of how to help him, or methods of counseling.[1] Or we can begin with approach and methods and study the dynamics as we are forced to them by our methodological questions. Having used both these approaches, I now believe the second to be quicker and more effective, because it follows John Dewey's general rule that we learn in proportion as we recognize our interests to be touched. All pastors know they have to counsel, and their first question is: How? If they find in the process of learning how that they cannot isolate this question from a knowledge of what is going on behind the scenes, they are following the same wisdom which makes the student of surgery realize that he cannot learn how to operate unless he knows anatomy and physiology.

We shall begin by looking at a particular pastoral interview. An interview is a kind of cross section. It is a cross section both of the parishioner and of the relationship between the parishioner and the pastor. When we study a single interview, it is like studying the cross section of a tree. We can learn much from it, but we do well to remember that one dimension of the tree is missing. A cross section is flat, and the real tree is not flat. Hence if we study interviews, we need later to correct the two-dimensional view into a three-dimensional one. The medical student begins by dissecting a corpse from which one dimension is missing, movement. When he later begins on sick, live people, he has to correct his previous perspective, but pity his patients if he has to learn his first anatomy from them. After all, the anatomy he learned was correct. He had to remember that the perspective later had to be corrected for the factor of being alive. What we have to recall in considering a single interview is that we later have to correct our perspective over a time period.

But what we can learn from study of a single pastoral interview is true, if we go about it properly.

ANALYSIS OF AN INTERVIEW

ONE of the methods I have used in the teaching of pastoral counseling is to make up a small, mimeographed booklet containing the report of a pastoral interview minus what the pastor himself said and did. Following the introductory remarks describing the conditions under which the interview took place, each unit of comment or action by the parishioner is placed on a separate sheet. Students may then write on the same sheet, below the parishioner's comment, what they would have said or done at that point. The device has its artificiality, but it is more successful than might be supposed. The interview with Betty Smith which follows was used with a group of about forty ministers in a seminar. It was presented to them in the first session so that the replies would represent their point of view unconditioned by anything they might learn in the seminar itself. The replies which will be given in the analysis all come from this group of ministers, who were at least average in general competence. Letters indicate specific comments which will be discussed.

The preliminary information given the pastors was as follows: Betty Smith has been a member of the Church for a number of years, has considered herself a Christian since an experience of conversion at the time she joined the Church. She is now in her late thirties. She has lived with her parents and two sisters, and has carried a good deal of responsibility for the home. Just a few months ago her father died, and her reaction to his death seemed at the time to be excellent; certainly she had her grief under control. Recently she wrote the pastor a letter, and followed this up with a telephone conversation— in both of which she said she wanted to talk about her faith and her father's death. An appointment was made, and the following interview took place.

MISS SMITH: I've had an awful time since Dad died. It seemed at first that I just had to go out and find him. I think I would have taken something, too, but I wasn't sure I'd land at the same place where he is.[4]

The following are representative replies which different pastors wrote they would make in this situation.

Pastor 1: "You were wise not to pursue that course."

Here, pure and simple, is agreement. The pastor believes he must agree or disagree with Miss Smith. The obvious result of his statement will be to make it impossible for Miss Smith to tell him any negative feelings she has, for he demonstrates that he knows no methods but those of agreement or disagreement. He effectively cuts himself off from the real Miss Smith, and the fact that his conscious intention is to give her encouragement does not alter that fact at all.

Pastor 2: "We all have these experiences sometimes."

This, simple if not pure, is generalization. Perceiving that Miss Smith has feelings of guilt, he intends to help her get rid of its overburdening power. He thinks this can be done by telling her she is not the only one who has had such difficulties. So he generalizes, thus convincing her that he is not interested in and does not understand her situation. Until there is understanding, help cannot be given. And so far he shows that he is not even sure there is something to be understood. For Miss Smith it is like nerving herself for a great leap over a fence, leaping, and finding there was no fence. But there *is* a fence.

Pastor 3: "What have you done, then?"

This pastor apparently feels that the important thing is to get on to action at once. So he moves immediately to that. And in doing so, of course, he entirely ignores her feelings. Miss Smith cannot possibly move on to action until she has had a chance to clarify how she feels. This pastor, we deduce, has a bit less than average sensitivity.

Pastor 4: "Your father lived *his* life, and you have *yours* to live."

This pastor assumes that counseling proceeds by moral judgments. Either a thing is right or wrong. Pastors help people to judge between them. "Sometimes people get worried about the wrong thing. Take this girl, for instance. Obviously she loved her father and took care of him. Nonsense for her to have this kind of feeling. Tell her so, too. After all, it's the future that counts." Such might have been the pastor's thinking. But his comment, well intentioned though it is, would push her into a corner. No doubt she is startled by the introduction of the moral element. Certainly she will be disconcerted and diverted. She sees that the pastor listens only that he may judge and then reassure or spank. He fails in understanding the first principle.

Pastor 5: "Yes, go on, perhaps we can get somewhere."

Miss Smith is startled. She had intended to go on, and had assumed they would get somewhere or she would not have come. But perhaps he means they will not get anywhere, and maybe she really should not go on. The pastor wants to make sure everyone knows he is there and in charge. The result is that he diverts and sows doubt.

Pastor 6: "I am sure your father's death has been a great shock to you."

Any time I have made a speech and the chairman says afterward, "I am sure we have all profited from this fine address," I know he did not know what I was talking about. This is a conventional phrase which, to the sensitive ear Miss Smith later showed herself to have, would suggest that the pastor not only did not comprehend it but also protected himself from understanding anything of this sort by having a supply of conventional comments and replies in stock.

Pastor 7: "I know it will take time for you, since you have suffered deeply. But we can have strength knowing these things are in God's hands."

Sermons are fine things from the pulpit. But their power to startle may be accentuated when used in interviews, especially after but one comment by a parishioner, and still more especially when that comment suggests a depth of feeling which wants and is perhaps ready to be unburdened. On Sunday noon Miss Smith might well say, "That was a fine sermon." But in the counseling period she would probably be too stupified to speak at all.

Pastor 8: "You've really been troubled."

Here is real understanding. Miss Smith has started on a confession, which is none the less real because she has paused to see if there is some understanding before she continues. The pastor's comment is brief, so that not even its length diverts her. It does not generalize, moralize, or try to help with an answer before there has been a statement of the question. The pastor catches the dominant feeling Miss Smith has been expressing in the effective word "troubled." It is his word, not hers. By using it he shows that he has properly translated, and hence understands, the central feeling she is trying to express. He does not unwittingly inject himself into the situation by saying "I'm sorry you've been troubled." He simply demonstrates that he understands.

Pastor 9: "Perhaps you'd like to tell more about how you felt."

This is cautious, a bit unsure, and may raise a bit of doubt in Miss Smith's mind; but on the whole it is a real encouragement to Miss Smith to go ahead. One might say that the pastor has the right approach to counseling but is unskilled in carrying it out. This suggests that even bad errors in technique are sometimes of minor significance provided the counselor has the proper attitude toward the process.[2]

The pastor whose interview it actually was gave an understanding

nod. This was good, not because no words were involved, but because
the need at this point was to suggest that the pastor understood and
to get Miss Smith to go on. It is a mistake to think that mere
silence or just fewer words are the key to counseling. But this was a
point where an understanding nod was sufficient.

Miss Smith: I feel better now, but I still don't know what I believe. I
   thought I was sure until he died, but I guess I've never had my faith
   tested before.[B]
Pastor: You now have some doubts.

The essence of Miss Smith's feeling is the suggestion that she is not
as sure of her faith as she once was. Without realizing it, she is
testing the pastor to see if he is willing to accept the fact that she has
doubts. His reply indicates that he is.

   Three other pastors in the group also did something effective at
this point. "This is a new experience, then" was another way of
accepting her doubts as facts. "Now you are facing uncertainty" was
a bit less effective because it might prematurely throw her thinking
into the future, but it was probably good. "You're trying to look
at faith in a new way" is also anticipative, but it certainly picks up
the thing Miss Smith is trying to say.

   Here are some unhelpful responses from certain other pastors.
"Just what is your faith?" is, to put it mildly, diverting. It ignores
entirely the parishioner's feeling and invades her personality in
heavy-footed fashion. "Was your father's faith all you expected it
to be?" is irrelevant. It probably expresses a wild and certainly mistaken theory of causation, according to which the girl's faith was
now ineffective because it had never been any better than her father's,
and yet she was content with it as long as it was as good as her
father's. Whatever the explanation, it would certainly bring down
the counseling house.

   "All of us meet such experiences, and I'm sure you will be
strong enough to meet them" is a combination of the generalizing
and moralistic approaches. Recourse to such tactics on the part of
a pastor must imply some deep fear that he will be found wanting;
thus he feels that he must always and immediately have the right
answer for everything in order to show he is not wanting. It is the
antithesis of expressing true understanding.

   "The tested faith is the only faith that is worth while" is an attempt at verbal reassurance when what is needed is understanding.
"You are beginning to grow in grace; just continue to have faith in

God" apparently comes from the conviction that anything is true and right and relevant if it can be put into theological language. The effect at this point is to divert.

MISS SMITH: Yes, I do. I still have them, and I think I'll always have them. I don't think I can ever believe as I did before. It's awful when you find that your faith isn't worth anything. I couldn't talk to anyone either. We don't talk very freely in our family, and I just couldn't say a word to anyone.

PASTOR: And you've wanted to talk this over with someone.

The essence of what Miss Smith is saying is that she has felt isolated.[3] She felt she was losing something of great importance to her, and yet she could not bring herself to talk about it with anyone. She felt cut off. Now she is talking about it with someone, but the sense of being cut off is still with her. How can she explain how she feels if the pastor does not understand what it means to feel isolated? The simple comment by the pastor shows he does understand the feeling she is trying to express.

Another pastor gave an expression of simple acceptance, "You felt your feelings were bottled up inside." And another, "You weren't sure anyone would understand." Both these indicate that Miss Smith is understood.

Not so with these. "Surely you could have found someone in whom to confide" is just an indirect way of saying: "Tut, tut, and fiddlesticks, my girl, you have no right to have a problem at all if that's the way you feel about it." "I always advise talking over such problems" is like the surgeon bringing the patient out of anesthesia in the middle of the operation to point out that he always advises an operation under these circumstances.

"When no one else understands us, God can" is a sentiment whose practical effect at this point will be to convince Miss Smith that no one else can. "All of us have doubts, the growing pains of a mature faith" will have the same net effect as if the pastor had said, "This isn't as serious as you think." What is gained by trying to get a person to believe his feelings do not matter as much as he thinks they do? Only a general depreciation of self-respect, which pushes the problems back where they are harder to get at and deal with.

MISS SMITH: Yes, but since I couldn't, I tried to find help by prayer, and that didn't help much either. Actually the first time I felt better was during one of your sermons. Something you said made me realize that perhaps if I got some other things settled in my life, this matter of faith would take care of itself.

PASTOR: I see.

A significant point in a sermon has struck home to Miss Smith, and has served to suggest to her that perhaps her feeling of losing her faith is not the whole trouble but is simply part of a larger problem of her whole relationship to the world, to people, and even to herself. She has not defined this for herself, but what she is saying is she recognizes that the difficulty may have something to do with her life as a whole. She knew this when she came into the room. Why then did she not start in by saying, "After my father died, I was greatly troubled by the feeling I'd lost my faith. Now I know that was only part of it. The trouble is with me, not just my faith"? The reason is that to say that would open up wide areas of her personality to be looked at. Before she can wholly trust the pastor with these, she has to feel that he really understands. By demonstrating that he does understand her feeling about loss of faith and loneliness, he convinces her that he can understand *her*. She has not consciously tested him, but that is the effect. Now she knows he can be trusted, and can go ahead. The comment by the pastor, "I see," is appropriate here, for it merely recognizes the fact that she has attained a valuable insight.

Another pastor said well, "You felt you'd have to face some things in your own life." Another, "You got a new slant on faith." And another, "Something I said struck home." These are all good.

Some other pastors were not so effective. "There's a lot in what you say" really means, "But I don't believe a word of it." "He who seeks earnestly shall find the truth and be made free" is our old friend the generalizer. "Tell me what the real trouble is" sounds like the sergeant who believes people will not notice he is around if he does not give orders. "What did I say in my sermon?" may indicate a forgetful mind, or it may indicate a pastor unable to resist any temptation to discuss himself or his sermons. "Good, what other things are you thinking of?" is the bulldozer in action. "You must have some serious problem in your life" is like saying, "Humph, sounds abnormal to me."

MISS SMITH: You said something I had never thought of before. You were talking about the woman who touched Jesus. You spoke of the people in the crowd who jostled him, but he didn't ask, "Who jostled me?" It was only in response to the deliberate touch that he said, "Who touched me?" I wonder if I've spent all my life up to this point just being one of the crowd near Christ, never having touched him in that deliberate way for myself.

PASTOR: You feel now that you'd like to have the closer experience.

Clearly the pastor has picked up the essential thing Miss Smith has been saying and has rephrased it in his own words.[4] This is not a trick. He wants to help Miss Smith help herself. To have the real entree to helping her he must understand what she is trying to communicate to him and make it clear that he so understands. This method of rephrasing a central thought or feeling, especially after a long statement, is the simplest way to demonstrate that one really has got the point.

Two other pastors who also got the point said, "You are feeling the need to give yourself completely to Christ," and "You have been more or less detached from the real thing?"

Here is the generalizer, "The great truth—and the hardest to believe—is that God cares for the individual." And the pusher, "Good, but are you willing to pay the price?" The sermonizer, "That is the weakness in many Christians." The arguer, "That may be true." The distracter, "You should remember that desire is the first step toward faith."

MISS SMITH: It would, I know, make an amazing difference in my everyday life. But do you think that a person working at an ordinary job, like me, needs that kind of experience? I can see where *you* need it, because after all that's your business; but perhaps *I* don't need it.[c]

PASTOR: You wonder whether you really need such faith.

Up to this point the interview has been plain sailing. Miss Smith has felt increasingly that the pastor understands, has revealed more of her inner feelings, has shown that she has gained one vitally important insight, and only now begins to reveal that she feels she has a conflict which even the new insight did not solve.

It is a very natural temptation for the pastor to feel goaded by the implication that his interest in faith is mainly a matter of good business and to tell Miss Smith off by saying that everyone needs faith. So one pastor said, "Yes you do. Jesus came to help regular people." And another said, "If *I* need it, then so does *every* follower of Christ." Although these responses are understandable, they are not helpful. For the first time Miss Smith reveals real negative feeling in herself by projecting it onto the pastor. His temptation is to react to this personally. But it is not really personal. It is just the way Miss Smith uses to try to prevent the unpleasant facing of the issue for

herself. If the pastor does not understand that, he does not understand Miss Smith. Hence however natural this reaction, it fails completely in the counseling situation.

Two other pastors responded in such a way as to show that they
could accept Miss Smith's conflicting feelings as a fact. One said,
"You're not sure it's for you; yet you are sure it would make a difference in your life." And another, "Then you're torn between wanting it and fighting it off. Both these responses are acute, and introduce an element which has not previously come into this interview.
Note that Miss Smith has expressed in her comment two sides of
the conflict: on the one hand the new experience would make a
difference in her life which she would value, and on the other hand
it seems to make a lot of demands on just an ordinary person. If
two feelings at least partly opposed to each other are expressed, then
understanding implies a recognition of both of them—as the two
comments of pastors immediately above actually do. But when this
is done, clarification is aided. That is as if the counselor were saying, "I understand how it is that you can have these two feelings,
though they pull in opposite directions." To hear the pastor re-
phrase in his own words the elements in the conflict leads toward
clarification of the nature of these elements. And that leads toward
the capacity to help oneself.

MISS SMITH: Yes I do, and I didn't realize how little I had until Dad
    died. I feel that I would have known how to meet that experience if
    I had had something like you spoke about in your sermon.
PASTOR: What you've been missing, then, is pretty important?

This comment comes out in the direction of the enlarged and expanded vision of faith, and not of the receding element in the conflict. The pastor rephrases the essential feeling again. Another pastor said, "Then you'd like such an experience of faith in your own
life." And another, "You want something deeper than you've had
before."

Here is a moralizing type of response, "It isn't too late yet." And
the hortatory, "We can get that experience by being loyal to the
best that we know. Don't you agree?" And the generalization, "It's
the hardest thing in the world to find faith." And the verbally reassuring response, "You are right." And the pastor who always
looks on the bright side of other people's troubles, "You may be
thankful that you've been awakened to the need for a deeper faith."

MISS SMITH: Yes, I think it is.
PASTOR: And it's something you'd like to have?

One pastor said a friendly nod would do at this point. A second said, "And you want to do what's necessary in order to have it?" A third, "You want it enough to seek it where it may be found?"

Some other poor responses: "Is your faith growing?" "Aren't you trying to live that way?" "Fine, together we shall explore the possibilities of fellowship with God."

MISS SMITH: Yes I do, but what would it mean? What would I have to do afterwards? That's what I'm afraid of.
PASTOR: You're a bit worried because there might be more involved than you're ready to give?

The pastor's temptation is to push Miss Smith in one way or another and try verbally to set her fear aside. But to do so is to fail to respect Miss Smith as a person and to deny her the right to have negative feelings like fear. Again Miss Smith in her comment is stating two aspects of her conflict. She is saying that she wants to go ahead but that she is afraid. A good response by another pastor was, "You rather wish you had the answer beforehand."

Here are suggestions on what *not* to say. "You would have to mean business." "You need not fear when you go all the way to reach Christ," which is another way of saying, "Don't you dare have any fear, because if you do, it shows you don't really mean this business about moving ahead." "Just put your trust in God and be willing to go forward with him" is like saying, "Just do as I say and don't ask so many questions!"

MISS SMITH: I guess that's so. I suppose that I must be willing to give myself and trust that what is asked of me will be the best for me. It will make a lot of difference in my business contacts if I really surrender myself. I've been a Christian a long time, but this would be different. Are you sure that I have to give myself in this way?
PASTOR: The answer to that seems to have made itself pretty clear in your own mind.[D]

Here the pastor was, I think, disconcerted. Until the last sentence it seemed clear that Miss Smith had definitely made up her mind to move ahead. When the doubt crept in again at the end, the pastor apparently felt he could get away with ignoring it. The fact that the interview does not move from this point on as significantly as it did before may be due to this action on the part of the pastor. He has recognized the negative feeling previously, and then it seems Miss Smith has dealt with it and come through on the positive side. Then the small negative comment comes in again, like backsliding. Metaphorically, the pastor turns his eyes away, and something is lost.[5]

One pastor made a better response, "You're convinced, and yet you can't help wishing there were an easier way." This continues to recognize the two sides of the conflict, which is, after all, not yet solved. Our friends, the commander, the moralist, and the generalizer, were all on hand for the occasion: "Yes! Go to church and seek God's guidance." "If you want to save your life, you must lose it." "Wholehearted commitment is the only road to full spiritual power." One may wonder if the last pastor ever saw a group of Nazi youths marching in wholehearted commitment to their Fuehrer, and thought of the kind of spiritual power that came out of that commitment.[6] The minute a counselor becomes more interested in something else —like a general truth, a moral principle, or next Sunday's sermon —than he is in the parishioner, the counseling begins to go off the track.

MISS SMITH: Yes, I know it has. I wonder if anyone else who heard that sermon was affected as I was?
PASTOR: I don't know, but it's clear that there was a special message there for you, isn't it?

Miss Smith's comment shows that she now feels a bit pushed by the pastor. His mistake in passing by her remaining doubt has borne fruit in the form of a new kind of doubt. She has apparently thought to herself, "Maybe there's something queer in my feeling drawn toward a new kind of experience, and maybe I took that sermon too seriously." The pastor does not quite get the import of this. His comment says in effect, "It doesn't really matter what other people got out of it; what counts is what it meant to you." A more accurate expression of her feeling would have been, "You rather wish you didn't have to face this new thing that came to you?" Another pastor may have been better when he suggested, "You'd feel a bit easier if you were sure you had some company in taking this step?"

This is the kind of point where the need for a parishioner to feel reassured can be easily confused by the pastor with verbal expressions of reassurance on his part. For instance, "We all have our needs. I am sure others responded too"; or "Different people are affected in different ways. Others may have felt it too"; or "I'm sure they were." In each instance the response is to the words, not the real feeling.

Miss Smith: I guess I would. I'm afraid I know what I must do, and it may cost a little too; but I still think that if I had had something like this when Dad died, I would have had something to hang on to. That was awful. Strange how I could go on all these years and then feel that I had been missing the real thing.

Pastor: But you feel you've found it now.

The pastor's comment expresses a bit more than Miss Smith herself suggested. When, a couple of comments back, he made the mistake of ignoring her remaining doubts, he set a course for himself which he is almost compelled to follow. In this comment Miss Smith almost says she has found what she is looking for, but not quite. The pastor is now clearly arrayed on one side of the conflict. This may, as the subsequent comments show, let Miss Smith leave with the conviction that everything is now fine. But there may be backsliding or new doubts because she has not dealt satisfactorily with her remaining doubts.

One of the pastors gave a superior response when he said, "You have a sense of having lost time in not discovering this before."

Miss Smith: I guess I know what I have to do though. I'm afraid that I have to get out of the crowd and really touch Christ in a new way. I know I have to do something about it.[E]

Pastor: You're convinced that you can learn to do it as you practice doing it.

This would be good if in the three previous responses the pastor had not refused to acknowledge the element of doubt which still persisted, and which cannot be downed merely by nonrecognition. Another pastor said, "You're ready to take action." A second, "You do see what must be done." But note the complete irrelevance of this one, "Yes, but it depends upon the crowd. Perhaps you could be a good influence on them." And the authoritarian tone of, "Then act upon that conviction." And the conception that the use of theological words has magical effect in, "Christ will make it possible for you to do it."

Miss Smith: Yes, I'm sure of that. I guess it's just a matter of being willing to do what is asked afterwards.[F]

Pastor: And you *are* ready to do it.

Here again Miss Smith hints at the remaining doubt which she has, but says nothing overt because her previous suggestions have not been recognized. Some such statement as the following, even at this stage, might yet keep the way open for Miss Smith to discuss the doubt that remains: "And you wish you were sure of your own willingness." The fact remains that if fear and doubt still remain, even though lessened by the earlier part of the interview, they will later cause difficulty for Miss Smith. And the fact that the pastor dealt only with the gross doubt and failed to acknowledge the remnant will make it less likely that when new difficulty arises she will come again to him. He has shown himself understanding and helpful about large things, so to speak, but also a bit impatient and one-sided after the large things have been discussed.

MISS SMITH: I think I know what I have to do.
PASTOR: Good.

Farewells are said. It is significant that Miss Smith's own summary of the situation is in terms of her obligation, what she *has* to do, not in terms of what she *intends* to do or *wants* to do. This is because the pastor, after demonstrating excellent understanding at the beginning and seeing that she is leaning toward the side he considers "good," decides to ignore from then on anything in her which does not reinforce the "good" decision. The result is that Miss Smith makes the decision he thinks she should, but not with the wholeheartedness and positive quality that would have been possible if the pastor had been willing to consider the small doubts as well as the big ones. Despite the pastor's obvious intelligence about counseling, therefore, the interview is only half successful. It is especially unsuccessful because doubts and difficulties Miss Smith is likely to have from this point on happen to be those which she senses the pastor will think too minor to be taken seriously; hence the chances of her coming back are small. The way is not left open.

TENTATIVE CONCLUSIONS

WE can at least tentatively draw some general conclusions from our study of the pastoral interview with Miss Smith. Our approach is not opposed to the drawing of more or less systematic conclusions. But it assumes that the general conclusions drawn are less important than an understanding of the processes through which their being drawn is justified. The systematic statement of conclusions may be correct and yet still correctable. Not only could the conclusions be accurately stated in a different way but they could also be qualified and made more inclusively relevant by comparing them with conclusions from other data. Nevertheless, the following seem to be the

tentative conclusions which can be drawn from this interview.
1. *The counseling process focuses attention on the parishioner's situation and his feelings about it.*[7] Conversely, anything done by the counselor which distracts the parishioner's or the pastor's attention from the parishioner's situation and how he feels about it impedes the process. Note again, for example, the response of Pastor 5 to *A*. She had begun her confession, and he said, "Yes, go on. Perhaps we can get somewhere." He was diverting her, partly by getting her to notice that he was there and partly by suggesting that perhaps they might not get somewhere. In contrast, Pastor 8 said, "You've really been troubled." Attention is centered on Miss Smith's situation and the way she feels about it—in so far as she has stated the way she feels about it. It does not divert. It gives the kind of encouragement that is needed, namely the sense that she is understood, that she is free to express how she feels, and that it is all right to concentrate on her situation and her feelings about it.

We may also conclude that this does not work if it is viewed by the pastor as a trick. For instance if he gets the idea that Miss Smith will think he is concentrating on her feelings provided he begins every sentence with "you," he is substituting shadow for substance. If the only choice one had were between sentences beginning with "you" and sentences beginning with "I," the vote would have to be for "you" in counseling. In this interview it is true that the effective responses generally began with "you." That is simply one of the easier ways for the pastor continually to remind himself that he is concentrating for the moment on the feelings of someone else, and not on something such as his own probable feelings if he were facing a similar situation. What is really significant about the actual pastor's responses up to *D* is that he is concentrating genuinely and wholeheartedly on Miss Smith's situation and her feelings about it, and in every response is demonstrating this to Miss Smith.

2. *The counseling proceeds through real understanding on the pastor's part of how the parishioner feels about the situation, and through communication of the reality of that understanding.*[8] This understanding has some intellectual element in it, but it is by no means primarily an intellectual matter. For instance, after comment *E* the pastor who said, "Yes, but that depends upon the crowd. Perhaps you could be a good influence on them," did not get the point even in an intellectual sense. But it is fairly obvious that even if he had, his whole approach was so at variance with the attempt to understand that he would still have made as gross an error. The pastor who said at this point, "Then don't be afraid to go and do it," missed

the emotional point, Miss Smith's real feelings, even though intel-
lectually he got the import of her words.

In addition to the pastor's understanding of what the parishioner
has been trying to express, there needs to be communication back to
the parishioner that he has been understood. He needs to be assured
of that understanding. When counseling experts say that reassurance
does not work, what they mean is that words which try to give reassurance apart from a demonstration of understanding are not in fact
reassuring. For instance, the statement: "You may be sure I understand your situation," is an attempt to reassure, but there is no demonstration with it. The pastor who says it may or may not be concentrating on the immediate feeling which requires understanding;
his statement does not tell the parishioner one way or the other.
Even so, such a statement is better than: "I certainly understand
what you mean. I've been through exactly the same thing myself";
or, "I see exactly. There was another woman in here just last week
who had the same problem." For these divert as well as generalize.

Even if we are interested in the person and concentrating on his
feelings about his situation, it is easy to slip into various patterns
which prevent us from communicating our understanding. Generalizing is perhaps the most widely used pattern of this kind. In response to A, Pastor 2 said, "We all have these experiences sometimes." This is poor, not only because it diverts but also because it
confuses a generalized statement of intended reassurance with the
communication of the fact of understanding. The pastor who, in
reply to B, said, "The tested faith is the only faith that is worth
while," was trying to reassure verbally by generalizing, and he obviously failed to communicate understanding.

3. *When conflicting feelings of the parishioner emerge in counseling, the pastor first aids the parishioner in clarifying the elements
of the conflict and their relative pull upon him.*[9] Although it is apparent from the beginning that Miss Smith is in conflict, is feeling
herself pulled in more than one direction, she does not begin to
state openly the elements in the conflict until C. Then she says that
if she had the deeper experience of faith, there would be a big,
and by implication a valuable, change in her life; but she says also
that she is not sure that an ordinary person needs such an experience.
One pastor's response showed that he not only accepted Miss Smith's
feelings as a fact and understood what she was trying to convey but
also communicated his understanding of the elements in the conflict in so far as she had indicated her own understanding of them.
He said, "You're not sure it's for you; yet you are sure it would make

a difference in your life." Both the recognition of the elements in the conflict so far as they were stated to this point and the verbal restatement of them contribute to clarification. This part of the process may be likened to helping the person put handles on tools he has already held up for inspection. The important parts of the tools are there, and at least some of them have been shown by the parishioner. But they cannot be used properly until they have handles, until they can be grasped far enough away from the cutting edge to permit them to perform their real function.

It is an entirely natural temptation for the pastor to treat a conflict like a train, and to hop immediately upon the car that looks best, or newest, or nearest, or rightest—especially rightest. Unintentional moralizing is our most serious danger at this point in counseling. In response to *A*, Pastor 1 said, "You were wise not to pursue that course." He did not intend to moralize. He just did not know any way to proceed other than through making a judgment on everything that came along. Pastor 4 drew a moral judgment more consciously when he said, "Your father lived his life, and you have yours to live." In both cases moral judgment was used as a substitute for understanding; and by the time these men reached the point where clarification was the required order of the day, they were so far on one side of the conflict that the other side could not even be mentioned. It is not surprising to find such a pastor saying after *C*, Miss Smith's statement in which she first began to define the elements in the conflict, "Yes you do. Jesus came to help regular people." After that moral judgment which has told her exactly how she ought to feel, and which implies that she is condemned if she does not feel that way, we can hardly see much incentive for Miss Smith to bring out the other side of her situation and ask for help in dealing with it. As the Bible says, "He that answereth a matter before he heareth it, it is folly and shame unto him." And, we might add, it is powerfully frustrating to the person he answers.

It is tempting to speculate on why we pastors have such a predilection for moral judgment even when its exercise clearly defeats our larger purposes. To some extent it is the expression of a general habit pattern built up partly out of our real concern to view what is right and wrong about the world in which we live and partly out of the fact that people unconsciously expect us to approach things through the avenue of moral judgment. We preach about the criteria of right and wrong, and properly so. But subtly, unless we are careful, this becomes our dominant perspective. We forget,

"Judge not, that ye be not judged," and become more concerned with the sin than with the sinner.

There is, of course, more to it than that. We let ourselves drift into something which is not far from a belief in verbal magic. We may end our prayers with "Through Jesus Christ our Lord" not for the proper reasons—to induce in us a renewed awareness that Jesus Christ is our Lord, that through him our prayers have new meaning in the eyes of God, and that even the very meanings and feelings we have been attempting to convey through our prayer are subject to correction through the gospel of Christ—not for those real reasons, but because it would not seem like a prayer if we did not use those words. We would feel vaguely uneasy or anxious if we failed to use them—just as we feel when we are out for the evening and our wives ask if we turned off the water in the kitchen. Actually it is not the phrase but the meaning that should accompany the phrase that is important.

Similarly we tend to have a vaguely uncomfortable feeling if a situation looks as if it required a moral judgment and we fail to speak up. Of course there are situations when we should speak out. But we may be suspicious when we hear someone who has spoken out say afterwards, "I just felt I *had* to get myself on record," or "I just *had* to clear my conscience." There may be deeply ingrained selfishness in the insistence on clearing one's conscience regardless of the consequences to other people. It may or may not be the thing to do, but there should be some standard involved other than the degree of tension which we feel inside ourselves. In counseling, moral judgments *in place of* understanding and clarification are especially likely to be disastrous.

The pastor needs to keep in mind one other fact about moral judgments in counseling. Atheists and agnostics seldom come to him; and when they do, it is not generally in a mood for counseling. In other words, the pastor's own stand where moral and ethical questions are involved is already fairly clear from noncounseling aspects of his work. He can assume, therefore, that the person who is willing and ready to discuss his situation with him has that fact in the back of his mind. Therefore it takes three times as much courage for someone like Betty Smith to tell the pastor she has doubts about the value of faith as it does to tell him that she wishes her faith meant more to her. If moral judgment is applied by the pastor the minute Miss Smith begins to state the negative side of her quandary, then the opportunity for her to learn how to deal with whatever it is that prevents her from having faith is cut off.

4. *The counseling relationship contains a special kind of freedom on the part of the parishioner, as well as a special kind of limitation.*[10] The better both of these are understood by both the parishioner and the pastor, the more likely is it that the relationship will be fruitful.

The basic limitation upon the parishioner is that he accept the pastor's task as helping him to help himself, and not as telling him what to do or precisely how to do it. In other words, the problem is accepted as his problem and is not shoved over to the pastor for solution. There are certain other limitations. There is some limitation upon time, mutually understood. An interview is rarely better and usually worse if the parishioner continues for two hours or more. There are limitations of various kinds, all of which center around the fact that the pastor cannot be "used."

The understanding of these limitations is important in counseling, and on many occasions the pastor can help by stating explicitly his limitations, as for example:

MR. RONALD: What I'd like to do is to tell you the story, and then maybe you'll have some suggestions on what I can do about it.
PASTOR: I'm free until three o'clock, and I'll be glad to hear the story. I've not found it very fruitful in my experience, however, to suggest to people what they ought to do. But it does seem helpful to aid someone to see his situation a little more clearly so that he has a better chance of handling it for himself.
MR. RONALD: I see what you mean. And I guess I wouldn't want to be told just what to do either. It's my problem, isn't it? Well, here's my situation . . .

It is not always possible to set the limitations on the situation at the beginning, or so clearly or explicitly. And yet, other things being equal, the more clearly they are understood from the beginning, the less likelihood there is of wasted motion.

But there should be in the counseling relationship not only the particular limitations described but also a special kind of freedom. The parishioner should be free to express or withhold any statements about his feelings When the word "free" is used here, it implies that no honest statement of feeling, whatever its content, will be the subject of condemnation by the minister. Betty Smith should be as free, so far as the understanding response of the pastor is concerned, to talk of her doubts about the desirability of faith as she is to talk of her desire for deeper faith. On the other hand, the fact that it is a counseling relationship should not be a kind of compulsion under which Miss Smith feels she has to state and discuss feelings which she is not ready to discuss.

Miss Smith said she had begun to realize that if she got some other things settled in her life, the question of faith might take care of itself. She said, in other words, that she knew her situation involved more than the question of faith. The freedom of the counseling relationship included her freedom not to discuss those other things if she did not feel ready to do so. As it turned out, she apparently wanted to focus attention on the faith problem—even after she had indicated that she knew it was but one aspect of a larger question. She was free to do so if that was the way she was prepared to go about it. On the other hand, if she had said, "Well, I have been worrying about my faith, but I know there are other things too. I think I'd like to discuss some of the other things," then the pastor would have left her free to do so, and not protested her leaving the faith problem before it was settled.

The question is often asked what the freedom and limitations are upon the kind of person who comes to the minister again and again with the same story and never makes any progress toward its solution. How, it is asked, can one permit freedom in a situation of this kind? As a matter of fact, this situation usually arises because of the pastor's unsureness in setting forth the limitations in the counseling relationship. The parishioner usually starts with something like, "I don't like to take your time, and I know you've heard some of this before, but I've just got to tell someone about it." The pastor thinks, "Well, I'd better resign myself and listen." He does, perhaps under the mistaken impression that merely permitting the lady—or gentleman—to get something off her chest is somehow beneficial in itself. He does not know why or how, but he does not know what else to do, so he hears the story.

At the end there is a question like, "Don't you think it's terrible? What would *you* do if you were in *my* place?"

"Well," he probably says, "it does seem difficult, but I hope it's helped a bit to tell me something of the situation."

And she says, "You mean you're not going to tell me what *you* think about it?"

If he wriggles out of that one, he will still have the same thing all over again next time she has to get it off her chest. The pastor's error is in not making clear the limitations of the relationship to the parishioner and, in a case like this, also to himself. He has rights as a pastor and as a counselor. If he doubts this or is confused about their nature, then the loquacious repeaters will continue to take his time with no profit to anyone.

After her first comment he could have said something like, "Of course you may tell me the story if you want to. But I think you should understand that it's not my practice to give advice or tell people what to do about individual matters. I believe each person has to decide about his personal situations for himself. Therefore I'm entirely ready to hear the story from you if you believe this can help you to handle your own situation better. But I don't think it will do either of us any good if you tell me a story and then ask me what is the right course of action for you to take." If this were done, it would do the parishioner far more good than what did happen, even if, as a result, she decided to leave without telling her story.

Three enemies of the freedom which is necessary in the counseling relationship have already been discussed, distracting, generalizing and moralizing. A fourth is coercion, or forcing.[11] In response to A, Pastor 3 said, "What have you done, then?" This is to ride roughshod over the emotions and souls of people. After B, one of the pastors said, "Just what is your faith?" which is coercive because it goes into the temple with shoes on. After D, which she concludes by asking whether she has to give herself through faith in a new way, one pastor said, "Yes! Go to church and seek God's guidance." Such a response is coercive. It seems to be founded on a pessimism which runs like this: "She seems near the top of the fence now; if I don't give her a push, she may fall down on the wrong side. Maybe if I do give her a push, I can manage to get her over on the right side." This contains not only the smug assumption that the pastor is dead sure of what is the right side—not just for him or in general, but for Miss Smith now—but also the pessimistic premise that if he does not "manage" her right, she is sure to go the wrong way. One can imagine that his image of the shepherd and the sheep is in terms of a superior being leading and pushing inferior beings.

Coercion may be direct or indirect, obvious or subtle. The response cited immediately above was direct and obvious. It is subtler and more indirect in the pastor who said, "If you want to save your life, you must lose it," but the intent is the same. For it must be plain by this time that despite the centering of our methodological discussion around words, words are not in themselves important except as they are vehicles for the expression of attitudes. If an attitude is coercive, that is, determined to produce a certain course of action in someone regardless of any circumstances or conditions whatever, it will come out somehow, whatever be the verbal vehicle chosen to convey it. Just because they are less easy to spot, the subtler expressions of coercion may be more damaging than the overt ones.

5. *The counseling process should include, on one or more appropriate occasions, that which will aid in consolidation of the insights achieved or the clarifications gained.*[12] There are some who believe that this consolidation is merely another phase of clarification, and I would not dispute such a classification. But whether it is done through words or is merely assumed, some kind of consolidation relating to the process of counseling always emerges, even though the pastor may not be aware of it.

In the case of Betty Smith the consolidation seems to have been largely negative. Will Betty come to see the pastor again? If not, do both she and the pastor understand that she will not? Is there a mutual understanding? As Betty leaves, we know that no arrangements for another contact have been made; and after our analysis of her feelings on leaving, we are inclined to believe it may be a long time before she comes back. If she has decided she is not coming back, or that she can now get along on her own without further counseling, or that for the time being she can do all right by herself, would it not be an important consolidation of whatever insights she has achieved if she said so—or said something which made her feeling clear about not coming back?

After *F* the pastor realizes she is almost ready to leave. He might well have said, "You're ready to move ahead now—on your own. Or would you like to go over this a bit more with me in a few days?" It is up to Betty to decide, but as the situation actually was handled, she had no chance to consolidate her decision about returning or not returning.

In addition to the consolidation—discussed or assumed—at the conclusion of interviews there come times when a conflict has been somewhat clarified. After this a kind of summary of progress in looking at the conflict is in order. The real significance of this point is more apparent later on in a series of consultations than in a first interview. Even so, the kind of response which would have been most suitable after *D* would have been of this character. In three or four previous comments she has been stating something about the two elements in her conflict. Now in *D* it is as if she is putting two and two together and seeing that together they make something she was not quite aware of before. This makes her draw back a little. We commended the response of one of the pastors as especially appropriate: "You're convinced, and yet you can't help wishing there were an easier way." The consolidating element could have been made a bit stronger if he had said, "You're convinced about the value of a new approach to faith in which you take initiative in a new way, but you still find yourself afraid of the demands it will make on you if you decide to move that way." Here the pastor would be picking up the several aspects of the two elements in the conflict which Miss Smith has brought out in several preceding comments and more or less summarizing them.

His consolidating does not introduce new ideas. It simply summarizes the elements in the conflict as Miss Smith sees them, on a broader basis than any single comment of hers has done. Hence it could enlarge the perspective in which clarification takes place. Such a procedure is still more appropriate in later stages of many counseling relationships.

Dynamic Psychological Understanding

Chapter Three IT HAS BEEN STATED EARLIER THAT THE CROSS-SEC-
tional road to the study of approach and method through analysis
of a pastoral interview has particular limitations which need to be
corrected if a true perspective in counseling is to be achieved. Two
more pedagogical steps are necessary to accomplish this, the first
of which will be considered in this chapter and the second in the
following chapter. Here we shall examine the place and function of
our knowledge and understanding of dynamic psychology in the
counseling situation. In the succeeding chapter we shall investigate
the elongated counseling relationship, special factors that have to be
taken into account in extended counseling and which cannot be
deduced either from study of a single interview or from the dynamics
of a life history.

The present chapter is divided in turn into two major parts. First,
what can we learn about the dynamic psychological factors going on
within a person from study of the counseling situation in cross section? And second, what are the most important things dynamic
psychology in general has taught us which are relevant to the counseling relationship?

Nothing mysterious is intended by the use of the term "dynamic
psychology." Equally effective terms for our purposes might be "personality psychology," or "psychology of interpersonal relations,"
or even "therapeutic psychology." The technical student will make
important distinctions among those phrases. But what they have in
common is so much more important to us than what separates them
that we may think of them almost interchangeably.[1] For what we
want to suggest is that the kind of psychological understanding
which is relevant to pastoral counseling is a social psychology of
personality in movement, moving and being moved, motivating and
being motivated, operating as a unit on a human social level as well
as on other levels such as the biological. There are important and
legitimate branches of psychology which have little to do with personality directly.[2] We are simply distinguishing the kind of psy-

chology that has something obviously to do with personality as we view it in the light of the pastor's counseling concern.

LEARNING FROM OBSERVATION

AFTER the worship service one Sunday morning, as a pastor was greeting persons at the exit of the church, he noticed a woman he had not seen before standing to one side, waiting for a more private word with him. Her opportunity came, and she asked if she could talk with him soon. He observed that she was twisting her gloves and that her voice appeared to be a monotone—as if she were holding its normal variations in check by a conscious effort. Interpreting these signs as indicating tension, he suggested an appointment for the next day, and it was made.

When Mrs. Finch, as we shall call her, came to his study, the pastor noticed more about her appearance than he had the day before. She seemed to be in her late twenties or early thirties, was of medium height and build, wore good clothes which, however, leaned toward an overstuffed look. Her hat was intricate and had a veil, and her short cloth coat had strips of fur at the bottom as well as around the neck. Her color scheme was striking without being garish. Her make-up was in good taste but noticeable. In manner she was nervous. Despite an invitation to take off her coat, she kept it on. She sat down in the chair without relaxing, took off her gloves, and began to play with them. She began to speak with no preliminaries other than the process of being seated.

MRS. FINCH: Your sermon yesterday was quite appropriate, though I'm afraid I can't recall the title you gave it.
PASTOR: "Beyond Suffering."
MRS. FINCH: Yes, that was it. You seem to have strong convictions about certain things over which a good many of us are quite confused (she pauses and watches the pastor, who nods; she continues). You talked about prayer, for instance. It's never helped me a bit in the hard experiences of my life. My mother died when I was ten, just when I needed her most. When I was in my teens I had a stepmother who hated me. After I married I thought things would be all right for me, but I had two miscarriages and then lost my first child when he was six months old. After I got on my feet again and had a child, I had to spend over four months in the hospital with a serious illness (she pauses). And now my husband is reported missing in Europe.
PASTOR: You don't think it's quite fair that you've had, and still have, such terrific suffering as this certainly is.
MRS. FINCH: "Quite" isn't the word. I feel terrible. What have I done to

deserve all these setbacks? If there is a God, why doesn't he do something about people's problems? (*Slight pause.*) And then if you kill yourself because you just can't take it any more, the church calls it a sin and says you will go to hell (*long pause*).

Let us pause to ask what the pastor should have learned thus far about dynamic psychology from Mrs. Finch. The first thing that is apparent is that Mrs. Finch is prepared to pour out her story, accompanied by a good deal of emotion, to a person she had never seen until the previous day. This suggests two implications. One is that she must have come to feel some kind of confidence in the minister as he preached his sermon. The other is that the tension inside her must be great if she, who is clearly not the kind of person who would buttonhole every stranger on the street to tell her story, can pour out her feeling of bitter frustration with no special help from the pastor.[3] In turn these suggest some more general truths. People are not inclined to open up their deepest feelings unless they feel some kind of confidence in the person to whom they are talking. Hence he who would counsel has to pay some attention to whatever there is in him which tends to give people such confidence, and also to whatever there is in him which tends to discourage such confidence. The other general truth would be that frustrations may pile up for a considerable time without a great deal of outward evidence of the fact; but when a certain point is reached, which is probably individual for each person, something has to be done.[4] When the wise step of letting it out to a counselor is selected, the counselor will find that for a time the pent-up emotion will rush out more or less regardless of what he says or does about it.

But Mrs. Finch has told us more than that. The central feeling she has been conveying could be paraphrased, "I feel that life has given me so many bad breaks that there can't be any meaning to it." Look again at the list of events: death of her mother when she was ten, a stepmother who hated her, two miscarriages, loss of her first child at six months, a long hospitalized illness, and her husband missing in action. It is a devastating list. But she does not cite these experiences like a list of discrete items; she explains her central feeling of resentment and puzzlement and then supports it by reference to these items.[5]

This is a person, a human being expressing a feeling rather than a lump of clay which has had various unfortunate experiences happen to it. The experiences *are* shattering, but this does not say that anyone who had these particular things happen to him would have the same response to them or feeling about them that Mrs. Finch has. Another way to put it is that we cannot necessarily infer from the external or objective facts of an experience—husband missing in action, for example—the way a particular person will feel about or respond to the situation.[6] What needs to be understood, then, is Mrs. Finch, a person. And she herself provides the essential element by not only telling us that certain things have happened to her but also summarizing her feeling about or attitude towards life itself. She is, she suggests, resentful and puzzled and discouraged.

She is also wistful. If she were resentful alone, she might have bitten her nails or taken to alcohol or turned on the gas. Instead she has come to church and sought out the pastor. For wistfulness means that although one is discouraged and inclined to be pessimistic, he cannot help hoping there is some resource which can meet the situation. Thus if the pastor heard only the resentful words and said to himself, "This woman is just angry," he would be stating but a half-truth. Life has dealt her terrific blows; she has reacted with a combination of puzzlement and resentment, but she will not give up hope that life may be more than confusion and frustration. This is her hope, and it is as important an aspect of her dynamics as is the feeling of resentment and puzzlement.

We are justified in some generalization from this. The dynamic meaning of a person's feeling cannot be understood from a mere statement describing its nature—for example, she feels resentful. A respectable executive who has been mulcting his stockholders for years and has just been found out, a minister who has had his salary cut because his congregation are tired of his sermons, and a small boy whose mother has prevented him from putting bacon in the frying pan all may have their reactions described as "resentment," but this tells us little or nothing about the dynamic meaning. Yet it is the dynamic meaning that needs to be grasped if the real situation is to be understood. Mrs. Finch suggests that the essence of it may frequently be apparent if we keep our eye on the entire situation— in this case the fact that she expresses resentment on the basis of experiences which by any standards are difficult and at the same time seeks help from the representative of an institution which professes to give guidance on the meaning of life.

Still another general truth is suggested to us by Mrs. Finch in the discrepancy between the kind of response she clearly expects from the pastor and the kind we know from our previous consideration of approach and method may be of help to her. Her statement is thrown out as if to say, "I defy you to prove to me that God is good, that religion means anything positive, that prayer can help, or that life has any meaning." She expects the pastor to say in effect, "If you understand these things as I do, you will see that they are good; you have the wrong slant on them." She expects, in other words, an authoritarian answer[7]—that is, an authoritative answer based so far as she can see on the fact that the pastor's views have not been shattered by the kind of tragic experiences she has had. She does not realize that another kind of answer is possible.

Why not? Because in her experience—and in the experience of an appalling proportion of the population—she has never enjoyed a human relationship in which she was fully and genuinely accepted.[8] It is not unreasonable to suppose, for example, that when her baby died, all her friends said with genuine sympathy, "It's really terrible, dear." And then they all added, "But you can have another baby soon." When she naturally felt only negative, deeply lost, no friend could so fully accept her as to share that loss without feeling impelled to drag in a supposedly silver lining. Her friends meant well. They were truly sympathetic, as one must be in such a situation if he is not a monster. But they were also embarrassed, that is, sufficiently preoccupied with their own feelings to be unable fully to accept hers. Thus Mrs. Finch infers somewhere underneath: "They are not sympathetic to *me*, but only to a woman who has lost a baby. They can't afford to understand how deeply lost I feel; for if they did, they're afraid they'd suffer as I do."

In any event Mrs. Finch does not expect from the pastor a kind of understanding she has seldom, if ever, experienced. And yet the very fact that there is a wistfulness, albeit mixed with defiance, suggests that something in her has not given up hope of finding understanding. She expects to be told how she *ought* to feel, but something inside her hopes against hope and experience that her real feelings may be accepted and understood.

A wife may ask us to help the family situation by seeing if we are willing to give her husband a lecture on the evils of drinking. A businessman may request that we believe him instead of his wife when he asserts that there's nothing personal between him and his secretary. A student may want us to tell him how to concentrate better when he studies and not to have his mind wander off to other things. The fact is that all these requests are impossible to fulfill on the terms in which they are requested—if we give the expected answer. For if we do, we will not be helping the person to help himself but reinforcing the illusion that the way to solve a problem is to get an authority to do it for us.

Yet the fact that the initial requests are made on such terms does not mean that the person is necessarily incapable of accepting help on the only terms which will do him any good, namely, those which enable him to help himself. He may turn out to be more or less receptive to these terms. That has to be explored. But the mere fact that the problem is stated so that there is a particular kind of answer expected does not mean that giving that answer, however ably, will really help. It is an index of what past experience has led the person to expect, not an index of his real need. If a man searching for a satisfactory writing instrument has tried out soft and hard and medium pencils, fountain pens with gold and platinum and iridium points, and ball-point pens and has still failed to find a satisfactory instrument, it will be natural and reasonable for him to expect, on his next try, to look for something which has the appearance of a pen or pencil. But the real answer for him may turn out to be a typewriter. We project from our experience. Our expectations are based on our experience. A new dimension may have to be added before our questions can be answered.[9]

We may tell a little more about Mrs. Finch:

PASTOR: It's hard to understand how there can be a good God if circumstances of this kind are permitted.

MRS. FINCH: That's what I mean. How can there? I've not belonged to a church since I've been married—my husband thinks all religion is the bunk. But I used to believe in it, and I guess I always thought I could come back to it some day. But when I need it most, then I find it isn't worth anything.

PASTOR: It hasn't helped you to make sense out of life.

MRS. FINCH: No it hasn't. But I wish it could, or something could. I didn't really expect anything when I came to the church service yesterday, but—well, I guess I did kind of hope for something. And what you said—it didn't ring true to me—but there was something in it. I thought maybe if I could talk to you I could see if there was anything. You seemed so confident. And what right have you to be confident when things like this are allowed to happen by a God you say is good?

PASTOR: You feel torn between thinking there is no answer, and on the other hand wishing you could find the kind of answer you thought I was talking about.

MRS. FINCH: Yes, I suppose I am. I do wish I could feel the kind of certainty you seem to have, that prayer would really mean something to me and help me, and that I could think God was on my side. I wish it, but I don't see how it can be. All these things, and now my husband (*she bows her head and holds her handkerchief to her eyes for a*

moment) . I just don't have anything left to go on with, with him gone.
PASTOR: It is tragic—and difficult. The last props seem to have been
knocked out from under you.
MRS. FINCH: Yes they do. It's really my husband far more than any of
these other things. After all, we were getting along well until he
went into the service—and was reported missing. He managed to do
well financially, and my future is secure in that way. I—I didn't want
children at first, after the miscarriages and Johnny's death, but later
I did, and I have a lovely little boy. My childhood was hard, but I've
survived. It's my husband. How *can* I get along? My whole life seems
to be gone.
PASTOR: If he were here, you'd feel entirely differently. But as it is,
nothing in life seems worth while, even though you feel you have
something you *should* want to live for.
MRS. FINCH: Yes, I *should* want to, but it's like ashes. You've been very
understanding, Dr. Blank, but I can't see why God lets such things
happen or how prayer could help me face it and live as if living
amounted to something.
PASTOR: You'd like to, but you can't quite do it.
MRS. FINCH: I do desperately want to. Oh, I know other men have been
killed. There's a friend of mine in the neighborhood whose husband
was killed two years ago. If we have a war, it's got to happen to some.
But why to me? Why does God pick out some and not others?
PASTOR: It *is* difficult to face when it happens to us.
MRS. FINCH: Maybe it isn't quite as impossible as I've thought. And
I guess God didn't make the war. But it's so hard to make any sense of
these things inside. I've felt as if God had it in for *me*. I—I think
maybe I see something I didn't see before. Could I—would it be
asking too much if I could see you again in a week or two?

The pastor's counseling method here is effective—not equally so
at every point, but it is so much in the right direction that Mrs. Finch
clearly gets some help. Her original expectations are not met. The
pastor does not repreach his sermon on "Beyond Suffering." But
what he does in the counseling situation is far more successful than
the sermon was in helping Mrs. Finch toward a new perspective from
which she can look at her life and its meaning.

What does this additional excerpt tell us about Mrs. Finch's
dynamics or about dynamics in general? From the counseling point
of view it is plain that the pastor has understood Mrs. Finch and
communicated this fact to her, as a result of which her perception of
her own situation is different at the end from what it was at the
beginning. She has not found a "solution" to her problem. But
because she is looking at things in a new way, she perceives her total

situation in what is a more realistic and ultimately more hopeful way. There has been no change in the externals of her situation, but there has been a considerable change in her perception of it. One might say that her capacity to perceive, or readiness to perceive, has been broadened to include a wider range of her actual experience.

Her previous readiness to perceive had been nearly overwhelmed by the series of tragedies. This had become generalized into a kind of cosmic framework in which there was a tendency or readiness to perceive the events and circumstances of life from a tragic perspective alone. And yet we have seen that there was within her a deep desire to find wholeness and integration, a wistfulness which is a hope against hope that something within herself may be so changed as to enable her to go on in the face of her difficult situation. She had expected the pastor to do this for her. Instead, he had understood her. This had enabled her to broaden her readiness to perceive to include a wider range of her actual experience, and in that sense to help her move toward wholeness and integration. The increased readiness for constructive action is an obvious by-product.

Two points may be generalized and are dynamically important. Both are similar to, but not identical with, points which have been emphasized by Carl G. Jung.[10] Jung said that personality difficulties can best be understood from the point of view of bias or one-sidedness, that we all have a tendency to develop one or a few aspects of our true selves at the expense of other aspects. We are then one-sided, and lose touch with important aspects of our selves. The regaining of psychic health can come only when we regain contact with these neglected aspects of the self. Jung's view makes the process appear a matter of quantity, as if the mere acceptance of an increasing number of aspects of one's experience into one's perspective would turn the trick. Actually, as we have seen in Mrs. Finch, concepts implying quantity have little to do with the matter. What has happened is that an interpersonal relationship of a special kind—whose outstanding feature is concentrated understanding—has helped to release the obstacles which were blocking the trend toward a more inclusive capacity to perceive and assimilate the totality of life experience. An interpersonal process has provided what might be called the setting in which a person can look in a more integrated manner at himself. We know that such a new view of the self inevitably means at the same time a new view of relationship with other people and with the cosmic framework in which we live. Hence a new view of the self means a new view of one's destiny. This point is obviously related to that of Jung, but it is not the same.

The second point, a corollary of the first, is that the potential resources for the cure of personality troubles may be understood to be within the person in the same sense and in the same degree that the troubles themselves are within him. As a matter of fact, the geographic metaphor is not very helpful except in one respect—to make clear that magical external intervention is no more necessary in finding resources to meet a situation than magical actions were necessary to create it. This is not to say that personal dynamics are to be understood as if they operated within an individual bounded by four solid stone walls. The troubles came about through interaction with the world without and so have the potential resources. Where they come from is one thing. The fact that they can be activated only on the assumption that they are potentially present is something else, and it is that which is the basic assumption for our purposes. The inner world contains more mud than we like to admit, but there is a sandy bottom beneath it. The demons do rage within us, but the Holy Spirit is much more effective at chasing them out than is an invading angelic army of occupation which does not know its way around this particular soul.

What has just been said assumes a point which has not yet been stated but which is logically prior: the meaning of the unconscious. What Freud meant—and his discovery is epoch-making—is that there is something within the personality, a part of the personality and not foreign to it, which is unknown and unrecognized and incapable of being brought into awareness by ordinary means, but which nevertheless influences the total conduct and behavior of the personality.[11] There are deeper levels of the personality which are no less influential upon our conduct because we are not aware of them. Freud tended to emphasize the darker aspects of the unconscious, and not without justification. But the magnitude of his insight is the very existence of these deeper levels not as things apart but as active though consciously unknown ingredients in every act and in our personality as a whole.

Mrs. Finch tells us little or nothing about the deeper levels of her personality. Almost by definition the content of these emerges not through ordinary means as in counseling, but by special processes of free association, dreams, and the like. But even Mrs. Finch tells us that there are dynamic forces in movement below the surface of consciousness, influencing her conduct. She thought she wanted to express resentment, to complain that prayer understood as a kind of magic would not work. But that was not all she wanted to do. Given the chance, through the fact of being understood and accepted, she wanted also to come to the point where she could begin to assert some of the positive and creative things which were pretty well buried under the depth of her suffering and resentment. We do not see her unconscious, but we see aspects of its dynamic operation in her total behavior. When she came to the pastor, she actually expected no real help. And yet she came, thus suggesting she had some kind of hope. She had expectations of what the pastor would do; yet at the same time she hoped he would do something different which would really help. There were two selves—and yet they were but aspects of the essential self.

The analysis of Mrs. Finch could be carried still further, but we can afford to leave a few dynamic threads still knotted. For the purpose of this discussion has not been to present a systematic account of psychological dynamics which is all-inclusive, but to suggest that we can learn while doing. Indeed, whether we know it or not, that is the way we do learn if we learn at all. If psychological dynamics could be learned only through systematic study, we could learn about them only as we drew up systems of our own or studied the more or less adequate systems of others; but we should then be turning aside from all our practical helping contacts as if they were only points where our knowledge could be applied, and not also points at which our knowledge could be advanced. Our counseling activity should be both. It should call upon every bit of sound knowledge we have gained about what moves and pushes and has power within the human soul. But it should and can be also a major and daily opportunity to add to that knowledge, refine it, correct it, and get the various elements into increasingly truer perspective.

One word of warning may not be out of place. To assert that we can learn from our counseling is one thing. To assume that learning is our major interest in counseling is something else.[12] More than one counselor has, before he realized it, developed such an intense interest in what he could learn from his patient or parishioner that his interest in helping that person has become merely subsidiary, until finally he has deluded himself that anything helps the person which increases the knowledge of the counselor. These two aims are not inconsistent in the sense that there is an inherent incongruity, for the most basic and important knowledge tends naturally to reveal itself as the genuinely therapeutic considerations are made paramount. Knowledge, in other words, ordinarily comes best as a by-product. If we give the best pastoral help we possibly can in a situation, concentrating energy and attention on that, we are far more likely to learn significant dynamics from later study of what went on than if we contrive some situation in which all we have to think about is what we are learning. For in the latter situation the true dynamics—especially the movement which gropes from the unsatisfactory to the satisfactory—may be completely lost to our view.

The dynamics of personality are not simple, and I would be misinterpreted if the inference were drawn that nothing is needed except to keep our eyes open while we are counseling. It is true that vastly more can be learned in this way than has been generally recognized; and since it is an avenue to knowledge open to all pastors, it would be folly indeed if we do not use it to maximum advantage. This is quite different from implying that because we can learn from our doing, no learning is important which does not come out of our doing.

Not only has the knowledge of personality dynamics increased greatly in recent years but also the essentials have been set forth in various written works in understandable and not too technical language. The volumes of Karen Horney, Gordon Allport, Karl A. Menninger, Erich Fromm, Fritz Künkel, Franz Alexander, Frances G. Wickes, and a number of other writers have been especially successful in putting complex facts into more or less sound and understandable form.[13] The technical scientific writing, found mainly in journals rather than books along this line, is on the increase. It is becoming more exact all the time. The skeleton is taking on flesh.

LEARNING FROM CLINICAL WORK

WE have already discussed what the day by day experiences of counseling may do to increase our knowledge of personality dynamics. Now a larger view of the nature of the problem is necessary before any answer can be meaningful.

Casual observers of the program of clinical pastoral training for theological students have sometimes been critical that some of these courses are conducted in mental hospitals. "We can understand," they say, "having such courses in a general hospital, for a pastor clearly has to deal with sick people all his life. But if he gets the mental hospital experience, he will have a warped view and will probably try to treat his parishioners as cases." Such a view assumes that the purpose of training in a general hospital is solely to teach how to deal with sick people. Quite properly, the clinical training movement denies that the purpose is so narrow.[14] It asserts that what is needed by the student is contact with people under those conditions best designed to teach him how to help them as a minister.

When a hospital is chosen as a center, the chief reasons are these. First, people can be seen more frequently than is usually true in a parish; thus there can be more contacts in the same amount of time. Second, people in a hospital are confronting difficulties; and if the student wants to learn how to help, he can learn much by understanding people at such points of difficulty as tend to make them open to new resources. Third, the supervision of training in a hospital is easier. And fourth, the student sees plainly that the pastor is not the only professional who can help people, that he needs to co-operate and work with the physician, the nurse, and all the others who come with various skills to aid persons in need.

These points are also, though not necessarily in the same proportion, true of the mental hospital, with one addition. Even patients in a general hospital tend to bring into the open feelings and emotions which might not be expressed in the routine course of events. In the mental hospital there is a sense in which the "psychic skeleton" is laid bare.[15] Or, to use another metaphor, the structure or framework of the building can often be seen in a mental hospital, whereas this is difficult to see if the complete building stands before us. All analogies have limitations, and this one is no exception. But if the depths and the heights of which human nature is capable have the close interrelationship which most theologians believe, there is an obvious point in observing one place in society where certain types of depths are accessible to view. If this were all one saw, or if there were no help from the pastor's point of view in interpreting what was seen, then training in a mental hospital might have questionable value for the clergy. But clinical pastoral training is supervised. Furthermore it is plainly not all the pastor needs to do a good job in helping people—which makes it no less important.

For what can make itself so indelibly plain to a pastor in the mental hospital is the dynamic importance of certain processes of personality which, though he might otherwise have acknowledged them to exist, would probably have been relegated by him to positions of secondary significance. A certain theological student, whom we shall call Clarence, was an attractive, outgoing, but still immature second-year student in a theological seminary. He was intelligent, but rarely used his full capacities because he found his charm could let him get by. One could imagine he was earmarked for a fashionable suburb in a few years. He had led a protected suburban life in a moderately happy home, and had had almost no first-hand contact with the grimy side of life. His good brains had told him the mental hospital training could be valuable to him, and in his attitude was a combination of fear of what he would see in the hospital and a fascination with what he expected would be bizarre.

At this training center each student, following an initial period of orientation and then duty as an attendant, was assigned several patients—with the co-operation and approval of the physician in charge, of course. Depending upon the need of the particular patient, the student would chat with him on the ward, take him for a walk and a breath of fresh air, take him outside to play in an informal ball game, or do anything else which might help meet the obvious human need of the patient for which the regular hospital services made no provision. Thus the patient got help—a walk outside once a day being a pleasant relief from the ward—and the student could hear whatever the patient chose to say, learning from it what he could.

Among the five patients assigned to Clarence was one considered by the doctors as having a poor prognosis.[16] Like the student, this patient was a young man, handsome and with a good deal of superficial charm. Most of the time he could engage in social conversation with convincing ease. But his thought forms always had a bit of a slant. They came out of his private fantasy. Despite the frequent reference to important things he was someday going to do, there was never any reference to what might be done now to lead to those things. Despite appearances, therefore, this patient was deeply withdrawn and going downhill rather rapidly.

The second patient was mute. He would walk, help take care of his own toilet needs when led into the bathroom, but that was the extent of his activity. He never uttered a word, would not make any motion to eat or feed himself and had to be tube fed, never gave the slightest sign that he heard or understood anything that was said to him. He had been in this condition for about two months before Clarence arrived.

When Clarence saw the first patient, he wrote a glowing account of the contact. Here was a young man of great promise. Perhaps he had once belonged in the mental hospital—Clarence conceded that he had probably not been railroaded in—but his deviation from normal health was very slight. During almost all their conversation it was just as if Clarence had been talking with a college chum; only now and then did something bizarre enter the conversation. And the patient had a lot of charm; he knew how to hold a conversation; he was nice looking. Perhaps what he needed was a friend to whom he could talk, and in short time he ought to be out in the world, getting ahead with his college work.

But when he saw Silent Sam, Clarence's report was all questions. What could he learn from a fellow who never opened his mouth? He had taken the patient out for a walk, but he had to nudge him to get him to go through the doors, and there had not been the slightest indication that there was any communication. He had felt embarrassed, Clarence said. At first he had thought if he kept talking of things, pointing out objects of interest and such, that he might get some kind of response. But nothing happened. When the walk was half over, Clarence said he could not stick it any longer, and he stopped talking except for directions on getting through doors.

A few weeks later Clarence turned in his final reports on contacts with the two patients. He had, he reported, been dead wrong in both cases. The mute patient, with whom spending a few minutes was a chore, had suddenly become himself again. He ate, looked after himself in all respects, conducted perfectly normal conversations, and—to Clarence's amazement—recalled to the last detail everything that had happened during the period of silence and negativism. The patient was immensely grateful for what Clarence had done for him, the walks outside which had broken the monotony, and the friendly chatter. Clarence was still further astonished when the doctor in charge told him his friendly interest had probably helped pull the patient out sooner than would have been true otherwise.

But it was the other patient who really shook Clarence's confidence in his own judgment. The rapid change which Clarence had expected had not taken place. He talked just as he had when Clarence first met him. And now Clarence saw that the little snatches of bizarre conversation were not set off by themselves as he had first supposed, but were part and parcel of a complete delusional system. He saw that the vestiges of the patient's charm and conversational ability were not, as he had first judged, positive and constructive in character but were defenses used to rationalize his drifting and withdrawal from the social world into the world of fantasy.

Clarence was shaken. He had been wrong in both directions. But since he had a good teacher, he made these miscalculations count in the long run. He really learned from them. He saw something of the dynamics operating in the lives of his two patients and that his initial judgments, while understandable, had been based on observations of the wrong things.

In one case he saw that his own valuation of charm and ease of social conversation had blinded him to the dynamic fact that this may be spontaneous and genuine and creative on the one hand or reactive and concealing on the other hand. He could never again be guilty of approving or disapproving a particular act of behavior solely on external grounds, without any knowledge of what it meant to the person concerned. If a parishioner later says to him, "I just can't feel that I am really loved and wanted," he will not assume this to be an irreducible datum requiring no further explanation. He will know that this may be, in Karen Horney's words, evidence of a "neurotic need for affection," that is, a kind of compulsive demand for affection in an unconditional fashion, which is impossible of realization unless insight removes the compulsive character of the demand. Or it may be, on the other hand, evidence that the person has patiently endured an unloving spouse for a considerable length of time.[17] It will require further observation to show what this means. But Clarence will know clearly that there is a radical difference between the two, and will have some idea of how to look for the differentiating factors.

When Clarence deals later with a parishioner who feels disturbed after just getting an advancement in his work and a raise in salary, he will have some idea of what may have happened inside this man, and not merely consider it queer that the merited advancement brings more anxiety than satisfaction. For he will know that whatever the individual factors producing the condition in this parishioner's background, the man feels that he is of value only in what he does, and not inherently. Therefore a promotion not only changes old patterns in which he had got by but also increases the chances for him to make errors and hence to be of no value.

Clarence will see immediately the distinction which Karen Horney makes between the "neurotic need for power, prestige or possessions" and the natural need to develop a sense of physical and mental strength or capacity, to be reasonably well thought of by other people, and to work toward acquisition of such possessions as contribute to the enjoyment of life by oneself and family.[18]

Through association with the second patient, Silent Sam, Clarence has learned a good deal about human communication and interpersonal relationships. Being on the outgoing side himself, he will naturally find it harder all his life to get close to shy people. But he now possesses a clue he never had before: that shyness can mean many different things. On the one hand it may be a thoroughly normal response of the person who does not feel that human communication is to be understood in back-slapping terms. On the other hand it may be, even in extreme cases such as Sam, an enforced withdrawal because experiences have led the person to feel that no one will value him if he is not extrovert, and unable to take that he has retreated into shyness. It is as if he said, "I want human relations intensely; but since I apparently can't have them except on a basis which is impossible to me, then I won't want them. From now on I *don't* want them."

When Clarence takes this knowledge into the pastoral situation, he can be vastly more effective in working with the shy people, judging his success in proportion as they are less shy with him. He will be less tempted to urge them into activity for activity's sake and more inclined to help them find such activity as really appeals to them. He will not act as if all shyness were something to be ashamed of, for he will distinguish the various meanings that the shyness may have. He may even think twice before he says something when he realizes that some silent ones may treasure up for months every detail without his being aware of it. In contrast he may learn that in evaluating his sermons and other verbal performances it is unwise to depend solely on the praise or criticism given them by the extroverts who speak right out.

We have been considering some important aspects of dynamic psychological understanding which may emerge from clinical pastoral training, and have suggested how they affect the viewpoint and insight of the pastor in his counseling and other personal relationships with parishioners. This is not to say that clinical training is the only avenue to such knowledge, though it is an important one. Wherever the knowledge comes from, however, if it is true knowledge, it can be useful in the pastor's counseling.

DYNAMIC PSYCHOLOGY IN COUNSELING

TO be more systematic, the following seem to be among the most important conclusions now generally recognized in dynamic psychology which have clear implications for the pastor's counseling.

1. *All conduct has meaning.*[19] No bit of behavior is merely capricious. Seemingly we all accept this; yet how often we are tempted to act as if it were not true. For example, here is a young college student who has come to the college chaplain to talk about his inability to concentrate when studying:

STUDENT: So it just seems as though every time I really started to crack a book, my mind wandered off to the Saturday night dance or something like that.
PASTOR: Do you think your study habits might be at fault?

STUDENT: What do you mean?

PASTOR: Well, I was wondering if you'd ever read a book on study habits. You know, some people have just never learned the mechanics of how to study.

STUDENT: I see. Yes, I did read a book like that some time ago, but it didn't seem to help. I tried underlining, and repeating the ideas to myself after I'd read a paragraph, and a lot of other things. But that kind of thing doesn't seem to help very much. I think if I could just get the hang of it once, I'd be O. K. from there on.

PASTOR: What about your hours of study?

STUDENT: I think I've set those pretty well. But if I could just find the right combination, I think it would all click.

PASTOR: Are you alone when you study?

The pastor can keep on throwing out suggestions for hours, and he still will fail to reach the vital fact because his assumptions are wrong. He is assuming that there is some detail the student has overlooked, and if that can be captured, everything will be all right. He refuses to face the possibility that the student's conduct has meaning as an expression of the student himself.

A woman in her thirties has become increasingly worried at her inability to say No to any man who makes her a sexual proposition. When she consults with a pastor she says, "I know it's wrong, and I know I don't want to do this, but I just can't seem to say No." As a matter of fact, only part of her "knows" that she doesn't want to be promiscuous; the other part of her does want to, and if she does not know both parts, she does not know herself. If the pastor tries to whip up her will, strengthen her resolution to change her behavior without changing her understanding of the conflicting forces within her, at best but a temporary victory can be won.

It is human to want to eat our cake and have it too, to want to believe that the "troublesome habit" can be changed without changing ourselves. Thus the alcoholic knows exactly how he wants to be cured. He wants to become a "normal drinker." The person who feels unloved knows exactly what he wants. He wants unconditional love, love which asks nothing of him in return and which is therefore not love but exploitation. The student wants to know how to concentrate without any changing of what he really is, as if a magic formula would turn the trick.

But all of this denies that conduct has meaning, that no behavior is capricious. Conduct has meaning, and personality—despite conflicts—is all of a piece. This is so obviously important for counseling that the implications state themselves. Instead of saying that a pastor should not be shocked or surprised by anything that comes to light, we may better say that if he knows all conduct has meaning, however bizarre it may appear on the surface, the mere appearance of the bizarre, whether we understand its meaning or not, cannot shock or surprise us. For we take it for granted there is meaning there. Similarly instead of saying, "You can't get anywhere by whipping up a man's will power," we may see that any desire, however noble, which does not represent the free and full concurrence of the whole personality cannot effectively take control. We are then protected from agreeing that a person does know all about himself and still cannot do what he wants to do. For if he can't, then he doesn't. All conduct has meaning.

2. *The meaning of conduct can be understood only if we look both at conscious awareness and at the deeper levels which influence personality and affect its acts, but which are not ordinarily recognized in consciousness.*[20] In other words, conduct has meaning only if seen in the light of both conscious and unconscious, or subsurface, aspects of personality. There has been a good deal of quibbling about the word "unconscious" as used by Freud, and it has defects etymologically. But the dynamic facts which Freud presented are what matter, and these are that there are moving and vital parts or aspects of the personality ordinarily not in consciousness which nevertheless influence conduct, including thought. Only through recognizing this to be a fact can we really believe that all conduct has meaning.

A student on his way to see the pastor goes by the library and notices that it is closed. This barely crosses his path of observation, and he notes the fact but casually. When he enters the study, he is whistling, and the pastor comments that he must be happy. Yes, he feels good, he says, but he doesn't know why.

They are discussing the student's personal problems; he has been on the surface a very good boy, always doing what was expected of him, seemingly on good terms with people. But recently he has felt anxious and has been slipping in his studies. In their conversation they return to the feeling of happiness when he entered the room.

STUDENT: I wonder why I had that feeling. I can't think of anything that happened while I was coming over here, and I remember I didn't feel that way when I left home.
PASTOR: You came the shortest way?
STUDENT: No, I came around past the library. That's the only thing I can remember—that the library was closed. I don't know why; I thought it was open today.

PASTOR: Did anything go across your mind when you noted the library was closed?
STUDENT: Why, yes, it did. It just flashed in my mind and was gone. I thought to myself: "Good, now no one can get any books out today and get ahead of me in my studies." Gee, and that made me happy.
PASTOR: It looks as though it took the disadvantage of others to produce happiness in you. Maybe we'd better look at that.
STUDENT: I guess we'd better.

From the level only of conscious intentions, this feeling of happiness on the student's part makes no sense. But when the new dimension is added, it makes plenty of sense. Actually this student is so full of fear that he can maintain the façade of good will toward all men only by strong efforts; none of it comes spontaneously. But he secretly and unconsciously welcomes anything which produces disadvantage for his fellows—who are really his competitors, not companions— so long as he does not have to take the responsibility of being the producer. He does not know this consciously, and only in the understanding counseling relationship can he put two and two together and face the fact. Once he does that, there is an excellent chance that he can clear it all up.

The literature of dynamic psychology, especially of psychiatry and psychoanalysis, is full of illustrations of this type.[21] Indeed one might almost say that the development of such psychology has come about through the building up of progressively relevant and effective theories to account for the observed phenomena. With the assumption that all such conduct has meaning, the problem is to discover that meaning, to disclose the connections that are assumed to exist. And the attempts are increasingly successful. If one meets some clearly fanciful theories from time to time in his reading, he should recollect that it is natural for poor as well as good minds to look at a subject so promising as this, and not conclude from one fanciful theory that all theories must be fanciful.

When considering the importance of taking the unconscious dimension into account, it is natural and often useful to seek out the bizarre or dramatic and show that it makes sense if we understand the meaning. For if the strange can be explained, how much easier to account for the familiar. There is a danger in this process nevertheless, for the uninitiated reader, meeting constantly that which is bizarre, may improperly conclude that dynamic psychology is concerned only with the queer, the abnormal, the recondite, and the esoteric. It is well to emphasize, therefore, that dynamic psychology can do just as much to illuminate the familiar as the unfamiliar. In fact it has sometimes been more useful in correcting our views about behavior whose meaning we were certain we understood because it was so familiar than it has been in explaining bizarre behavior.

3. *Personality growth proceeds through the constructive handling of conflict, not through the absence of conflict.*[22] This sounds reasonable, and we tend to accept it in the abstract, but we belie it in many concrete ways. Here, for example, is a lawyer who has been going through a difficult domestic situation. The most casual observer senses that it must be very difficult to have to live with such a wife as the lawyer has. For years the lawyer has struggled with the situation, doing what he could to meet any demands of his wife, which could, by any stretch of the imagination, be considered legitimate. But the situation has become worse, not better. Since he faces the double duty, as he sees it, of appeasing his wife and of feeling responsibility for the whole thing to the degree that his appeasement is unsuccessful, he is in a vicious circle. He eventually finds himself tense and anxious, sleepless, and halfhearted in his work and other activities.

The suggestion is made that he might at least improve his own peace of mind by going over the whole situation with a good psychotherapist. The lawyer is horrified at the thought. "I just couldn't bring myself to do this," he says. Logically he would have nothing to lose and much to gain. Psychologically he might have much to lose. For he might discover that the Herculean appeasement efforts have been but shadowboxing with himself; that actually he has been proceeding on the assumption that the way to deal with inner conflict is to deny it, keep up the front, be courageous, in other words do anything except face the reality of the conflict and seek to find a constructive way out—let the chips fall where they may. He condemns himself unnecessarily to permanent unhappiness, with no resultant compensation to his wife or to the maintenance of their family situation. His failure to seek help is much more likely to disrupt the family than would be anything at all he discovered through therapy.

Why, if we believe that conflict is a permanent part of life and is fruitful if we can find constructive approaches to it, do we have static views of heaven or any other kind of paradise? The truth is that this is one of the easiest points in dynamic psychology to see in general and one of the most difficult to believe in particular.

At least so long as we live in a complex society in which different and frequently conflicting claims are made upon us, so long is it inevitable that there will be inner conflicts which cannot be so much solved as resolved. What we shall require is not such a clear settling of issues that we never thereafter admit doubt but rather a basic direction in which we move and a method for constructive handling of specific conflicts as they arise. Dynamic psychology shows us that the various claims made upon us tend to become internalized as aspects of our personality; and in so far as these conflict in the world outside, they conflict also in the world inside. They may or may not have relationship to our biological needs or our essential human needs. Their mere presence as driving forces within us does not tell us their correspondence with truth or reality. The fact remains that they have a truth and a reality for us, and must be dealt with on that basis.[23]

Recent careful observation of young children suggests that their growth is through three observable recurrent phases.[24] A stage of equilibrium is reached; then this stage is broken up, and the child appears to slide backwards; then there is a new thrust, and a new stage of equilibrium is reached, with behavior at a more complex level than previously. This means that children's growth is through a process of recurrent equilibrium, with intermediary stages in which there is a kind of disorganization necessary if there is to be growth to new and more complex levels and not mere fixation at an old level. One might say that this shows growth to be a zigzag process rather than a straight-line-upward process. To illustrate, children at two years of age are, on the average, at a period of temporary equilibrium. They tend to be happy, play pleasantly by themselves, but like to have other children around while they are doing it. If they are to become social and learn to play *with* other children, the pattern of merely playing in the presence of other children must be broken up. Six months later, children usually tend to be more disorganized. They act as if they did not know what they wanted; they may not be happy playing by themselves with other children around but do not yet know how to play with other children. By the age of three, on the average, they are happy again, and enjoy a much higher social level of playing with other children. The apparent backsliding period is just as important to the process as are the two levels of equilibrium in which a new-found capacity remains until it is mastered.

There seems to be a sense in which all human growth is characterized by something of the same zigzag quality, though in adult years the mere fact of chronological age is not a determining feature, as it tends to be in childhood. The other major difference would seem to be that adults may arrest the process in any phase, something which is vastly more difficult for the child because the biological aspects of his growth impel him to change even though he might try to cling to an old pattern.

If an adult is to continue growth, he needs to have sufficient flexibility or resiliency that he is not tempted to stop completely at any point of equilibrium and say, "I shall never permit any change any more." On the other hand he is also becoming fixated if he refuses to halt momentarily at any of the points of equilibrium in order to collect his resources and hold discriminatingly to those which will continue to prove valuable while he prepares for change in those which will not be permanently helpful, as if to say, "Since I must change and move again, I cannot rest at all."

Broadly speaking, the basic attitude of a person toward growth and toward inner conflicts tends to be the same phenomenon. We can distinguish two major types of attitudes: on the one hand, those which tend to compromise by somehow denying that conflicting forces are at work which must be dealt with, or which tend to fixate at some stage in the growth process in the fashion suggested above; on the other hand, those which tend to face conflict and the elements in it and resolve it sufficiently that progressive movement is possible, or which alternately rest and move.[25]

Some investigators point to neurosis as an intermediate type of approach—a sort of psychological fence-sitting. As such it brings both suffering and satisfaction. For example, a person under the illusion that he is valued only in terms of external achievements may work like a beaver, because only through enormous production can he attain even a modicum of peace of mind. But in working hard, he gets no satisfaction from his work. He fears facing the conflict and the elements in it; yet he suffers so long as he does not. He is trying to eat his cake and have it too. And although he suffers, he has something which the "rigid-normal" person, who has become completely fixated at a self-satisfied level does not have—hope, or the feeling that somehow something better is possible than everlastingly unfruitful compromise.[26] So it is that one may gird his loins and welcome it when a neurotic trend in himself is recognized. His recognition did not put it there, for it was present already. He is not glad to be neurotic, as if recognition permitted him to become fixated there. But he looks on it exactly as we look on sin—the specific perception of its reality is to be welcomed, not shunned, in that it is a sign of hope of extrication or of salvation.[27]

These are but a few of the enormously important points in the dynamic psychology of inner conflict which have a clear bearing upon pastoral counseling. To see counseling as a process whereby people are aided to grow, in the sense here indicated, helps us to see more exactly the "bridge" function which counseling can perform. Problems are opportunities; suffering is not to be sought, but it is to be used as opportunity; the people alert enough to sense that something better is possible are more truly right than those who sit back complacently. Consideration of the real meaning of inner conflicts helps us to be more understanding, more clear, and more accessible to people through counseling.

4. *Other truths of dynamic psychology.* Space does not permit anything but a skeleton outline of some of the ways in which dynamic psychological understanding illuminates the aims, approaches, methods, and meaning of pastoral counseling. We may merely mention a few additional points without elaboration or illustration.

The "real person" is always more than the specialized aspects of the personality which have been consciously recognized and encouraged. Psychic health will always be greater when the aspects emphasized have not been too narrowly selected, or when through counseling or actual life experience perceptions are broadened to include a greater totality of one's experience.[28]

By proceeding on the assumption that the creative dynamic forces which can produce needed change are potentially present within the individual already and do not have to be "poured in," the only lasting results are achieved.

The most vital question about a person always is: In what fundamental direction is he moving? Is it compromise, concealment, fixation, projection; or is it, however small the achievement be in a quantitative sense, in the direction of growth through constructive dealing with conflict?[29]

There is a sense in which the life road of no two people is the same. There are basic temperamental differences and many differences on a distinctively human and social experience level. Unless the person accepts the necessity of discovering his own road—though he may need help—he may remain permanently sunk by inner conflict, whether recognized as such or not.[30]

The meaning of an event in a person's life can never be clear merely from study of the event itself, but through observation of its relation to his personality as a whole, to his character pattern. We can understand him only if we understand his frame of reference.

The character pattern is not a list of traits or an aggregate of anything, but an integrated conception of the direction a person is taking. The best indices to it are found in study of what he perceives and fails to perceive and what he really seeks, whether it is what he professes to seek or not.[31]

The character pattern has antecedents which are largely traceable, but the dynamic elements which are constantly at work in it are present now. Counseling, therefore, may or may not deal with the past history of the person. If it does, it is to illuminate still present dynamic patterns. If not, it is because those patterns become plain without much historical review.[32]

SUMMARY

IT is hardly possible to do more than skim the surface of dynamic psychology in one chapter. But all other chapters of this book try to show evidences of its use, though these are not always explicitly pointed out. There is value, however, in lifting our sights for one chapter and looking more or less systematically at the relation which dynamic psychology bears to pastoral counseling.

I have tried to show on the one hand that dynamic psychology is not merely something which we apply in counseling. It is also something we learn from counseling. A generalization gained from someone else, however valid and thoughtful, has still not been assimilated until we take opportunity to judge both its truth and importance from our own observations. And the leaders in the field of dynamic psychology would be the first to say that it is just such observations, seen and then reflected upon critically, which can continue to keep dynamic psychology dynamic.

On the other hand, it would be folly to ignore the tremendous importance of what is already known about the dynamics of human character. There are various ways of acquainting ourselves with and grasping the meaning of this knowledge, but, however acquired, some basic minimum is essential to even the least pretentious attempts at pastoral counseling. In this chapter an attempt has been made briefly to indicate some major points of clear pertinence to pastoral counseling.

The Pastoral Counseling Process

Chapter Four WE HAVE CONSIDERED THE WAYS OF DISCOVERING proper methods in pastoral counseling and the relation of our knowledge of psychological dynamics to counseling. We are now ready to correct this picture for the time dimension. It is as if we had examined the cross-section of a tree in some detail and are now to look at the tree in all its height. Or we are like the medical student who has studied the make-up of the body in the dissecting room and now examines the fourth dimension of time by seeing how the body works in living beings. The correction is vastly important, even though the knowledge gained previously is true. That is, the correction does not relate to an error of fact but to a merely partial point of view. Now the broader point of view will engage us.

Pastoral counseling is a process. It is to be viewed not merely as something we can examine by viewing the relationship between pastor and parishioner at any given moment of time but as what happens within that relationship over a time span.

Pastoral counseling, we recall, is the attempt by a pastor to help a parishioner help himself, granted that certain conditions are present. The counseling process is going on when the parishioner directly or indirectly requests help, realizes in some measure that something about the problem is within himself, has at least some desire to alter what is in himself in order to move toward a solution of the problem or situation, and understands that the pastor's job in the process is to help him help himself.

In later chapters we shall consider the precounseling pastoral work of the minister, which constitutes a good measure of his personal work. Roughly speaking, it involves his personal work with parishioners who have a problem, or face a difficult situation, but who have not requested help, or who do not realize that anything can be done by looking within themselves, or who have little or no desire as yet to alter anything within themselves, or who want the pastor to solve the problem for them. That is, much of the pastor's personal work is dealing with people who have not yet come to the point—either led by insight or driven by desperation—of realizing the conditions under which the pastoral counseling process itself could proceed.

In this chapter we shall consider the actual counseling of the pastor, with special reference to understanding it as a process that occurs over a time span. This means that we shall distinguish between counseling over a relatively brief span of time and counseling over a more extended period of time.

BRIEF COUNSELING

ALL the illustrations given in this volume so far have been about relatively brief processes in counseling.[1] As a rough and ready indicator we might say that seeing a parishioner two or three or six or perhaps up to a dozen times within a total period no longer than a few weeks could properly be called brief counseling. Seeing the person once a week for six weeks, or twice a week for four weeks, or every other week for ten weeks, and so on, would not be extended counseling.

For the most part, little needs to be said in addition to what previous chapters have pointed out to give the proper correction on brief counseling. At the end of this chapter we shall consider what does and does not distinguish brief from extended processes in pastoral counseling. But that can be done more easily after we have given attention to what is involved in the more extended processes.

There are two main and rather obvious reasons why most, if not all, the pastor's counseling work is of the brief type. The first is his limitation in time. In addition to pastoral work and pastoral counseling he has to conduct worship services and preach sermons, run an educational program, lead the social outreach of his church into the community, administer the business and group-work programs of the church, seek to evangelize those not in a church, and sponsor programs of missions. To the outsider the pastor's job often appears to be a hodgepodge of miscellany, because the organizing principle is not apparent to them. This will be discussed at length in Chapter VII. As a matter of fact the pastor's job is a unit, but it is like a diamond with several facets, or, better, like a horse with four legs. All the legs are necessary; all are a part of the same animal. The horse has a hard time if he tries to hobble along without using one of them, but he has an even harder time if he tries to locomote with but one leg.

Some pastors who have been especially successful both in their counseling itself and in integrating it as a part of their total ministry report that only rarely do they see a parishioner in a particular series

of counseling contacts more than four to six times, though at any particular period they may have one person whom they are seeing up
to a dozen times. Eight to twelve hours a week is probably near
the limit which the pastor of a medium or large-sized church is
usually able to devote to counseling if he is not to neglect his other
equally important duties. Some may do more. Many, in fact, do far
less. But the pastor who tries to spend thirty or forty hours a week
in counseling, unless he is one of several ministers in a large parish,
will either neglect most of the rest of his work or else endanger his
health through an eighty-hours-a-week schedule. Limitations of time,
then, usually suggest to the pastor that most of his counseling relationships be brief.

The second reason why most pastoral counseling should be confined to a relatively brief process is the pastor's limitations in training.[2] It may well be asked: If the pastor is not trained to do extended
counseling, how is it safe for him to do even brief counseling? Part
of the answer to that is that he has counseling thrust upon him, if he
is not so impossible as to warrant withdrawal from the ministry altogether. A second answer is that he does have at least some minimal
training if he has graduated from a good theological school, even
though he and we may consider it far from what it ought to be.

The third and most important reason is that some things happen
in extended counseling which do not generally occur in brief counseling. We shall consider some of these differences in the section
which follows. Here we merely note that the pastor's training does
not include the kind of guided experience which would make him
an expert in the more extended type of counseling, except in rare
instances. We may note that a few pastors have had such training
and do possess such expertness.[3] In those cases somewhat different
issues are involved, and these are not discussed here. But if it is true
that extended counseling tends to bring out more complex matters than does brief counseling, then it is clear that at least most pastors are wise not to get into water over their heads.

There seem to be three basic functions which brief counseling can
perform with different people. The first, something we always hope
for, is to enable the parishioner to "turn the corner" in reference to
his situation. Near the close of the third interview which a certain
pastor had with Mrs. John Keating concerning a possible divorce
from her husband, she said:

MRS. KEATING: I guess that's about the way it is. It would be so much
    easier to make a decision one way or the other if John ran around

with women, or got drunk, or did anything except what he does do—just withdraw himself. But it's helped a lot to talk this over with you.

PASTOR: If it would decide itself, things would be simpler.

MRS. KEATING: Yes. But of course I know I can't look for something magic to make the decision—or try to fix things up between us, either. Right now I don't know what I'm going to do. But I think I see that I've been goading John for a long time without realizing it. Maybe if I'm better in my approach to him for a time, it may make some difference.

PASTOR: If you saw some steps moving toward better understanding, you'd wait a while to make the decision?

MRS. KEATING: Yes, I would. Yes, I think I will see if what I've got here makes any difference. It's just possible it might make a lot.

We cannot be certain from this, but there is a chance that Mrs. Keating has turned her particular corner—even though we still do not know what her decision is going to be in relation to the particular problem which she brought to the pastor. She came to him not to discuss ways of getting along with her husband but because she had religious scruples about divorce, even from a man who she had decided was impossible. Now, there is a good chance that whether some increase in her insight and consequent effect upon her husband will have much influence or not, she will have a new perspective in which the whole question can be seen. She may have turned the corner.

Turning the corner means that the direction has been changed. Many of the problems that come to the pastor's attention are life-situation problems, that is, they come close to being statistically normal, in the sense that they are understandable if we know the person's background. They are then made worse because the point of view, which the person assumes is the only one he can take toward the situation, is narrow and inadequate. If he can turn the corner, clarify the conflicting forces involved, gain a bit of insight into why he feels as he does, then he has a new point of view or a new place on which to stand. Even brief counseling can often do just enough to bring a slightly new perspective, hence altering the approach to the situation and giving a chance for spontaneous successful handling of it by the parishioner. This is what we hope will be accomplished in most brief counseling.

But there are types of situations which, while they may contain the elements appropriate to counseling, are different from the turn-the-corner, or achievement of insight, type of counseling. These may be summed up under the phrase "supportive counseling." [4] This is what the pastor does when some heavy or catastrophic change has upset the parishioner's world. It is what happens in the early stages of bereavement, or when a business has crashed, or when a marital partner has been deserted. The pastor counsels because the elements of pastoral counseling are there. The person recognizes need; knows that in a measure he must deal with his own feelings and not merely with the external situation; realizes that someone else can help him, but that this is through helping him to help himself. But he does not mainly need insight or clarification—at least not now. What he does need is support, the assurance that he and his feelings are understood, that someone is truly standing by with him.

This might also be called "reactive-emotion counseling," for the situations are those in which emotion has been brought to the surface through the agency of some life event to which reaction is natural and expected. At first, supportive counseling is what is needed. Insight counseling may be appropriate later on, but not at first.

It can hardly be expected that brief counseling will make a significant dent on all situations. Properly carried out, it does either support or help turn the corner, more often than we used to believe was possible. But since many of the personal problems and inner conflicts with which the pastor will be called upon to deal are deeply rooted in a character pattern which started to grow malignant during the person's early life, we can hardly expect even a corner-turning in such cases after a few counseling contacts, however skillful the counseling.

What can brief counseling do in such situations? It can, as Hippocrates said medicine should do first and foremost, "do no harm." That is, it can take some care that it does not make the situation worse. Provided the principles and methods already discussed are consistently followed, and there is no coercive probing, only honest understanding of what the person is ready to discuss, it is but rarely that even brief counseling can do harm.[5] And if it does no harm— that is, if the parishioner can say something about his situation and how he feels, not becoming worse thereby but having the feeling that he is understood—then it is fair to say that something positive has happened. For a beginning has been made in the kind of process which is necessary if eventually he is to get hold of any deep-lying trouble. If he is no worse, he is then closer to being able to go over his difficulties with a depth psychotherapist if that opportunity is open to him. If it is not, then at least he knows that there is something he can do again if the inside pressure later on becomes too high—talk about some of it.[6]

A woman of middle age was in a hospital for surgery. The chaplain made a routine call on her, saw evidences of very high tension,
and through two or three brief calls prior to the operation helped
her by playing a supportive role. After the operation, when she was
plainly on the mend physically, she talked with him and was very
anxious to have him return as often as possible. However, all her
conversation—which became increasingly fluent—was general and
even vague so far as herself, her feelings, and her background were
concerned. The chaplain did not probe or press. On the day she left
the hospital she said to him:

PATIENT: You certainly have been a great help to me. Would you pray
with me again today before I go? I'm—well, I guess I'm a nervous
kind of person and—well, I was hoping you'd ask me questions and
all that. I thought maybe if you did I might be able to talk. But I
guess I'm glad you didn't. I—tell me, what can a person do when
they realize something is awfully wrong with them inside?
PASTOR: You mean when you're pulled in different directions inside?
PATIENT: Yes, and when you discover you've been pulled that way for
a long time without knowing what was happening.
PASTOR: And you'd like to get hold of those things so that you could
run them instead of their running you?
PATIENT: Yes, that's it. I really think if I could talk with someone—but
if I started I'd want to finish it. I was going to talk to you, but then
I knew I'd be leaving here.

The pastor then explained what psychotherapy was, that a good
therapist would not have any fixed length of time, etc. It is plain
that had the pastor probed, something more would have come out.
But it is an open question whether this would have done more
harm than good. In this instance his skillful handling led the way
to work by the patient with a good psychotherapist. It is worth noting that this pastor was more interested in seeing that the patient got
help than in helping her, and sometimes the two are not the same.[7]
In summary, brief counseling constitutes the great bulk of the
counseling work of the pastor. With some parishioners it attempts
to help the person turn the corner through insight and new understanding. In other cases it plays a supportive role. Even in those instances where the counseling never gets beyond oblique references,
it may indirectly be of help by making the person more ready for
expert help.

EXTENDED COUNSELING

THERE seem to be three ways in which extended counseling differs from brief counseling. All are based on the assumption that in more extended counseling the relationship between pastor and parishioner has deepened so that something constructive is happening—and that it has not dribbled off into negativism on the part of the parishioner.[8]

The first difference in extended counseling is that after a certain point the counselor can risk more by way of method if he is confident the relationship has been cemented. There is no magic about this. A child who is deeply certain his parents love him can take from them a lot of restraint and discipline which would produce inner turmoil on the part of a relatively unloved child. So in an extended counseling relationship, where the parishioner has become deeply convinced that the pastor is ready to understand anything, details of method become less important than a proper assessment of the state of the relationship. Ultimately, of course, this means assessment of the growing capacity of the person to face the totality of himself.

This is especially important in dealing with "patterns" of personality.[9] From our knowledge of dynamic psychology we recognize that a person who has become disturbed, for example, and sought help because he finds himself unable to make a certain vocational decision, in all probability has this as a part of a whole pattern of personality and is therefore unable to make decisions in many other areas of life. The other areas may, however, have been so dealt with that they present no immediate problem; hence he comes for help only on the vocational decision, believing that is his problem. Any good counselor will, of course, begin where the parishioner wants to begin. But the fact remains that since the difficulty is more pervasive and is a pattern of personality, not merely an area of tension, the parishioner would be much further along the road if he were able to recognize the pattern instead of merely "turning the corner" in relation to the vocational decision.

In the discussion of counseling methods we have seen how great a danger there is in the pastor's telling or even suggesting to the parishioner his idea of the pattern which is behind the problem. Imagine the consequences below, for instance:

MISS CASEY: Well, that's the story. There was no trouble at all about public speaking until I was almost eighteen, and I won all those debates. Then after that time I almost lost the debate to Mary

Conover, I just couldn't speak at all in public. It's got worse, so that if there are more than three or four people in a group I just can't open my mouth, even if I have practically memorized in advance what I want to say.

PASTOR: Surely this isn't confined to the field of speech.

MISS CASEY: Why, what do you mean?

PASTOR: You see those boats you have on your printed dress? You and I can look at those which are in the front. Now you know, and I suspect, that if you turned around, I would see the same kind of boats on the back of your dress as I now see on the front. There's a pattern. If you have had this kind of difficulty about speech, isn't it likely that if we turned you around to the back we would find the pattern in other areas of your life?

MISS CASEY: Well, perhaps so. Thank you very much, Dr. Jones. I'm afraid I've taken too much of your time.

No wonder she tries to get out fast. He has scared the wits out of her, though the full effect of this will not be apparent until she has left. The pastor has real psychological insight, but he uses it like a jack-in-the-box. Few brief counseling situations can create a relationship of such depth as to stand hammer blows like this.

Suppose, however, that the pastor has had extended counseling with Miss Casey, that they started with speech and then Miss Casey moved on to consider other areas of her life. At a certain point in the counseling she herself might put two and two together and say she thought there was a connection between her feelings over making a speech and her feelings about men. A little later she might say she felt it wasn't just her relationship to men; it was her relationship to people. She has started tracing the pattern. Suppose her conviction that the pastor really understands becomes very deep-seated. Then we can well imagine something like the following:

MISS CASEY: Funny how I could have been so good at speaking and getting along superficially with people and a lot of other things— and yet not know that I didn't really think I was any good—until I faced what seemed to be some real competition. Then it kind of blew up in my face. It was the speaking I worried about, but I can see it went all through my life.

PASTOR: In other words, you begin to see a pattern of your personality which ties together a lot of threads.

MISS CASEY: Yes, and I begin to see why I have had it and why I couldn't even begin to face it.

The pastor still does not jolt her, or moralize or generalize or make any of the other counseling errors discussed previously. But

—and here is the point—words and ideas from the counselor which could be disastrous in a brief relationship may be clarifying and helpful in an extended relationship. Indeed, the real test is accurately described not by speaking of brief and extended counseling but through accurately assessing the actual relationship. Nevertheless, experience shows that the time factor is a vital element.

Professional psychotherapists, who give their full time to extended counseling and psychotherapy, differ as to the degree to which they believe it safe and helpful to reveal patterns of personality to a patient if he does not, step by step in the therapeutic process, discover and set them forth himself.[10] They differ on many complex matters which are of interest to the special student. But in essence they seem to agree that what can be risked in the counseling situation depends on the character of the particular relationship, which in turn depends on the person's view of himself. And the time factor is one important element here.

The second difference in extended counseling is that, other things being equal, the longer the period, the deeper the material that tends to emerge. Whatever one's theoretical view of the unconscious, it is true that in extended counseling more and more private material tends to come out. A pastor once told of a man he did not know who sought an interview with him, and whose first words were, "My trouble is that I can't shoot quail." But the problem turned out to be very real. The gentleman, who had made a hobby of collecting shotguns, and who loved to roam the state forest and sight birds, was completely unable to pull the trigger when the season was on and he had his sight on a bird. The pastor reported that he was able to give only a minimum of help in this situation. And indeed, if the desire to kill and the still more powerful inhibition in regard to killing were as much in conflict as we might imagine, it seems unlikely that anything short of thoroughgoing extended therapy could do much about it. We would hardly expect our man to follow up the quail remark with, "Of course, I realize given the kind of father I had, the dominating old so and so, my inner eye really sees him across that gun sight every time I really start to pop a bird." Certainly not, because if that was the origin of the difficulty, and he could discuss it in that way, he wouldn't be lost between his viscera and his trigger finger. We may well expect that nothing short of extended counseling would have enabled him to see that his whole pattern of relationships with people and even with inanimate things was preoccupied with a precarious balance between feeling vengeful and denying to himself that he wished harm to anyone; that this pattern had real antecedents which are capable, in their outlines, of being traced; and that he would get well by tracing them with help.

This should suggest why he who would dip his hand deeply into the pot had better make sure he is wearing an asbestos glove. The deeper material requires special knowledge and skill in handling simply because it has been more deeply held back previously and therefore presents a greater threat to what the person has always considered to be the organizing center or supporting pillar of his life.[11] It is not dangerous because some of it is immoral. The maiden lady who finally confesses she has occupied half her daytime hours with sex fantasies may not be revealing something as deep as does the aggressive business man who finally brings forth repressed spiritual or aesthetic tendencies which he buried without ceremony during adolescence. It is not the moral or immoral quality of repressed material that requires special skill in handling it. It is the fact that the more deeply it has been repressed, the more it threatens the present organization of the personality—whatever its content may be. Clearly this is no field for amateurs, and such we pastors are —unless we have had the special training required to deal safely in such realms.

The third difference which extended counseling shows in contrast to brief counseling—always remembering that the focus of all three differences is the character of the relationship between pastor and parishioner—has to do with what the parishioner expects of the pastor. To put it in other words, the way in which the parishioner treats the pastor differs in extended counseling from what it is in brief counseling. Feelings of the parishioner which have been long and deeply repressed may tend to emerge in extended counseling, and may then be fastened temporarily on the pastor. Thus considerable hostility or affection or fear may be manifested. Even without illustration it is clear that some special training would be required in order to know what to do with these long-concealed emotions once they come into the open, and especially once they fasten themselves on the pastor himself.[12]

These three differences between brief and extended counseling, all tied up with the nature of the relationship, have been set forth not to encourage or discourage pastors in relation to extended counseling but to show precisely why extended counseling is not to be entered into lightly by anyone, pastors included. And yet there is no inherent reason why extended counseling could not be a part of a pastor's work—if he were trained, had the time, and did not in the process step out of his role as pastor. That is, extended counseling is not inherently foreign to the pastorship, but in a practical sense it is rarely wise or appropriate for most pastors to engage in it. We can, however, be helped in our brief counseling if we are clear on the ways in which it differs from extended counseling.

Brief and extended counseling are not two entirely different things; and yet there is a sense in which extended counseling is more than brief counseling elongated. We have tried to suggest in a general way the kind of change in the relationship that may, or should, occur in extended counseling. This produces, for all practical purposes, new qualitative problems after the fashion that has been indicated. Yet there is no sharp dividing line. What the pastor knows, therefore, about extended counseling may stand him in good stead in brief counseling. For there is no law that prevents a parishioner from getting mad at him in the fourth rather than the fifty-second contact, or that restrains another from identifying him with her long-dead father in the third interview.

Extended counseling is not more coercive, pushing, or directive than brief counseling. It is not necessarily more helpful to the parishioner than brief counseling, for that criterion depends on the nature and depth of the need, not upon the number of hours spent in counseling. If one parishioner turns the corner after six contacts, then he is on a new road, and help has been mediated. If another requires 145 hours to turn the corner, assuming the counselor has been effective, then the difference is a comment upon the depth of the need at the beginning.

SITUATIONS CALLING FOR EXTENDED COUNSELING

WHEN is the pastor justified in using, or when is he obligated to use, more extended methods in counseling? There would seem to be four types of situations in which he might be both justified and obligated.

First, when no other better trained therapist is available. Include whom we will, the number of trained professional psychotherapists in the United States is still small, and they are rarely to be found outside large cities. Furthermore they are now enjoying a landslide business, with people on their waiting lists. Often, until the supply increases and the distribution is wider, the pastor may find that he does not have access to such a person except perhaps for diagnosing roughly the degree of the difficulty—which it may be important to do even if the therapist does not have time to follow through on it.

There will also be occasions on which the pastor will be the only one with psychological access to the parishioner. The latter may resist the idea of a psychiatrist, or even a social worker or other counselor. This means that psychologically speaking a trained therapist is not at the moment available to the person.

If the pastor has carried on brief counseling with the parishioner and found the following factors in the situation, then he may be both justified in proceeding and obligated to proceed with further counseling:

1. When a therapist is not physically or psychologically available
2. When the counseling to date has not done harm
3. When the pastor has had enough training so that he will know at any point if it seems to be getting beyond his control or his training.

A second situation in which extended counseling may be done is when the pastor has had special training which qualifies him to do it, and when he is in a position where extended counseling will not compete with his other pastoral work. For example, a pastor with thorough training in extended counseling who is one of several ministers in a large church, and who is assigned to devote his time to counseling, may well do extended counseling as particular need suggests. Or such a pastor on the staff of a local council of churches who is charged with responsibility for counseling with persons referred by other pastors of the community may perform valuable service with some extended counseling. Or a well-trained mental hospital chaplain who may have psychological access to some patients the psychiatrists cannot reach, and who may have special skill in making contact with the hidden creative powers of the particular psychotic person, may engage in extended counseling. In other words, pastoral specialists may well exercise their specialty if they have been trained to do so.

The third situation in which the pastor may carry out extended counseling is in collaboration with professional therapists. This may be illustrated. James Naylor was an artistically inclined bachelor in his early twenties, an office worker and ardent church member. The church and its activities were almost a hobby with him. He began to have dreamy spells, occasionally gazing into space for several seconds even while someone was talking with him. His pastor noticed this, having been for some time a bit worried about Naylor, and invited him to his study for a chat. There the pastor, in whom Naylor had much confidence, told him that he had noticed this once or twice and thought the best way to do was ask him openly about it. Naylor said he had noticed himself doing it, and it had so scared him that he had not been able to bring himself even to mention it to the pastor. The pastor said he thought a thing like this should be looked at as we would look at a boil—it may heal itself, but it's a good thing to get expert guidance and make sure. With Naylor's full consent the pastor got in touch with a psychotherapist friend, whom Naylor then saw four or five times. He concluded that the trends in Naylor were not so malignant as might have been possible in view of the symptoms; and, further, he found it difficult to establish the proper relationship with Naylor, which the pastor already had. The psychiatrist recommended to the pastor that he carry on with Naylor, seeing him once a week and checking back with the psychotherapist once a month. This was done for over three months; then Naylor turned the corner. This presupposes some real skill and knowledge in the pastor. It also demonstrates a useful type of co-operation.

It is possible that a fourth situation should be added in which extended counseling might be done—the field of "spiritual direction," as the more priest-minded churchman calls it.[18] This need not imply the hearing of formal confession. Essentially it implies that a pastor or spiritual director acts as a kind of spiritual public-health man, aiding the person at chosen intervals to review and examine his spiritual life and helping in the application of therapy where that seems indicated. Such a relationship does not need to be sentimental or dependent, nor does it have to be directive, in the "tell them off" connotation. As one of the able spiritual directors of the Church of England puts it, the best way to direct spiritually is Don't.[14] In other words, the methods of counseling contained in this volume may and should be applied.

There is more to this suggestion than is apparent at first. We are to see our dentist twice a year, our doctor once or twice a year, to make sure things are all right, or if they are not, to catch the trouble while it is still young enough to be easily repaired. An analogy in the spiritual field makes a great deal of sense. Even though such a plan does not bear promise of sweeping the United States like wildfire, the pastor may find a parishioner from time to time for whom the kind of support it offers can make an enormous difference in his life.

Even so, such counseling might not be extended counseling—except in the sense that the person anticipates periodic return. In that sense it would differ from the brief counseling which is precipitated by a particular problem or situation or feeling, and in which the parishioner does not anticipate further counseling unless further problems present themselves.

As early as 1929, a Church of England priest, T. W. Pym, in a volume called *Spiritual Direction,* illustrated the method of spiritual direction with script interview material. The great temptation for the parson, he wrote, is to be dominant. Yet the mere assertion of our authority does no good. The priest is in a position where he is tempted to "dictate on matters of conduct and conscience." To the question of how to direct, the answer is Don't. "Normally the business of a director is to help people to help themselves, and to help them find God or find God more." [15]

He writes of two ways in which to handle a seeker of help, or enquirer. The first:

ENQUIRER: I think my greatest weakness is failure to concentrate in prayer. I find I'm so frightfully liable to wander in my thoughts.
ADVISER: You probably pray when you are too tired.
ENQUIRER: Yes, that must be it.
ADVISER: Well, choose another time. What about 6 P.M.?
ENQUIRER: Yes, I could manage a quarter of an hour then. Do you wish me to do that?
ADVISER: Yes, that would be better.

The second:

ENQUIRER: I find I'm so frightfully liable to have wandering thoughts when I'm trying to say my prayers.
ADVISER: Why do you think that is so? How does it happen?
ENQUIRER: Well, of course, I have to stop up working pretty late, and when I start going to bed I relax my effort and then seem unable to secure concentration again; I'm so tired.
ADVISER: I suppose we all find it harder to pray when we're very tired. Have you thought of a way out of the difficulty?
ENQUIRER: No, I thought you would help me with some suggestion.
ADVISER: I will, if you wish. But a suggestion of your own would be worth more to you than one from me.
ENQUIRER: Well, I suppose I might try and fit in some other time, a bit earlier.
ADVISER: That's not a bad idea. But what time could you choose?
ENQUIRER: Well, I might manage a quarter of an hour at 6 P.M.
ADVISER: Well, think it over. Don't decide in a hurry, but if you come to the conclusion that you could and should do that, then make up your mind to it and go through with it.

The difference which Pym is attempting to portray is clear to us and is in line with what we have attempted to state.

SUMMARY

PASTORAL counseling is a process, whether it last ten minutes or a hundred hours. The actual counseling begins, following the pre-counseling pastoral work, when the person recognizes a need, knows some of it is in himself, directly or indirectly seeks help in understanding it, and senses that the pastor's job is to help him help himself.

In aim, approach, and method the pastor proceeds as earlier chapters have indicated. Ordinarily he will not see a parishioner more than a few times at any one period. He will accept feelings as facts; understand, and convey his understanding; aid in clarifying conflicting feelings; help insights to be consolidated—all to the degree the parishioner is himself ready for counseling. But he will not make mechanical application of methods. He will not confuse understanding the parishioner with starting every sentence with "you." Nor will he conclude that the trick in counseling is merely never to introduce any ideas of his own. He will be concerned not with ideas as such but with their feeling content—what they mean to the parishioner. And he will not be interested in tricks of any kind.

He will find it helpful to study an interview record from time to time, for an interview has some thickness and is not merely a two-dimensional cross section. But he will keep his eye mainly on the nature of the relationship. If he has made what he later concludes was a bad error and no harm seems to have resulted, he tells himself truly that this is because the relationship was strong enough to sustain the error, not that his previous ideas of method were all wrong. He knows that the foundation of method is attitude and approach, that being accepting, understanding, receptive, nonmoralistic, and specific is more important than methodological details. He realizes that a firmly cemented relationship can stand a degree of directness which might shatter chances in a first or second interview. But by and large he will see that understanding concentration upon the parishioner's feelings about himself and his situation is the key to counseling of any duration with any person.

Chapter Five COUNSELING IS AN ACTIVITY, NOT A PROFESSION. It is a process of relationship between one who seeks and one who gives help, carried out as a more or less prominent, more or less time-consuming, aspect of the professional activities of the helper. What distinguishes all counseling from manipulative procedures is that the help required is of such nature as to imply initiative on the part of the person seeking help. If a man's appendix needs to be removed, the doctors give him an anesthetic before they go to work on him. But if he wants to know why he cannot make a decision, or how he can get over saying Yes to his wife all the time, or whether he should be a preacher or a plumber, manipulative measures will not do. He as a person must not only co-operate but also assume leadership.

The generic aim of counseling is new insight, with proof in action. That is, if a person is troubled about his situation or some aspect of it and seeks a helper through counseling, the end which all such professional helpers have in common is to aid the person to get a sufficiently clear view of his situation, with the conflicting trends and pulls and motives and ideals and desires, that he may then see his situation in a freer, clearer, more objective way and consequently be able to act in a similar new fashion. Beyond such a general statement the specific aims and assumptions of counselors may differ, and often do so. We shall later return to the differences.

Some may object to the definition of counseling as a process occurring between an individual and a helper and suggest that there is such a thing as family counseling and group counseling. It is true that the insights and knowledge and skill which have been developed through personal counseling are applicable in many ways to group situations.[1] And it is legitimate to call such activity group counseling if it serves anyone's strategic purpose to do so. But the ordinary connotation of the term counseling is, and with justification, the relationship of a person who seeks help and a helping person— even though the fruits of the help may be very influential upon a family or other group situation.

The development of counseling as we know it today did not be-gin by any particular professional group setting out to develop some thing which they thought of as counseling. It began when various professional groups, in seeking to help people solve the types of pre-sented problems which were supposed to be their specialty, stumbled upon the significance of that which we have come since to call coun-seling. Freud set out to find a way to cure hysteria, paranoia, and other types of symptoms which were commonly agreed, a half cen-tury ago, to be the province of the physician. The early social work-ers set out to give the greatest degree of efficiency in the use of public and private funds to help particular kinds of personal and family trouble.[3] The vocational group set out to place people in jobs where they would be most productive and happy.[4] The industrial counselors set out to make workers more productive.[5] And so on.

It may be worth noting that the rise of the various professions which now carry on counseling was not motivated initially by an unadulterated social concern for the welfare, happiness, and creative expression of the individual person. At first these groups were pro-tectors of society. Psychosis, poverty, or inefficient workmen were threats to certain group interests. Only later have we begun to see more clearly that a partial reversal of this position is necessary in a democratic society.[6] We do not believe men exist for the state or for the corporate society; neither do we believe that a frustrated or sick or destitute or puzzled man should be cured of his particular diffi-culty solely to prevent him from bothering his neighbors. Society has an interest in his welfare, for his own sake as well as for its sake. And the best protection of society is the best promotion of his in-terests for his sake.

When the various professional groups, each in its apparent field of expertness, came up against problems which could not be handled by manipulative methods, they turned with varying degrees of thoroughness to studying what lay behind the particular type of problem with which they were dealing. There were tremendously important leaps of imagination. When Adolf Meyer failed to find the causative clue to mental disorders in microscope slides, he turned to the study of "psychobiology," watching the function of the total human organism from both the psychological and the biological points of view.[7] When social case work failed to help a lot of people even though a perfectly logical plan had been worked out by the case worker, the workers stopped explaining it away through saying the family refused to co-operate and began to study why they would not, thus introducing marked changes in case-work method.[8]

When vocational placement experts found a man had skill and aptitude, but did very inefficient work, they came to realize that this might be due not only to inaccurate tests or the "cussedness" of human nature but also to attitudes and past experiences in the man himself.[9] When pediatricians found that the problems of babies were mostly the problems of mothers, and then discovered that telling a mother what attitudes she should have did not turn the trick, they moved after a time from public castigation of parents to study of what made parents misbehave.[10]

From these many points, which we now see to be converging, there was first preoccupation with the symptoms of a presented problem; second, a manipulative attempt to handle it without knowledge of the processes of its causation; third, an exploration into the processes of causation; and fourth, an application of the new causative knowledge as if it were the exclusive property of the group that had found it out. This is a thoroughly natural progression, and the fourth point is as understandable as the others. A child who learns to use a new word is quite uninterested in the number of times it appears in the Bible or Shakespeare or even a Donald Duck cartoon book. The fine distinction between the word as *his* new word and the word as a part of the social tradition which includes both word and child is entirely too academic to serve as the road along which his new discovery may run with enthusiasm.

After all, psychiatrists have learned what they know by studying what their teachers have called psychiatry. Social workers have learned what they know by examining something represented to them as social work. Educational counselors have acquired their knowledge by exploring what was probably called educational guidance or student personnel work. How could it be otherwise than that the more closely they reach to the true dynamics of the subject, the more they and the others should feel a greater degree of exclusive ownership?

If each group has developed a proprietary attitude toward the causative or background knowledge on which it operates, it is natural to expect that a similar attitude would emerge in therapeutic or other helping methods, and it has. One by one each group has developed a helping method increasingly eductive—drawing more and more of the solution to the situation out of the creative potentialities of the person needing help. Is it not natural also that this discovery should be regarded in a proprietary fashion, as it has been?

What has been said should not be interpreted as implying that there have been no differences in the degree to which various professional groups have penetrated various strata of truth. Some have reached much more deeply than others—and some have been much more proprietary than others. But in some measure all of us have shared the proprietary fallacy, both in understanding the causes of human conduct problems and in the therapeutic methods for helping people who have them.

Nor is it to be interpreted as suggesting that there are or should be no differences in the knowledge or technique which various professions should have. A social worker does well to have a little knowledge of the human kidney, but she would need vastly more if she were a surgeon removing an injured kidney. Her friend the surgeon had better have some comprehension of the difference between a patient who has come from a luxurious home and contented husband, and one who spends her days humoring a psychotic aunt and her nights defending herself against an alcoholic husband. But he would need a great deal more knowledge of social background if he were going to help her with her family affairs. The surgeon and the case worker—and all the others—have different fields of specialized knowledge, and herein lies the efficiency, actual or potential, of the modern world. But, whether the specialists know it or not, there is a body of knowledge and a body of skills which they have in common, which belongs to no one group as against another, which can help all in proportion as all recognize their mutual, and therefore nonproprietary, interest in it.[11]

Here is where counseling comes in. If the surgeon knows something about psychological dynamics and counseling method, he can help his patient as a whole more effectively than if he knows nothing of the matter. If the vocational counselor is alert to his client as a whole person, he may be able to do a first-class counseling job over and above the technical one of giving and interpreting tests. A similar point is true for all, including the pastor.

What professional groups do counseling? How deep and far does each go? How much of its time is devoted to counseling? What training does it provide in counseling? What is its point of view?

THE DEPTH THERAPISTS

WE begin with the professionals who spend the greatest amount of time with their patients, who dig most deeply into psychic and emotional life, who attempt to produce the most radical transformations of unsatisfactory patterns of personality. They might be called the vacuum-cleaner group of counselors, as against most of us who are sweepers, dusters, or perhaps on occasion dust blowers. Or, to change the metaphor, they are the surgeons of the psychic life, while the rest of us are first-aid men, or spot-out-of-eye-takers, or public-health workers who remove the cause of the diseased condition so that an operation is not necessary. At any rate they dig the deepest, which is sometimes also the highest.

There are several denominations of depth therapists, distinguished from one another in various degrees from very small to very large. The distinctions are not all of the same kind, however. Some differ on the type of training their practitioners must have; others, on their underlying philosophy; and still others, on their theory and practice of therapy itself. While it is not a very safe procedure to classify them, especially in a few words which are bound to be partly unfair to any particular group, it is highly desirable that the pastor have in mind some of the essential facts about the different groups. In presenting what seem to be major differences, however, it should also be emphasized that the more progressive groups are just now in the beginnings of a kind of ecumenical movement of their own. While the groups on the stand-pat side have shown few signs of deviating from orthodoxy, or at least of admitting deviations from orthodoxy, most of the others are moving toward ecumenicity. They recognize that there may be values in somewhat different approaches, and they are also increasingly impressed with the common core of either theory or practice, or both.

All the groups stem from Sigmund Freud in two senses. Freud was the first to disclose the possibilities in systematic exploration of the inner psychic life by methods that recognize the reality of the inner forces which influence personality but which do not operate in consciousness. Further, all the groups are first or second or third generation offshoots from Freud's original psychoanalytic movement.

The term "psychoanalysis" was for a time restricted to the group which continued to be the orthodox Freudian group, partly to distinguish it from the early splits made under the leadership of Alfred Adler, who spoke of individual psychology, Carl G. Jung, who founded analytical psychology, and Otto Rank, who was clever enough to avoid the creation of a system or a label.[12] During the twenties, when the greatest enemy of psychoanalysis was a faddish public interest in a badly distorted Freudianism, the movement had also to fight the "psychoanalysis free of charge" or "psychoanalysis in two lessons" quacks, from which we are still by no means free.

During the past few years there have been other splits from the orthodox stem, the major one being that initiated by a group under the leadership of Karen Horney about ten years ago.[13] In turn, a split from the Horney group joined forces with the William A. White Psychiatric Foundation and formed the Washington School of Psychiatry, under the leadership of Harry Stack Sullivan.[14]

The split into groups should not be taken lightly, or glossed over on the ground that psychologists should be able to put their house in order—any more than we can say that Protestants should have reformed Roman Catholicism instead of forming a new church, or Arminians should have acommodated their convictions to those of Calvinists, or Baptists and Episcopalians should find a common denominator instead of insisting on different forms of worship and church government. Significant differences are represented. The new groups are no more cults than the original Methodists were a cult. They may be more or less right or wrong, but they generally stand for important convictions.

Membership in the orthodox psychoanalytic societies in the United States is confined to medical doctors who have had certain training in addition to their medical education, including a personal psychoanalysis done by an accepted member of the group, psychiatric training and internship, and special courses in psychoanalysis in one of their own training centers.[15] The distinctive characteristics of this group are (1) medical training; (2) confining the concept of psychoanalysis to a long-continued therapeutic process rarely taking less than a year or two hundred hours; and (3) retention of the psychoanalyst's couch and compulsory free-association methods in therapy, together with certain other details of the original Freudian method. Some of these things are being modified in practice. For instance, many do therapy of shorter duration, without the couch, on a different schedule than an hour every day—but they may not call this procedure psychoanalysis. Recently the able group at the Chicago Institute for Psychoanalysis, under the leadership of Franz Alexander and Thomas M. French, have made large moves against the former specific orthodoxies and continue to retain the psychoanalytic label for their work.[16] Whether this will result in a new split from the orthodox group is not yet apparent, but it may well not do so, since the entire group has so far made more change in practice than it has acknowledged in theory.

The Adlerian group was originally an ideological protest against Freudian doctrine. Because it was based on relatively superficial premises, and such sound ideas as it had were later assimilated by other groups, it has not been perpetuated as an influential group. One generally hears about it as a contemporary force only from those without specific acquaintance with the historical development of the psychotherapeutic movement.

The Jungian group is a clear entity, standing apart in a sense not wholly unlike the pietistic groups of church history.[17] Unlike the Adlerian movement it was a basic revolt from the Freudianism of some thirty years ago, and was in a sense a philosophic rebellion rather than a methodological or technological protest. Like the pietists, the Jungians thought they could get along better by keeping to themselves; and, so long as the philosophy of mechanism dominated orthodox Freudianism, they may well have been right. To the outsider many points in theory and practice of psychotherapy now seem to be very similar to those found, for example, in the Horney group or the Sullivan group; but the Jungians have not demonstrated interest in the ecumenical possibilities—with, of course, individual exceptions.

Karen Horney did not intend to break from the orthodox psychoanalytic group but only to reform certain aspects of its theory and, later, its practice. Like many a prophet before her, however, she found that her insights conflicted with establishments, and a new group became inevitable.[18] The issues surrounding the subsequent split between the Horney group—the Association for the Advancement of Psychoanalysis—and the Sullivan group—the Washington School of Psychiatry, with headquarters both in Washington and New York—are obscure to the layman. In theory the groups are very similar. One point of difference is that the Horney group admits only medically trained persons to membership, while the Sullivan group admits a few nonmedical people of exceptional talent and training.

There are certain other "schools" or "groups" which practice long-term or depth psychotherapy, but none seems sufficiently important to receive consideration in a sketch of this brevity.[19] One group which is not organized should, however, be noted. This is the group of psychiatrists—physicians who have specialized in psychiatry and then taken psychiatric internship and residency—who in private psychiatric practice combine the short-term treatment of some patients with the long-term treatment of others. That is, they do long-term or depth therapy as they feel the diagnosis justifies need. But they do it without having had two of the elements which all the psychoanalytic groups feel are essential aspects of total training; namely, a personal analytic experience and practice in depth therapy under supervision. From the point of view of the analytic groups such men have not had adequate training in deep psychotherapy.

From the point of view of these men themselves such special training may be considered either unnecessary or harmful. To the casual
eye there seems to be a strong tendency for most such psychiatrists
eventually to take some special training in deep psychotherapy and
affiliate themselves with one of the analytic groups. Whatever laymen
may at times say, with justice, in criticism of physicians or of the
medical profession, we should not forget the devotion of most doctors to the exploration of and schooling in new methods and approaches if these demonstrably produce more therapeutic results.

One of the questions depth therapists face all the time, with the
form changing from year to year, is to what degree the practice of
deep psychotherapy is a medical matter.[20] Nearly all would agree that
it is not a medical matter in the sense that any physician, or indeed
any psychiatrist, is automatically qualified to practice it. But should
anyone practice it, even if he has had the very best training in depth
psychotherapy itself, if he has not had medical training? The groups
differ on this point. One of the chief arguments formerly used in
confining this to physicians was that without medical training the
therapist would be unable to recognize medical complications.
Since all good nonmedical depth therapists now are careful to keep
in close liaison with a physician, some of the weight from this conten-
tion has been lifted.[21]

Since the solution to this issue may eventually have much significance for the public interest, we may consider it a little further.
Suppose that Mrs. Sadie Boling, aged forty-three, married and the
mother of two children in their later teens, realizes one day that a
stiffness has been growing in her arm. She is worried, but attributes
it to lifting a suitcase in the attic last week and decides to wait a day
or two to see if the soreness will subside. Instead it becomes worse.
So Mrs. Boling goes to her doctor. He cannot find any organic condition to account for the stiffness and soreness, and tells her so carefully in words she can understand. He suggests a psychiatric examination, but she thinks of mental hospitals, and declines. Her doctor
prescribes packs as a palliative. Mrs. Boling tries the packs, preparing them herself. Her husband, as usual, is at his office working in the
evening and so is unavailable to assist. The packs seem to help a
little, but the stiffness progresses. After several more days Mrs. Boling,
red-eyed from weeping, telephones her doctor again. She agrees to
see the psychiatrist.

The psychiatrist at the clinic has an interview with Mrs. Boling
and makes an appointment for an additional contact. But he sees
that the root of the difficulty goes much more deeply than he can

deal with in a few contacts, so he explains the meaning of depth therapy to Mrs. Boling. Talking with the psychiatrist has helped a little, and she decides she will wait and see. After a few days of partial relief the soreness becomes worse than ever. She returns to see the psychiatrist. He does not himself practice long-term therapy, but he knows how to refer. When he discovers she is willing to have therapy of a longer-term type and can pay a reasonable amount for it, he tries out his medical therapists one by one. All are busy, with their time filled to capacity—the usual condition in recent years.

The psychiatrist ponders. He knows the medical complication in this case to be purely symptomatic; that is, if good psychological therapy is given, the physical difficulty will disappear. The treatment required has nothing to do with surgery, medical apparatus, drugs, and the like. Furthermore, here is a woman ready for extended therapy. If she can wait a few months or a year, perhaps a place can be found for her on the docket of one of the medical therapists. But that waiting is dangerous; for a functional condition of this kind, he knows, may over a period of time produce structural change as well, so that at some later time, even if the psychological causes of this disorder are dealt with satisfactorily, the structural and organic condition might at least in part remain.[22] So time is a factor.

He thinks of a certain psychologist who does extended therapy but whose training in therapy itself is unexceptionable. He privately considers this man to have deeper knowledge and skill than many of the medically trained psychotherapists. Because of certain factors involving a change of residence, he knows the psychologist still has some free hours. Shall he refer Mrs. Boling there?

This is not the whole issue, but it typifies the focus of it. As the well-trained psychologists would say, can the public or the medical profession run the risk of having Mrs. Boling's functional arm difficulty become structural merely to protect the abstract principle that no one can do extended psychotherapy except a physician? And, once Mrs. Boling's difficulty has been adequately diagnosed, what is there in its treatment which is distinctively medical? If she wrung her hands and worried about the sins committed in her adolescence, would the physcian consider her a medical problem if she had no organic difficulties? Probably not. But in that event how does Mrs. Boling differ? Patently her physical trouble is but a symptom of something else. And doctors are not doctors when they fail to call a symptom a symptom. The case, to the outsider, seems strong.[23]

At any rate more people trained in psychology but not in medicine are doing extended therapy year by year. At first these were persons who, many of them trained in academic psychology of some years ago, were dissatisfied with confinement to the research and teaching and testing roles which were as close as they could then respectably approach to therapy. They sought such knowledge and training as they could get from the depth therapy groups, finding various degrees of help available. Some had hoped to get around the basic question by doing counseling or psychotherapy in a college, for example, or at least on a salary rather than a fee basis. And some did just that, bringing fruitful insights into academic psychology. Others took the plunge and went into consulting practice on a fee basis.

Meanwhile the psychology departments in the universities became more interested in personality and, eventually, in counseling and psychotherapy.[24] In the past few years counseling has become a major concern of a large number of psychologists, and the past president of the American Psychological Association, Carl R. Rogers, has had more to do with the development of this trend among psychologists than anyone else. The psychological group may be differentiated in several respects from what we have called the depth therapists. It has engaged in objective research and explored the values of various kinds of tests in revealing personality patterns as well as skills and aptitudes.[25] Perhaps it would not like to see itself mentioned in a section on depth therapy. But it is worth mentioning because even though it rarely does extended therapy and always makes references to psychiatrists as needed, there is something so significant in its research method that this is bound eventually to have a wholesome effect upon depth as well as other psychotherapy.

Depth therapy may be compared with surgery in more ways than one. For example, the untutored eye cannot conclude from a mere observation of external symptoms whether or not a certain procedure is necessary in a particular situation. But, as the previous chapter has suggested, when a pastor has engaged competently in brief counseling and yet discovered that no change has occurred, he may conclude that in all probability only a deeper type of therapy can be successful. This is merely a rule of thumb, but it has the fingerprints of truth on it.

When a pastor has decided that a particular person might profit from deep psychotherapy, what kind of therapist will he want? He will be concerned not only that the therapy be competent but also that the parishioner's religion, so far as it is constructive, be met by the therapist on that basis, and not treated as if all religion were negative.[26] This he has a right to expect. If he is fortunate enough to find such a therapist who also has a positive Christian point of view, he can be still more grateful for that. There are an increasing number of these therapists around.

My observation is that from the pastor's point of view there is no school or group of depth therapists mentioned herein which does not have at least a few representatives to whom the pastor may with considerable confidence refer parishioners. It must be admitted that the proportion is much higher in the progressive psychoanalytic groups than in the orthodox. It must also be admitted that the pastor who gets a parishioner successfully in contact with a Jungian analyst does well to be prepared for the possibility of seeing the person at least during a certain stage treat Jungianism as a philosophy of life rather than a therapy.[27] And if he refers to a nonmedical therapist, however well trained, some of his orthodox medical friends may not approve. But as the ecumenical trends in therapy increase, and as there is an increase in the number of therapists available, some of the now difficult questions should become easier to answer.

The pastor has no right to expect a depth therapist to do his work for him. It is not the therapist's business to put religion into a person or to get him interested in religion. What the pastor legitimately can expect of the therapist is that he deal with religion as a fact of life, helping the patient to disentangle his neurotic or destructive religious ideas and feelings from those which are positive and healthy, showing him how to release himself from those aspects of his religion which are compulsive, obscurantist, moralistic, or otherwise warped and to become free to act according to the insights of those other trends in his religion which are creative, sustaining, integrative, and healthy. It is to help him move from a basis on which he can understand his religion at worst as hatred, or at best as ambivalence, to a foundation upon which a religion of love becomes genuinely possible. If the psychotherapist can help his patient get his religious potentiality to that point, then it is the pastor's job from there on out.

THE STRATEGIC-PROBLEM THERAPISTS

IF the group which has just been described is to be known as depth therapists, what can we call those persons who carry out counseling or psychological therapy which does not have the characteristics we have called "deep"? We can hardly call them "surface therapists." But there is something which several professional groups have in common. They do counseling as a more or less important part of their job, yet their counseling is different from the work of depth therapists. For each of these groups there is some field of knowledge in which they are expert, and this field has an important function in relation to their counseling—though the counseling is always more than the field of expert knowledge.

The term "strategic-problem therapists," or "strategic-problem counselors," may be used to describe these groups collectively. That is, they are known to the public chiefly through the specialized field of knowledge with which they deal. From the point of view of each as a counselor this specialized area represents his channel of access to the person.

If what worries someone is the feeling that he may be maladjusted in his job, he is likely to look for a vocational counselor. In addition to—and indeed as a prerequisite of—aiding the man in the area of the presented problem, the vocational counselor, if well trained, will do general counseling; that is, he will help the person with *any* areas of his life and personality which the person wants to discuss and understand more clearly. Thus vocational doubt would be the strategic problem by which the counselor is able to move in the direction of helping the person as a whole. Hence the vocational counselor is a strategic-problem counselor, as are all the others who will be considered here.

Some *psychiatrists* belong in this group. A psychiatrist is a physician who has specialized in mental and emotional illnesses and difficulties. He may do depth therapy, or he may not. If he does not, then he is a strategic-problem therapist in regard to those patients with whom he carries out brief psychotherapy. They may tend to come to him if they fear they are "going crazy," or if they have physical symptoms for which their general physician can find no organic cause, or because they think the problem is sexual and they believe the psychiatrist is an expert on sex.[28] The psychiatrist, like every other good counselor, must be sensitive to the needs and patterns of the personality as a whole, not merely to those areas in which he has expert knowledge. But if there is, for example, a sex problem involving the attitudes and emotions of the patient, the psychiatrist will not conclude that this is merely a "sex problem" and deal with it as if sex were something apart from the whole personality. Instead he will realize that the sex problem is one aspect of a total personality problem. He will also realize it is his avenue of access to the total person. In this sense the psychiatrist in other than depth therapy is a strategic-problem therapist in the same sense as the others to be mentioned below.

The *psychologists* who do counseling but not depth therapy are also strategic-problem therapists. Their channel may be similar to the psychiatrists', or it may be through tests of ability or interest or personality. The *vocational counselors,* most of whom are psychologists by profession, are explained by their very name.[29] It is important to realize that all these groups have both a special field of expertness and a channel of access to the personality as a whole.

The *educational counselors* have various subtitles conferred upon them, depending on their specific means of access within the educational system.[30] There are the personnel people, the guidance group, the student-health group, the religious-counseling group, and others. All have in common an expertness in dealing with persons of a certain age group in some kind of formal educational setting. Depending on how they are placed in the school system, and on what the students believe to be the function of each in terms of expertness, they find their respective channels of access to the students.

This would appear to be the point at which a parenthetical word on "roles" is in order. The public may believe that a psychiatrist deals only with psychotic people, that a good vocational counselor can tell exactly what job any one should take, and that a school guidance man deals only with naughty children. We know such concepts of the various experts' roles to be fallacious. But the fact remains that this is the kind of thing which brings many people to different types of experts for help. This would seem to suggest two things: first, better "public relations" over a long period of time to help the public understand what the roles and the particular expertness of various types of counselors are; [31] and second, a much stronger stressing of the fact that all good strategic-problem therapists deal both with their special field of expertness and with the personality as a whole.

There are the *physicians,* especially those who carry the principles of psychosomatic medicine into their practice.[32] The pediatrician, who is a general physician for children, has been at the forefront in considering the whole personality as well as the presented problem. Internists—specialists on diagnosis of the "insides" and such treatment as does not require surgery—are becoming more psychosomatically minded as a group. The internist, many believe, may well become the general physician of the future—not like the old country doctor in his lack of technical knowledge, but with the same kind of interest in his patients as persons; not a general practitioner, but a super general practitioner, so to speak. Surgeons, allergists, ophthalmologists, gynecologists, obstetricians, urologists, and all the other specialized clinical practitioners are increasingly taking into account the relation of psychic and somatic factors. Even the nonclinical doctors, the laboratory and research men, are realizing that their work must be geared to the realities of man as a unitary organism, of which his body is but one aspect.

The *industrial counselors* and *labor union counselors* are other strategic-problem therapists who, while now relatively small in number, may be larger and more significant groups in the future.[33] The channel of access in all these is the counselor's special knowledge of the problems of industrial workers, of industry itself, and, we may hope, of managers. Increasingly such counselors are unconnected with personnel work in the usual sense; that is, no reports are made to the industry or the union. Where this is true, workers come in larger numbers for help. Some of these counselors have had their training in psychology; some, in social case work; but now an increasing number are being trained specifically for such work in industry. In view of the way all studies of the value of such counseling, which began about twenty years ago at the Western Electric Company, have shown money saved to industry—over and above increased personal happiness of workers—the layman wonders why so few industries have as yet put in such counseling departments. At the present time the trade unions seem to be doing more pioneer work than the industrial concerns themselves.

Another group of strategic-problem therapists are the *marriage counselors*.[34] Very few personality problems or difficulties are unconnected with marriage and the family. But just as some person would go to an industrial counselor who would not go to him if he were labeled a psychologist or social worker, so others who would not go to a case worker or psychiatrist will go to a marriage counselor. While marital counseling is not a profession, it has been found to be an important strategic-problem area. A number of marriage-counseling centers in the large cities, the Association for Family Living, in Chicago, for example, have on their staff workers of various professions. Hence they operate in team fashion, like the out-patient department of a hospital, or like a child-guidance center or a mental-hygiene clinic. There is certainly a field of expert knowledge around marriage and the family, but there can be no question that one of the important merits of marriage-counseling centers is that they provide access to persons who would not think of getting help from other types of clinics or centers.

In some respects *social workers* are strategic-problem therapists.[35] As we shall see below, social workers have also another field of operation, and the nature of their work demands that we consider them under both categories. As strategic-problem counselors their channel

of access is defined by the specialized function of the agency or institution for which they operate. For example, a social worker who is
with a public assistance agency has access to her client through the
client's financial need. But like all other strategic-problem therapists
she will find many occasions when counseling is necessary if the
person is to be helped and hence will deal with the total person,
having started with the financial need. Or another worker, with an
agency dealing with families, will have as her channel of access some
family problem—desertion by the husband would be an example—
and will also have to go into other factors of personality than those
defined by the presented problem. The general public, not having
yet accepted the fact that group workers and community-organization
specialists are also social workers, believes that social workers
deal only with poor people. As the social workers keep pointing out,
their skills equip them to deal with all kinds of groups. It is true that
a majority of the places where they work still have some connection,
direct or indirect, with financial need. But it is interesting, for example, to see some of the family service societies offering counseling
on family problems on a fee basis to those who can pay as well as to
persons with economic problems.

The counseling done by the social case worker is fairly obvious
from what has been said above. But the group worker—for example,
the professional worker in a settlement house or the Y.M.C.A. program director—has unusual opportunities for doing counseling,
with the function of group leadership serving as the channel of
access.[36] Large group-work organizations, like the Y.M.C.A., are now
emphasizing the value of and need for both specialized counseling
or guidance services on the one hand and the counseling incidental
to group leadership on the other hand. Since the number and
type of agencies in which social workers operate is large, their specific
channel of access to the person in need is also very broad and varied.
What has been said illustrates, but does not exhaust, the strategic-
problem counseling function of social workers.

There is an important sense in which the *clergy*, too, are strategic-
problem therapists or counselors. The pastor, like the others, has
his area of special knowledge and expertness. But if he too is to help
a person, he will often utilize the role of religious expert as a channel
of access to the whole person. What has been said in earlier chapters
should make clear what is meant by this.

By and large, there is little evidence that the *legal profession* has
begun to realize its function in the strategic-problem counseling
sense.[37] The opportunities are there, but they have been less utilized

than in any other group here mentioned. In the work of the legal aid societies, which give or arrange for free or minimum-fee legal advice service, according to financial need, there is a more progressive attitude in this respect than elsewhere in the profession. But lawyers as a group seem to have salved their conscience by saying that their function was completed once they were sure the proper technical advice had been given and the proper moves made in connection with a court or in some other formal way—and have felt that anything having to do with the whole person was out of their field. This is about the point social work had reached forty or fifty years ago, when it said of its failures, "I did my job, but the clients would not cooperate." If progress is to be made in the direction of having lawyers see beyond their strategic-problem area as a thing in itself and view it as a channel of access to a whole person who has personal as well as legal troubles, it will have to come from within the profession. Since the chief intelligent idealism in the profession is found in the legal aid societies, it is probably from them that the impetus will come for training lawyers to recognize their social and human—and therefore counseling—responsibilities as well as their technical legal adviser function. After all, they are known as counselors.

The pastoral reader may have found little or no new information in this section about vocational counselors, lawyers, psychologists, industrial counselors, and the rest. But he may not previously have realized that all of them are—whether they know it or not, whether they are trained for it or not, whether they do anything about it or not—also counselors. Their particular field of expertness, defined partly by what it really is in their minds and partly by what the public thinks it is, is what makes people come to them for help. Their expertness is in the field of the problems presented to them. And such expertness is of enormous importance, as anyone knows who realizes that the skill and knowledge required to perform a surgical operation might be classified as a type of expertness.

But in addition to operating in the field of their expertness, all these workers find, unless they arbitrarily close their eyes to the fact, that they have a particular channel of access to other phases of the personality than those involving the presented problem. Whether they know it or not, what they do has an influence on the person—as well as upon his vermiform appendix, or his knowledge of his occupational skills, or his capacity to manage a budget.

It is not being suggested here that all the groups named need to attain the same degree of expertness in dealing with the problems and difficulties of personality by the method we call personal counseling.

Manifestly there can be different levels of understanding and opera-tion. But it is equally clear that no professional group such as those named can be equipped to do its job in our society if it does not have some understanding of the functions of its area of special knowledge as a channel of access to personality and not merely as an isolated field of expertness.

Sensitivity to this fact, with at least minimal training on how to use it for the good of those we try to help, becomes still more impera-tive when we consider those trends in society which heighten the individual's sense of isolation, make him feel lonely and set apart, give him the impression that no one can truly understand more than a part of him. If, for instance, he has been worried for years by a facial disfigurement and finally gets up courage to go to a plastic surgeon, his expectations will be in terms of advice as to whether there should or should not be an operation, how much it will cost if there is to be one, and the like. He will not expect that the surgeon will be interested in having him tell how he has felt all these years about the deformity, the way in which he has felt pulled this way and that, the agonies he has had about girls when he felt affection might be but a cloak for pity. If the surgeon is completely unin-terested except in the details of plastic surgery, our would-be patient does not know enough to hold it against him. But the patient *should* know enough to do so.

The surgeon on his part has probably but rarely met a patient who really expected such understanding and treatment. This kind of thing needs to be broken through wherever it occurs. If any of us would help people, we need to keep our minds on people, not merely upon the particular field of expertness which happens to give us access to people.

ENVIRONMENTAL-RESOURCES THERAPISTS

ENOUGH has been said of the nature of counseling to demonstrate why merely manipulative procedures are not counseling itself, even though there are certainly occasions on which manipulative pro-cedures are essential preconditions of helping people to help them-selves. An illustration would be hospitalization of a psychotic to protect himself and his fellows and to provide a setting in which both mechanical and psychotherapeutic means can be used, as called for by his particular situation, in order to help him. But the aspects of the total process over which he can exercise no initiative are, while sometimes important, not parts of the counseling or psychotherapeutic process itself. They belong, in my analysis, to the precounseling situation.

At any rate, counseling itself is not to be found in manipulation. We do not counsel when we say to this man Go, and he goes—to a mental hospital or a vocational counselor or a marriage counseling center—or to that man Come, and he comes—to an out-patient clinic or a school psychiatrist or a clinic for alcoholics. It is not counseling if our man goes merely because we say he should, or if he lets the prestige of our expert knowledge persuade him in spite of his own judgment. That is, the use of environmental resources may or may not involve counseling, depending upon the situation, the skill of the worker using them, and his conception of how important it is to have the person understand what any particular resource may mean in terms of helping him.

The use of environmental resources may, however, in many situations and in the hands of a skilled worker, be a very important form of counseling itself. Because it differs from both deep psychological therapy and strategic-problem therapy, it is being considered in this separate section.

For the most part it is only the social workers who have made themselves experts at counseling in connection with the use of environmental resources.[38] But some psychiatrists, pastors and others have come to see the significance of this and, while leaving the center of the field to the social workers, have attempted to incorporate some of the knowledge and procedures into their own practice. This would seem to be a desirable development.

What is meant by environmental resources? The term could mean helping a small boy through counseling with his mother, or aiding an alcoholic to come to the point of desiring treatment by counseling with his wife, or conducting a group to which people might come if they happened to find out that this was the group they needed. Such things are important, and they are environmental resources. But they are sufficiently covered in what has been said in previous sections.

What is meant here by environmental resources is the selective use of whatever resource the community offers in order to meet most efficiently a particular need. And by counseling through environmental resources is meant the process whereby a person is helped to get the benefit of the proper resource, with a sufficient understanding of why it may be able to help and in what respect.

Suppose that a social worker in a family service agency suspects that an eighteen-month-old child may be mentally deficient. There is a way of finding out for sure, but the technical procedures are things the case worker herself cannot manipulate. There may be a psychologist in her own agency equipped to help, or she may have to get help from another agency or person. In any case, she must know where the best help is available in view of all the factors in the situation. This is a special field of knowledge and an important one, in which case workers are our chief experts.

But it is not enough to have such knowledge in her head. It would be bad case work indeed if, on suspecting the child might be mentally deficient, she said, "I think that boy of yours may be mentally deficient. Let's give him some tests and find out." Mothers have enough natural reasons to weep without the creation of unnecessary artificial ones. The following is more like the way a good case worker would approach such a situation:

WORKER: You know, I'm just a bit concerned that Johnny hasn't learned to use his spoon yet. I wonder what you've thought about it?

MOTHER: Oh, Miss Barden, I've worried a lot about it. There seem to be quite a lot of things like that. Of course, the book says every child is different and parents shouldn't expect the same thing of every one, but I am afraid Johnny is different.

WORKER: You've given it a lot of thought as well as worry.

MOTHER: Yes, I have. I've even been afraid to talk about it with my husband, though. I'm afraid he'd get mad just at the idea, or else pooh-pooh it.

WORKER: It's harder when you can't talk about it.

MOTHER: It certainly is. Sometimes I think if I knew Johnny wasn't quite—average, it would be better than thinking about it all the time.

WORKER: At least you'd know what to do for his welfare.

MOTHER: Yes, I would. But it's so hard to think of, if we really found out that is true.

WORKER: It certainly wouldn't be easy to face.

MOTHER: What would we have to do if we wanted to find out?

WORKER: It isn't difficult. We could make an appointment with the psychologist who comes to our agency on Wednesday afternoons, and you could bring Johnny down there. Dr. Brook is very thoughtful and nice with children, and what he would do to test Johnny's intelligence would be fun for Johnny.

MOTHER: Well, that may be the thing to do. I suppose I ought to talk to my husband about it before we go, though.

WORKER: So that you would both be in on the decision together?

MOTHER: Yes, and so that if anything is wrong, he wouldn't be too much shocked by it. But I hate to bring it up with him.

WORKER: Not an easy decision to make.

MOTHER: No it isn't, but I guess I'd better. When will you be coming out this way again?

WORKER: Let's see. Day after tomorrow I think I'll be in the neighborhood. Would you like me to drop in then?
MOTHER: Yes, I would. Oh, Miss Barden, this has helped a lot. I know
we should do this, but I've just put off admitting it to myself. I love
Johnny so much, but it is so hard to think of.
WORKER: It certainly is hard. Good luck on your part of this, and I'll
be back to see you day after tomorrow.

This is environmental-resources counseling as well as good personal
counseling. Not only does the social worker have to aid the mother to
come to grips with the situation; she also has to know, or be reasonably sure she knows, what outside resource can most appropriately
be called on for help in this situation. And she has to interpret this
to the mother, not in technical detail, but in such a way that the
mother's approach to it will be consistent with the kind of help that
it can give. Even a general physician who refers a patient with eye
difficulty to an ophthalmologist should make use of methods similar
to those used by Miss Barden. What makes the Miss Bardens unique
is their extensive knowledge of all kinds of agencies and services in
the community and their discriminating diagnosis of which can be
most useful in a particular situation.

John L. Mixon and I have written in detail elsewhere of how the
pastor, with the help of the social worker, may best use community
help on pastoral problems.[89] Here we are noting not the details
but the way in which the social worker especially—but most of the
rest of us in some degree—may profitably give some attention to
how counseling enters into the proper use of environmental resources.
We do well to remember that even though we have built up considerable knowledge of our own, that of the social worker is likely
to be much greater and more extensive, and we may therefore
profitably call upon her more frequently for this kind of help than
we often do.

THE PSYCHOTHERAPEUTIC OR COUNSELING TEAM

COUNSELING as it has been described here is a special kind of
process occurring between two persons. An attempt has been made to
indicate what the various professions which do more or less counseling have in common, and also what kind of expert knowledge is distinctive to each. It should be clear from what has already been said
that there is importance in the specialized knowledge which each
professional group has, for a channel of access as well as for technical
purposes. But it should also be plain that, human problems being as

complex and far-reaching as they are, an approach to them which involves the explicit co-operation of two or more professions may be able to accomplish things impossible for the professions acting independently or with only a nodding acquaintance with one another.

In recent years we have seen the development, in various ways and under numerous auspices, of psychotherapeutic teams—centers in which there are associated workers from different professional groups.[40] There are mental-hygiene clinics, guidance clinics, and child-guidance clinics, in which a physician, a psychiatrist, a psychologist, and a social worker are usually to be found. Marriage-counseling centers usually include approximately the same professional personnel.[41] The psychiatric or neuropsychiatric clinics connected with many general hospitals are coming to have at least the same four groups represented. Guidance centers or departments within some public school systems sometimes include the same four professions, though in others the medical work is carried out under different auspices. Some social-work agencies have added personnel from other professions, including psychiatry, general medicine, psychology, nursing, and education. And it should not be forgotten that the healing or rehabilitative institutions of society which deal with psychological and social cure or change—such as mental hospitals, correctional institutions, and the like—have increasingly been working out a teamwork basis of treatment and rehabilitation. For example, all the larger federal penal and correctional institutions have on their staffs one or more physicians, psychiatrists, psychologists, educators and vocational-training experts, librarians, chaplains, and social workers.[42]

Broadly speaking, there are two types of theory which underlie the work of these psychotherapeutic teams. The teams resulting from these two types might be called the "fixed-role" teams and the "fluid-role" teams.

The fixed-role team could be illustrated by the mental-hygiene clinic in which the function of the psychiatrist is defined as treatment, that of the general physician as giving medical care, that of the psychologist chiefly in terms of testing, and that of the social worker as making family contacts and dealing with relatives. The assumption is that the particular field of expertness of each worker is almost the sole determiner of his function on the team.

In the fluid-role type of team, developed more recently, an important place is left for the expert knowledge and skill of each profession represented on the team. But in the mental-hygiene clinic attention is paid to which worker—psychiatrist, psychologist, social worker, or other professional—is best able to carry on the continuing counseling with a particular person. If because he has reached a better relationship, or because his schedule permits, or for other good and legitimate reasons the psychologist rather than the psychiatrist is assigned major responsibility for a particular patient, then he proceeds with the counseling, calling on the other members of the team as occasion suggests but carrying the main therapeutic load himself. Such a process would be impossible without clear recognition of the common core we have discussed, and without training in counseling on the part of all the professional groups involved. Under other circumstances the fluid-role type of team clearly would not work. Army and navy and Veterans Administration experience, face to face with the necessity of psychotherapy on a wider basis than had ever before been conceived, has helped to break down artificial barriers which have stood in the way of co-operation of this kind.[43] Their work cannot properly be called fluid-role team therapy entirely, but it has been moving in that direction—especially in the Veterans Administration.

The place of the pastor in relation to psychotherapeutic teams has not yet begun to receive the attention it deserves.[44] The place of the pastor on the team has been increasingly recognized, first in correctional institutions and more recently in hospitals. But so long as the job of each professional worker is defined solely in terms of his field of specialized knowledge and there is no real team in an active sense, the pastor is in a difficult position, even in institutions. For he must then define his role solely in terms of its making a "religious" contribution—in a rather narrow sense of that term. If fluid-role team therapy were in operation, the chaplain would evaluate his work partly in terms of what he did with many men as a religious worker in the narrower sense and also in terms of what he did in a counseling way with a smaller number of men to whom his religious role has given him special access.

Consider, for example, the clinic for alcoholics and for other persons with alcohol problems. There is evidence to suggest that a large number of persons can be helped by such a clinic containing a fluid-role team who could not be reached by some other type of center. It is generally agreed that religion, in either a positive or negative sense, plays a considerable role in the lives of many, if not most, alcoholics. Pastors have probably been about as successful as doctors in helping alcoholics. Alcoholics Anonymous states clearly its therapeutic rootage in religion. Suppose that a pastor is skilled in counseling, and in addition has had special training in dealing with alcoholics; is it not probable that working on a fluid-role team he could find the channel of access to some persons who could not effectively be reached by psychiatrist, psychologist, social worker, or even the ex-alcoholic lay therapist? [45]

The nation is in great need of clinics and treatment centers for persons with alcoholic problems.[46] Not more than a handful of communities now have such centers. If such centers are developed in the next few years, as they should be, should not trained pastors have a relationship to them? If a problem of this kind is not considered now, then such centers may be developed without reference to the pastor; and twenty-five years hence churchmen may be complaining of an increasingly secularized society, citing alcoholic clinics as illustrations. A few decades ago social-work agencies began to develop the form now familiar to us, and the Protestant churches considered only the issue of whether these should remain under Church control or not. That was an important question; but after it was, for various reasons, answered mainly in the negative, Protestants did not go on to ask in that case how the church representative could properly belong to a social agency team. As a result none of the general private community-service agencies known to me accords a staff or formal consultation relationship to a pastor even today— although psychiatrists, physicians, vocational counselors, nurses, and many others have been added to the staff or given formal consultation connection.[47]

This history may well have been inevitable. But it would appear that the time has come to challenge the basis on which this practice has grown up. As psychiatric and nursing and other consultants have been added to social agency staffs, it has become clearer that an exclusive fixed-role approach to therapy or rehabilitation is arbitrary and inefficient. There seems to be now a slow but general movement in the direction of the fluid-role approach. This is, and quite properly so, cautious. Too many values have inhered in the fixed-role type to warrant a complete change overnight, and no one can yet be sure of how far the move should go in the direction of fluid-role teams to get best results. The more fluid in practice teams become, the clearer it will be that the pastor if suitably trained, has a distinctive contribution to make to the work of the team—and the more difficult it will be for the pastor to get by merely on the ground that he is an expert on religion in any sense which does not include concrete knowledge of human personality and counseling methods for helping human beings. Indeed, in this development the stakes for the Church are a good deal higher than might be thought at first glance.

SIMILARITIES AND DIFFERENCES

THE pastoral counselor has, to use George S. Stevenson's phrase, a particular "focus of function." [48] This should be defined in two ways, both important. First, the pastor's focus of function in counseling is as a representative of the Christian fellowship, ideas, ethics, and concepts of human destiny to people who have various assumptions—right or wrong, clear or unclear—about what these things mean. That is, his focus of function is around what people think religion is—whether or not that is what the pastor considers religion to be. An alcoholic may fight a pastor because he associates the pastor with the father who dominated him in his childhood. Or a particular woman of middle years may, because of an inner need to believe the world and all that is in it is sweet and lovely, think that as the representative of God's love the pastor must be Dr. Sentimentality himself. One may say that the pastor's role in this sense is what people project onto him, rightly or wrongly. He needs to understand this and in his counseling accept it as a fact—which is different, however, from agreeing with it. He has sermons and other ways for attempting to help his people see his focus of function more nearly in the same light in which he sees it himself.

Second, the pastor's focus of function in counseling is human destiny. While he has no monopoly on this interest, he is clearly committed to the long-range view of the purpose of living. Can a person be helped to face a particular problem? The pastor will be as interested in this as is the social worker or doctor. But in his mind's eye this will be one step in a long staircase—with heaven at the top and a very real and very human hell at the bottom—and he will be concerned with the solution to the particular problem in the context of what it means for the upward or downward movement on the staircase. The pastor ought to be an expert on the human soul, especially on its hitherto unreleased potentialities, which, in theological language, become possible through the operation of the grace of God in the process of salvation. But every observation shows that he cannot be an expert in the heights unless he has some acquaintance with the depths. The Apostle's Creed says he ascended into heaven, but not before he had descended into hell.

We need to confess that the interest of the pastor in human destiny, in the long view of life's purposes, does not necessarily mean he is best qualified to deal with the specific problems of human destiny as they arise. One responsible psychotherapist suggests that perhaps half of all the people in New York City who seek out pro-

fessional therapists are troubled, at the root, by the meaning and destiny of their life and the life of mankind. Specific symptoms of various
kinds constitute the presented problems and impel these people to
move. But the root problem is deeper and higher than the immediate
motivating irritation. Yet pastors have been around, have been hard
at work, and at least theoretically have what is the true approach to
the answer. It may be that we have been so preoccupied with the
ends and goals that we have not taken seriously our obligation to
learn the means.

Meanwhile counselor starting from various professional and
ideological points of view have reached beneath their field of technical expertness and discovered the rich soil of the dynamics of human
personality. They are now coming to realize how much they have in
common in this underlying realm, and how fallacious they have been
in putting up "no trespassing" signs on what is really the village
green. As the most thoughtful workers in the various fields have
taken all of this seriously, they have expanded their horizons, and
are now coming close to dealing with questions of human destiny in
their patients or clients. Not so many years ago someone could say
that mental hygiene and ethics, for example, dealt with quite different things; hence there was no reason for conflict and no need for
rapprochement. That was much too simple.

More power to the pioneering therapists, whatever their professional field, who are discovering problems of human destiny and are
not afraid to study them. I could feel happier if more of these persons
of insight were committed basically to the Christian view of life.
But it is inevitable that they must eventually deal with this dimension of life if they are to help their people, regardless of their personal convictions on such matters. They are not usurping the pastor's focus of function in doing so any more than the pastor is usurping the psychiatrist's focus of function by recognizing sex or hatred
as among the facts of life. But human destiny is where the pastor
starts. If pastors are to help people find their destiny from a Christian point of view, we do well not to be so preoccupied with the
goal as to pay only incidental attention to the steps necessary for
approaching it.

What, then, is the pastor's special knowledge in counseling? It is
what it *does*, not merely what he wants it to be, in his helping relationships with his people. We see his focus of function as that which
brings together both his role as representative of a tradition and his
role as guide to human destiny. Much of his knowledge and much
of his skill he shares with all other groups which attempt seriously

to help people through counseling. He uses both in his role as pastor, with a pastoral focus of function. If he becomes so interested in what psychiatry or psychology or social work can do that he wants to do his counseling from the focus of function of one of them, then he may wish to change professions. With the Protestant concept of Christian vocation, that all men may serve God equally through honorable labor, he can be as useful to the kingdom of God there as in the ministry.[49] But in doing so, he need not believe that these are inherently superior approaches to helping people. He may see that they better meet certain inner needs of his own, which in another person could be better met through the focus of function of the ministry.

On the other hand, the pastor does well not to become so enamored of that which is distinctive about his own focus of function as to think that if it is not distinctive, it is not his job. If religion touches all of life, then he cannot assert that the presence of a sex or vocational or financial problem in a parishioner's situation puts it categorically out of the field of his concern—solely on the ground that his field is religion. Naturally it does not mean on the other hand that he should necessarily do all that is to be done about it. It does mean that in discriminating analysis of what he as an individual can and cannot do, is and is not trained to do, he will decide on the merits of the particular situation what he will do, how far he can go, and where he should seek help. He will realize that the core of knowledge and skill which he shares with other counselors is as important to him, and is as much the creation of God, as that which is distinctive to his practice as a Christian pastor.

In the first chapter we have already discussed the basic assumptions which various counselors hold: the social-adjustment view, the inner-release view, the objective-ethical view, and the Christian-theological view. Every shading of these views is to be found in every one of the professional groups which does counseling. True, more social workers and psychiatrists than pastors stop with the first two. But sometimes differences about assumptions are as wide within any of the professional groups as among two or more groups. The pastor is clear that he wants all four of these views properly included in the basic assumptions of all who help people through counseling. But it is just as well to remind ourselves that an effective obstacle to movement in that direction is arrogating the third and fourth assumptions as if they were our peculiar property, and interpreting any movement toward them as implying that other groups are now joining us. Surely we have had enough experience with churches professing to desire Christian unity but interpreting this as having all others join them to prevent ourselves from slipping into such a psychological error.

As to counseling methods, the general point is that once the process of counseling as defined in the previous chapter has been started, the basic methods of the pastor and of other counselors is so nearly similar as to be almost identical—if the counseling is good. No counselor dealing with Miss Smith in Chapter II could be moralistic, general, distracting, coercive, or flip, and be of help to her. In this sense, and it is a fundamental sense, basic methods and approach are the same once counseling itself has begun.

But this is not to say there are not important differences between pastoral and other counseling in terms of method. Had Miss Smith gone to a psychiatrist, what she would have presented initially would probably have been different, even though the basic personality situation in Miss Smith would have been the same. This difference alone, representing the differing roles and foci of function of different counselors, is in itself sufficient warrant for special training in pastoral counseling as against the false conclusion that since the basis of counseling method by all professional groups is the same, therefore all can be taught the same thing together.

But the most important distinctions between method of the pastor and method of other counselors lie not so much in the counseling itself, once begun, as in the precounseling situation. These differences will be discussed later. Much less study has been done on them by nonpastoral counselors than has been done on counseling itself, so that our comparisons will be less exact. Even so, we know enough to make some statements about precounseling in connection with the minister's function and that of other counselors.

There is desperate need for counseling. It is not a procedure to be undertaken lightly. God did not see fit to make the human soul less complex than the human body. Training is essential. We need more good counselors in every profession mentioned in this chapter, and all need to realize the importance of others. At the same time, the one-big-happy-family approach is not enough. There are too many sibling rivalries and parent-child misunderstandings without adding to them by attempting to minimize differences.

But a kind of ecumenical movement—co-operation without concession—is essential if counseling needs are to be met. Most Protestants have discovered that in the process of common action toward objectives which can be better achieved in co-operation than in separation, they have found vastly more of a common faith than they ever realized they had. Those who have worked successfully together on counseling are taking the surest road to a similar objective, better appreciation both of one's own contribution and that of the other fellow. Theoretical agreement rarely if ever precedes practical co-operation in a democratic society. While I have not hesitated to talk about the equivalent of "faith and order," I remain convinced that the road to ecumenicity in counseling is "life and work."

PART II: *Preparation for Pastoral Counseling*

Chapter Six ONE OF THE COMMONEST QUESTIONS WHEN PASTORS discuss counseling is, "When is the pastor justified in taking the initiative in counseling?" It usually turns out that the situation which the questioner has in mind is somewhat like the following.

A couple in early middle age, whom we shall call the Stephen Boltons, are members of the First Church in Kalopolis. Mr. Bolton is a lawyer, specializing in trusts and real property. He belongs to several clubs and organizations in the community, but cannot be considered either as a leader in civic affairs or as a convivial joiner. He belongs to the Church, attends worship about once a month, does not participate in other church activities. One suspects that all his extrabusiness activities are being undertaken as "good business." Mrs. Bolton, on the other hand, is active in church affairs, especially those of the social type, and attends worship regularly. Her two children are now in school away from home, and her days tend to be a stream of welfare activities, women's clubs, bridge clubs, and other activities which bring her into contact with people. She is not light-minded, and her welfare activities have been handled with skill and conscientiousness. But one suspects the activity is more important to her than the results.

In the upper middle-class suburb of Kalopolis where the Boltons live, it has been a whispered rumor for some weeks that Bolton has been seen at Seaside City on a weekend with a young girl from his office. The good-looking young lady in question is married, without children, and her husband has six months more to serve in the occupation forces abroad before he will come home. He had come home once, and had re-enlisted for the special tour of duty, the reasons not being generally known.

The news comes to the ears of the pastor. Shall he do anything about it? Shall he interpret his function as sitting tight until either of the Boltons comes to talk with him? The girl is not a member of his church, so he has no entree there. Or as the spiritual adviser—whether they realize it or not—of the Boltons, does he have some obligation to take the initiative? Suppose he does take it. Would this be sure to rouse the Bolton ire and make things worse? Or is there a way in which it could be done with some chance of success?

Here is the way Pastor Breen reasoned: "These are my people, the Boltons. They are members of that segment of the Christian fellowship of which I am shepherd. Whatever the truth or falsity of this rumor, it is spreading throughout the community. It is likely the Bolton home life is not on the firmest of foundations. If it is not, now may be the last chance to save it by getting the Boltons to help themselves. If the rumor is false, though that does not seem likely in this case, whatever misunderstanding that might exist between the Boltons may be so intensified by this that there will soon be little chance for anyone to do anything.

"Clearly nothing will be accomplished if I barge down to Bolton's office and excoriate him as a philanderer. If the rumor is true, there may be provocations which should be understood, not merely condemned. His wife's schedule doesn't sound like the best way to make a man comfortable and happy at home. If the rumor is not true, then a bawling-out from me would, quite properly, incite him to throw me out. And then where would we all be?

"Yes, I must fulfill my obligation as pastor, but I cannot do so by acting as judge, either overtly or subtly. If I bring up this subject with him, merely saying I've heard of it and what about it, he will himself cast me in the role of judge—and no doubt proceed either to throw me out or defend himself. No, that won't do. The only way I can keep from being cast in the role of judge is to define a different role—a shepherding role—in such a way that it's clear to him and he accepts me in it. That will take some doing.

"But there is a plan, and it's the only one thoroughly consistent with my role as a shepherd. I'm going to try it."

BOLTON: Hello, Dr. Breen. Sorry I haven't been able to get to church for the past few Sundays. Things have been at their peak here in the office, and I've been working part of the time over weekends.
BREEN: One look at me and you think of church, I take it.
BOLTON: (laughs) Well, you do remind me of it. When you telephoned, I supposed you wanted to talk with me about something like that.
BREEN: Mr. Bolton, I'll put my cards on the table. I want to raise a question with you. Sometimes a minister feels obliged to do things he'd rather not do, and this is such an occasion. When I've spoken my piece, if you want to ask me to leave, you should feel free to do so.
BOLTON: I don't think I know what you're getting at.

BREEN: It's this. There's a rumor which has spread very widely through the community that you are seeing a good deal of another woman, that you have been spending weekends with her. You may know this rumor is going around. If so, you have probably decided already what you want to do about it. On the other hand, the people concerned are often the last to know that such rumors are in existence. Now I want you to understand that I am not here to ask whether the rumor is true or false, and I am not here to condemn you if the rumor is true. The rumor is a fact, in the sense that it is circulating through the community. If you and your wife know about it, you may be able to decide what you want to do. But no good purpose can be served if you don't know about it. As your pastor, I have felt an obligation to make sure that you knew of this. If you want to talk with me about this in any way, I'm here; and, of course, anything we say is between us. On the other hand, if there is nothing to be said, I will leave here now, and even the fact that I've been here will be known to no one but you. It's your situation, not mine. If I can help, I shall want to; but the decision is yours, not mine.

BOLTON: Why, I had no idea—

BREEN: I thought the news of the rumor might be a surprise to you.

BOLTON: (disturbed. He sits thinking for several seconds). You don't believe there's any truth in this, do you?

BREEN: Frankly, I have no idea, and that isn't the concern that brings me here. More than one man has got into such a situation without actually intending to, and it usually turns out that there are reasons for it which aren't apparent at first. On the other hand, a good many have been maligned by vicious rumor that has had no foundation in fact. I'm not here as a judge, but as a pastor. As your pastor, I can't permit you to be ignorant of what the community is saying.

BOLTON: (bitterly) Why can't people mind their own business and keep out of other people's affairs?

BREEN: A lot of things would be easier in life without rumor.

BOLTON: Dr. Breen, I don't know what to do. This floors me. I know you have good intentions in coming here. But it's none of the community's business what I do. If it weren't for the old maids, over at your church too, waiting for juicy bits of scandal, a story like this would never have started. I can see why you've come, and I suppose it hasn't been easy for you. But it is my business, as you said.

BREEN: (rising to leave) Yes, it is, and I appreciate also your understanding what has prompted me to come.

BOLTON: This is between ourselves, isn't it?

BREEN: Completely.

BOLTON: (as Breen goes) This has been a shock, but thanks.

Two days later Bolton telephones the pastor to ask if he may talk the situation over. When they get together, Bolton's first statement is, "I resented it pretty badly when you came to the office the other day. But I've been thinking it over since then—I haven't had much sleep—and I think I'd like to talk over the whole situation. That rumor *is* true. The girl is in my office, but I am no more in love with her than she is with me. The real trouble is in my home." And the discussion proceeds on a counseling basis.

The question with which we began was, "When is the pastor justified in taking the initiative in counseling?" Is what has been described an instance of taking initiative in counseling? The pastor has transported himself geographically to the parishioner; he has raised the question, not waited for the parishioner to raise it. Is this taking the initiative in counseling?

The answer to this question seems central in our understanding of pastoral work and personal counseling. Counseling, in our definition, does not begin until Mr. Bolton telephones Pastor Breen and opens their discussion with the sentence quoted above. By this point Bolton has the attitudes which, in some measure, are essential in any counseling situation; he recognizes and admits there is something wrong, that this has something to do with himself, that help in connection with it is possible through another person, and that the essence of this help is in aiding him to help himself, not doing something to or for him. Whatever happens prior to such a point is not counseling as such, but precounseling activity.[1]

The interview which is reported, therefore, is not to be judged as a counseling interview. That is, we get nowhere by applying the principles of counseling to this contact. If we made such a literal comparison, we should say that the pastor talked too much, did not wait for the parishioner to bring up the problem, represented a particular point of view, and the like. But to compare a true counseling contact with this precounseling contact in literal fashion would be like equating apples with oranges.

This is not to say, however, that the principles involved in pastoral counseling and those involved in precounseling pastoral work are essentially different. Indeed, they can be translated into each other. But idiomatic, and not literal, translation is needed.

PRINCIPLES OF PRECOUNSELING WORK

WITH our eyes focused on Breen and Bolton we may examine more systematically what happened in the precounseling relationship.

1. *Breen offered help in such a way that it could be refused.* That is, Breen took the geographic initiative in telephoning Bolton and

going to his office and the factual initiative in bringing up the rumor, but he left the psychological initiative entirely up to Bolton. After Breen had made his long speech, Bolton might have said, "It's all a dirty lie. If you want to peddle it around, go somewhere else." And Breen would have gone. Or Bolton might have said, "I know you mean well, and it's better I know this rumor is going around. But I don't want to talk with you about it now or later." And Breen would have departed. When Breen said, "If I can help, I shall want to; but the decision is yours, not mine," he really meant it. It was not a mere trick to get Bolton talking. If it had been, the entire psychological situation would have been different. Breen left the psychological initiative up to Bolton.

If the Boltons of this world choose—as they often do—to keep quiet or seek compromise solutions, then the pastor has to accept this attitude as a fact. This is not because he agrees with what they have chosen. But, in metaphorical language, his only chance of keeping them from going to hell is to begin by accepting their right to go to hell if they insist on it. This may take off enough pressure so they will stop and look around, and such a look may in turn lead to something constructive. Even if it does not, their hellward journey is more under their own conscious steam, and is likely to slow up a trifle.

2. *Breen made it clear he would understand any attitude Bolton had.* The crucial point came when Bolton said, "You don't believe there's any truth in this, do you?" Suppose Breen had replied, "Oh, I'm sure there isn't." That would have implied, "I have come to help you, on the condition that this rumor's a lie. Tell me it isn't true, and then perhaps I can help you." But such conditional understanding is no understanding at all. It is tantamount to saying, "I can understand you if you're a good boy; but if you really have any problems, well, I don't associate with bad people."

Suppose the rumor had been false. Breen would have had to understand Bolton's proper indignation, and would have had to make clear in advance that he would understand it if this were the case. Or suppose Bolton had been in such a state of mind and emotion that he had immediately said the rumor was true. Breen would have had to understand that—and make his probable understanding clear in advance. As it was, Bolton partially understood during the contact that Breen was understanding; but not until he had sweated further with himself did he realize what that willingness to understand really meant.

It might be well to indicate another way in which Breen might have demonstrated lack of understanding at the point where Bolton asked, "You don't believe there's any truth in this, do you?" He might have replied, "Well, I'm afraid I must believe it. The evidence from two independent witnesses who saw you together at Seaside City is too clear to be taken lightly." The effect of that would have been to throw the discussion into the realm of evidence—content instead of feeling. Whether Bolton then tried to refute the evidence or defend himself or admit everything, the psychological situation would have passed out of the pastor's hands. Bolton would merely be reacting to Breen.

Understanding means here, as we have already seen in the counseling situation itself, the willingness to understand, the fact of understanding, and the communication of that fact to the parishioner. Without it nothing constructive can occur.

3. *Breen denied explicitly the incorrect expectations Bolton was reasonably sure to have had without the denial.* Is Breen there to judge and condemn? Like it or not, we must admit Bolton would have assumed so without Breen's specific denial. Has Breen really come to find out whether or not Bolton will admit the truth of the rumor? Bolton will assume so unless Breen defines the situation otherwise. Is Breen going to insist, however subtly, that Bolton must discuss the situation? Bolton will assume so if Breen does not make it clear that talking or not talking is up to Bolton. Is Breen trying to get some word he can pass on to the Ladies' Aid Society to stop the scandal? Bolton may think so unless the real purpose is made clear.

In counseling itself we saw that a definition of the situation, so that the parishioner comprehended what the pastor could and could not do to help him, was important. It is also important in a situation like this. But the application of the principle requires some imaginative assessment of the total situation, and not a slavish verbal imitation of what would be effective in a true counseling situation. It may be charged that Breen went rather far in defining the situation in this case, and there would appear to be some justice in such a criticism. However, better to err on that side than permit highly probable misconceptions to exist.

4. *Once the situation had been defined, Breen was willing to wait.* When it became clear that Bolton did not intend freely to discuss his situation at this time, but wanted Breen to leave, the latter left. At the conclusion of the contact he might have defined explicitly his desire to help at any time Bolton felt he wanted it; but Breen apparently concluded this could be taken for granted in view of the attitude he had demonstrated throughout the contact. Especially in

this case Breen wanted to be sure that any later request for help would come from Bolton, and not from any pressure that Breen had put on Bolton apart from the nature of Bolton's situation itself and his feelings about it. Breen was willing and ready to wait, and Bolton apparently sensed this.

5. *Breen was alert to evidences of Bolton's wanting help, but he did not exploit them.* When Bolton began to consider the implications of the rumor as a fact, his reaction was anger against the disseminators of the rumor collectively—"Why can't people mind their own business?" Breen could see that this was a fumbling attempt to deflect the problem, and therefore in a sense, by its very fumbling, a partial indication of readiness to have such an excuse brushed aside. Psychologically that is so. But suppose that Breen, alert to the possible meaning of this, had replied, "That's a very understandable feeling you have. But even as you say it, you know it's not the real problem, don't you?" Such a reply would suggest some understanding, but understanding, so to speak, of something Bolton is not yet ready to have understood. The net effect would have been coercive. On the other hand, had Breen not sensed the psychological significance of Bolton's statement, he might have been tempted to reply, "Come, now. That won't get us anywhere," thus demonstrating no understanding and refusing to accept Bolton's resentment as an understandable fact under the circumstances. What Breen did was to be alert to the partially hidden evidence of desire for help without exploiting it.

COMPARISON OF COUNSELING AND PRECOUNSELING PRINCIPLES

IT may be clarifying if we restate here the general methodological principles already enunciated in relation to counseling itself and see how they compare with those of the precounseling situation. In counseling we have these principles:

1. The counseling process focuses its attention on the parishioner's situation and his feelings about it.[2] This is identical in the precounseling pastoral work as demonstrated by Breen and Bolton.

2. The counseling proceeds through real understanding on the pastor's part of how the parishioner feels about the situation and the communication of the reality of that understanding. This is the same in principle as the second point in the counseling list, but the details are different in the precounseling situation. In precounseling the whole situation is either undefined in the parishioner's mind or else defined differently from what it would be in a counseling re-

lationship. Hence the understanding is not merely of what the parishioner says and the feelings he thereby communicates. It is that, but also something else. It suggests that any honest feeling which exists can be expressed, and an attempt will be made to understand it. In a sense it is anticipatory understanding. Not too much should be made of the anticipatory element; but the Breen-Bolton contact suggests that Breen's explicit definition of his interest in the situation anticipated in a proper sense his capacity to understand anything that Bolton chose to tell him, and also to understand if Bolton chose to tell him nothing.

3. When conflicting feelings of the parishioner emerge in counseling, the pastor first aids the parishioner in clarifying the elements of the conflict and their relative pull upon him. Such conflicting elements emerge verbally, with a consciousness of what they are, only in the counseling situation itself. Hence they do not emerge in the Breen-Bolton contact as they would later on, after Bolton had reached the point of wanting counseling. At this point a literal translation would be fatal; but a free translation of the essential principle is sound. For the precounseling situation this would read: When a person is in difficulty but has not yet reached the point of wanting counseling help, acceptance of his conflicting pulls about whether or not to try to get help is essential if he is to reach the point of clearly wanting that help. Breen did this with Bolton.

4. The counseling relationship contains a special freedom on the part of the parishioner as well as a special limitation. Again literal translation would be pointless; but idiomatic translation is relevant. A parallel in the precounseling situation is: When a person is in a situation in which counseling could help, but he has not understood and accepted that fact, whatever can help him define accurately the nature of help which is mediated in the counseling process will aid him to reach the point where he can seek that help. In other words, both counseling and precounseling involve definition of the situation in which help can be given or mediated. The details of how this is done differ.

5. The counseling process should include, on one or more appropriate occasions, that which will aid in consolidation of the insights achieved or the clarifications gained. This relates to later stages of the counseling relationship, and hence is not specifically relevant to the precounseling situation. But the essential point behind it—that is, no hidden motives on either side—is also relevant to the precounseling situation. It is a specific instance of definition of the counseling or precounseling situation.

Thus there is nothing basic in the counseling situation which is foreign to the precounseling situation. Acceptance of the parishioner's feelings as a fact, understanding them so far as he wants to disclose them, absence of coercive pressure, moralizing, generalizing, or distracting are all involved in both types of situations. But in the precounseling situation there are some things which need to be especially stressed because of the nature of the situation itself—that is, it has not yet become a counseling relationship.

We may return to being systematic, and consider the different emphases in the precounseling situation:

1. Help is offered in such a way that it may be as easily refused as accepted. We cannot be sure that a person really needs or is ready for counseling. Anything that is done to make counseling serve in his eyes as a club over his head, or to augment his feeling of guilt, makes that much less likely his ever turning to this kind of help. Hence this point, which is almost taken for granted by the time a person has reached the stage of requesting counseling help, is of enormous importance in precounseling situations. If there are any strings attached to the offer of help, if it cannot be refused as easily and with as little sense of guilt as it can be accepted, then the potential counseling relationship has been made less likely.

2. The incorrect expectations which the parishioner is reasonably sure to have of the nature of counseling help are, as occasion warrants, explicitly denied. In the counseling relationship, which begins with some kind of expressed desire for help, this process usually takes place in response to something the parishioner has expressed, as if he were to say, "Here's my problem. I want to tell you about it, and then I want your advice on what I should do." In the counseling relationship the pastor will point out what the parishioner should and can expect instead of giving advice on what he should do. In the precounseling relationship, as in the Breen-Bolton case, the definition is both more explicit and more subtle. Remember that Bolton does not even know he wants help. Breen says in effect, "Here is why I have come to you. It is not, as you might naturally suppose, because of A, B, or C reasons, but as a pastor I am concerned for D reason. If you feel in view of this that I can help, fine. If not, I will leave, and this is still between ourselves." This is definition of the counseling relationship in advance of the development of the parishioner's attitudes to the point where that relationship can be established. It therefore defines in advance as a means toward creating that relationship—if the parishioner needs it. The "if" is important too.

3. Once the pastor's role in the situation has been defined to the parishioner as well as possible, the pastor is content to wait. In the counseling relationship, once initiated, something takes place; at least the two persons see each other. In the precounseling situation once the pastor is reasonably sure he has defined his place, as did Pastor Breen, he waits. This does not mean that he can or should complete his defining of the situation in one contact. But he should recognize the difference between a contact in which he is seeking to define what role he would have if the person decided that help was wanted and a contact in which the parishioner understands that perfectly well and says, "No, thanks." In the latter situation he waits. And in the case of a church officer who has been making things miserable for everyone for years, or of a woman who has just divorced the fourth husband in a series when all four have been psychological blood brothers, he may wait a long time. But if he knows dynamically what he is doing, then the waiting is fraught with understanding and not impatience.

4. The pastor is alert to evidences of the desire for help, but he does not exploit them. Once the counseling relationship has got underway, the desire for help takes care of itself if the counseling is well handled. But in the precounseling situation this point is of great importance. In the Breen-Bolton case the rumor was going around the community, and it took no great wisdom to sense the possible disastrous consequences if the Boltons did not face up to it. In many other situations the evidence of desire for help will not be so obvious. Here is what may be called the pastor's "detector" function, which is not so much seeking out evidences of disorder as being alert to evidences of desiring help of the kind counseling can give on life-situation problems. Here is an illustration.

Pastor Oaks, in a new parish, is calling upon a family who, he has been told, have no church affiliations. His purpose is to sound out their interest in the Church and see if he can get them to his church or some other. He is the kind of pastor who truly means the "other" if that turns out to be best. He finds Mrs. Pine at home in an upper middle-class house, surrounded by evidences of unobtrusive luxury. After explaining the purpose of his call, the following conversation takes place:

OAKS: We're not interested in taking anyone away from another church, but we are concerned about people who have no church home and children for whom the parents have not yet found opportunity for church training.

MRS. PINE: I see. I do feel the children should be getting some training. We are having some trouble which I don't care to discuss just now.
OAKS: I understand.
MRS. PINE: I am getting to feel that any church training is better than none. Even if they should change to their own church when they get older, it would still be helpful.
OAKS: I should think so too.
MRS. PINE: My husband doesn't feel the way I do about this. In fact he doesn't believe in church at all. By the way, where is your church, exactly?

The pastor had not gone out looking for counseling contacts. But in this conversation he not only sensed a defensiveness on the part of Mrs. Pine but also found two overt evidences of her desire for help. The first is in her reference to the trouble with the children, and the second is in her husband's attitude toward the Church. These are subtly veiled appeals for help, as if she were saying, "Of course I can hardly expect help from a young man like you, and anyhow I'm too proud to admit I could get help from anyone except maybe big city specialists. But I surely wish someone could help on this situation of the children and my husband. We're all in a bad way, if the truth were known."

The pastor had a clear reason for his call, and he defined the situation in those terms. He sensed the evidences of desire for help, but did not exploit them, indicated his understanding of her reticence in relation to the problems with the children. He noted her quick change of the subject when she had mentioned her husband's lack of interest in the Church. It was a precounseling pastoral work situation. Some day he might be called on to help. For the present his job was to be alert to evidences of the desire for help but not to exploit them.

FURTHER PRINCIPLES IN PRECOUNSELING PASTORAL WORK

WE began with the question, "When is the pastor justified in taking the initiative in counseling?" And via Breen and Bolton we have seen that however sparingly the pastor should move in on such situations, he can with reasonable safety do something about them when his obligation is clear. We have seen further that our initial question is too simple, that we have to ask instead: "What do you mean by initiative?" Our conclusion has been that the psychological initiative must always and invariably be left up to the parishioner. But the pastor's task implies that he will not infrequently take the initiative,

if by that is meant raising a question or going to call on someone—
in short, geographic and factual, but not psychological initiative.

We turn now to some broader aspects of precounseling pastoral
work. What about this situation? A middle-aged man is dying slowly. He is under good medical care, but the doctors have decided to
leave him at home rather than take him again to the hospital. His
wife and her sister have taken care of him in the long illness. The
wife is very tired after the long strain. During the pastor's brief call
one afternoon he notices how near the breaking point she seems.
He has known the family for many years. He says he would like very
much to come back after the church meeting that evening and take
care of the husband during the night. The wife protests that he is
busy; but after making sure that she has no objection to his doing
it, but only to what it will take out of him, the pastor says he will
return, and does. The wife gets a little sleep for a change, and she
and her sister are very grateful to the pastor.

While this can hardly be recommended as a nightly practice, there
are certainly occasional situations when nothing can be so helpful as
direct physical service. The pastor knows the women are worn out
but, because the death is near, feel they cannot leave for a moment or
trust someone new in the situation. But the pastor is not new, and
hence their feeling about him is different.

One would hardly expect the pastor to think of this merely as
precounseling activity. There is a sense in which it is done just because it meets a need then and there. But death will come, and
grief, and the readjustment to a new kind of life. The pastor will
play a role then and later, when the plans for a new life are being
made. If he helps now, he can help still better then. In this sense he
prepares the way for the counseling to come later on.

A great deal of pastoral work is anticipatory in this sense. Pre-
marital counseling is important for what it does here and now for
the couple contemplating marriage; but it is equally important for
the relationship it may set up in which, as problems and difficulties
arise later on, there can be a feeling of freedom about returning to
the pastor. And so on through the whole duration of life. This
volume is not analyzing these tasks separately, though such analysis
is important. It is our purpose to see all of these pastoral work activities in their context of precounseling activities. In that sense
they are a unit.

The situation concerning the dying man leads us to certain other
general principles of pastoral work as precounseling activity.

1. *Playing well a supportive role may lead to counseling when it*

is needed. This has been illustrated with the dying husband and his wife and sister. Often the pastor stands by—with a relative when there is illness, with a mother whose son has been sent to a correctional institution, with a man who has just lost his job, and in many other ways. He may spend time with such folks; they may or may not talk with him. This is not the time for counseling as such. This is the time for friendly pastoral support merely through presence and interest. A little later may come the time for counseling. The supportive job is to be done whether it leads to counseling or not; counseling depends on the need of the parishioner. But what the pastor does in the supportive function should, at the least, not make it impossible for him later on to perform a counseling function.

The supportive role, be it noted, is usually especially necessary when "reactive-emotional situations" are involved, that is, when some event has taken place in the outside world which affects the equilibrium of the parishioner and is therefore something to which his emotions quite naturally react. Perhaps the person should have seen it coming; the wife knew her husband would die before long, or the mother knew her son could not be picked up many more times by the police without drawing a reformatory sentence. But the reality is different from the anticipation.

The nature of the supportive function likely to be most helpful at such times has had light thrown on it by recent research on grief at the Massachusetts General Hospital.[3] As reported by Erich Lindemann, the special interest in this problem began at the time of the Cocoanut Grove fire, when many patients brought to the hospital had lost relatives or close friends in the fire. When some of the patients failed to make progress in recovering from their burns, the surgeons and physicians called in the psychiatrists, who in turn suspected that grief might have something to do with the retardation of physical healing.

They gave attention to the patients who were not doing well, but, wisely, they also studied those who were. And their findings, especially when published later in more systematic form, should be of help to pastors not only in dealing with grief situations but also in understanding the meaning of supportive help in the face of reactive-emotional situations.

The patients who were doing well had uniformly followed a fairly well-defined process of learning to live with the "image" of the deceased relative or friend lost in the fire. Spontaneously they had called before their mind's eye the deceased person on the day of his death and gone through in memory the relationship with the person on that day. "We went to this place together, and then he said to me . . . And I said . . . And then we went to . . ." Then they did the same for the day before, and on back. The process was not mechanical, but it had a certain progress about it. The memory was participative (*with* the deceased person) and not merely objective (*about* him). It was exceedingly painful, but the person came to be able to live with the pain for short periods of memory. Then he would think of something else, and back again to painful recollection. Where such a process was followed, before long the image and memory became more supportable. That is, the pain in memory and imaging was lessened. Despite the psychic pain there was no evidence that such a procedure lessened physical recovery. In fact such recovery was astonishingly quick, apparently in some proportion to the degree of direct handling of the grief in this fashion.

On the other hand, those patients who were unable to stand the pain of seeing the image at all, or those who were trying to concentrate on new plans before working through the grief, or even those preoccupied with consolations before facing the reality of their loss, were having difficulty. In a number of such situations the psychiatrist was able from his knowledge of successful grief to aid the person to view and talk about the image of the deceased person in a participative way. Where the pain could not be stood, or the short-circuit ways of handling were too deeply imbedded, this did no good and perhaps some harm. Any kind of coercion, even going through a process the psychiatrist knew to be necessary to recovery, tended to backfire. But if the other trends were not too deeply rooted, the psychiatrist found he could help; and he observed that the chaplain or a nurse or a good friend sometimes enabled the person to face the image of the deceased when it could not be done satisfactorily in the mind's eye alone.

Further research on grief has suggested that weightier consequences than have previously been realized can come if a person does not learn how to work through the grief situation when it occurs. The hospital has the record of a young woman who developed ulcerative colitis within a day or two after her father's death, never having had it before. Less extreme instances are numerous in which the failure to work through a grief situation has had a fairly clear effect upon the development of somatic difficulties even up to one or two years following the bereavement.

The pastor is in the midst of such situations. His function then is supportive. The bereaved person may or may not want, or be able, to tell him how she feels. But if he stands by, is not under compulsion either to discourage or encourage the flow of emotion, his supportive task may be of even more importance than he has previously realized. Incidentally but significantly, such studies suggest to us how even in our traditional pastoral function of helping the bereaved there are incidents and situations in which our work can be greatly aided by the expert knowledge of other professional groups.

2. *Counseling with one member of a family may serve as precounseling pastoral work in relation to other members of the family.* This requires only brief illustration. Mr. Buxton is not an alcoholic, but his drinking is making heavy social and financial inroads upon the family. His wife consults the pastor, and a half-dozen counseling contacts are held. The net effect is Mrs. Buxton's realization that she has been concentrating so hard and so negatively on Mr. Buxton's drinking that she has failed to pay attention to Mr. Buxton. The latter senses a changed attitude in his wife, asks her about it, and she tells him of her talks with the pastor. Buxton is worried about himself, and with this background decides himself to come to the pastor.

3. *Requests for information may have importance as precounseling pastoral work.*[4] Russell, aged sixteen, comes up to the pastor after a young people's meeting:

RUSSELL: You know, Dr. Locust, I graduate from high school next year, and I wonder what you think is the best college around here. I will have to stay at home because of finances. But we've got several colleges here, and I wonder what one you think is the best.

PASTOR: I suppose Chickasaw University has the best all-round reputation across the country.

RUSSELL: Yes, I know that. But the trouble with it is it's so big. I suppose I could get along there. But I've heard the classes are so big the teachers don't give much attention to the students. What do you hear of Cherokee College?

PASTOR: Very good things. Certainly it's smaller than the University.

RUSSELL: Yes, that side of it would be a lot better. But do you think the teachers there are as good?

PASTOR: From what I've heard most of them are very competent. They aren't as well known as some of the Chickasaw men, because the University does a lot of graduate work and research. But I understand they are just as good, as teachers.

RUSSELL: Well, what I've really been trying to decide is between Cherokee and the Arapaho Institute. It's so much nearer, and it would be a lot easier to go to. But I think I'd get a much better education at Cherokee.

PASTOR: Would you like to come and talk a bit more about it some day soon?
RUSSELL: Yes, I would, if it wouldn't take too much of your time.

Rarely is a request for information merely that and nothing more. Occasionally it is, and should be so treated. But it is more likely to be, as in Russell's case, preliminary to something else. If handled according to good precounseling attitude and methods, it can lead to counseling—by the pastor if it is within his scope, or by referral to someone more competent if it is not.

4. *Discussions of religion may be significant as precounseling pastoral work.*[5] Here is the report of such a discussion, used through the courtesy of a theological student in charge of a young people's group in a church. One night a visiting minister talked to the group on the subject "What's the Point in Being Christian?" After the meeting a young student of nursing sought out the theological student, and their conversation was as follows:

THEOLOGICAL STUDENT: That was some discussion, wasn't it?
NURSING STUDENT: Yes, but I think he hedged the real issue. As a matter of fact, I don't think he proved anything at all.
T: How is that?
N: Well, he told how some people might experience Christianity, but gave no reason. He didn't give any reason why people should read the Bible, either—at least none that I agreed with.
T: Why do you think people read the Bible?
N: In the first place I don't think people do read it. The people who do read it do so more as a pious exercise than to get anything out of it. You know, a chapter a day.
T: Don't you think that people can benefit from it in that way?
N: No.
T: Don't you think it could develop a good habit?
N: What good is a habit if you don't get anything out of it?
T: Do you know anyone who reads a chapter a day and doesn't get anything out of it?
N: No, as I said, I don't know anyone who reads the Bible (*pause*). A girl down the hall does read it a lot, now that you mention it. But she's kind of queer. She prays a lot, too.
T: Is there anything you admire about her?
N: I guess so. We sort of respect her. None of us swears in front of her very often.
T: Yes.
N: I guess it's because she's different that we respect her. I have never seen her angry, and she never gripes when she gets dirty work.

T: Do you think reading the Bible might help in developing those desirable characteristics?

N: I don't know (*pause*). You know, they gave us all Bibles with references for particular situations in the back. I never use mine, though, because I'm never in those situations. I suppose if my father died I'd read the Bible.

T: Don't you as a nurse ever face any difficult situations?

N: No, we seldom find any opportunity to talk to people.

T: Don't you ever feel disturbed when one of your patients dies?

N: No, we really don't know our patients.

T: Doesn't life mean anything to you? Does it make any difference whether you know them or not?

N: How can you, when you know lots of people would be better off dead?

T: Aren't there other cases?

N: Yes, but what can you say to people when they ask you why their kid has to suffer or die? You can't do much but try to comfort them.

T: Don't you think the Bible could help?

N: Yes, I guess so. But you'd have to know where to turn—or have memorized some verses. You'd have to know it real well.

T: Well?

N: I guess you're right about that. If we nurses read the Bible a lot more, then we might give a lot more comfort than we do now, I guess.

T: Yes!

N: I guess the Bible says it better than we do, too. Like the twenty-third psalm—you know, the valley of the shadow of death. Maybe you're right there.

T: Well, that calls for a lemonade.

While we are dealing here with a theological student, not a pastor—and an honest one if he can tell stories like this on himself—the story illustrates pretty well what not to do in such general religious discussions if we think that a person may have real religious needs which could profit from counseling.

The theological student got results of a kind. He got the student nurse finally to admit there might be something in reading the Bible and that this might have some relevance to her work as a nurse. But he made her *admit* it, give in to him in an argument. People who have been forced to admit they were wrong do not generally set up creative relationships with whatever the other person has proved himself right about.

The student fixed his attention on the intellectual content and rode roughshod over the student nurse's feelings. He tried to put his point across, made no effort to understand how she could have come to feel this way. He interjected things which, while logically relevant, were psychologically irrelevant—as when he reached the end of his patience and asked, "Doesn't life mean anything to you?" He permitted the childish elements in the nurse's religion to go unclarified, as in the swearing reference. He did not follow her leads at any time, but drove through in sledge-hammer style to prove his point. He persistently rejected the negative feeling of the girl in relation to the Bible and religion, merely treading it down heavily. And he misjudged the results, believing that because he had drawn an admission from her, he had accomplished something important.

Reconstruction is always risky and involves guesswork. But the following would seem to have been possible had this alert student made the contact at the end rather than the beginning of a course on counseling.

THEOLOGICAL STUDENT: That was some discussion, wasn't it?

NURSE: Yes, but I think he hedged the real issue. As a matter of fact I don't think he proved anything at all.

T: Off the beam, huh?

N: *I* thought so. He just told about how a lot of people find Christianity and find it helpful. And about the Bible helping them. But he didn't show how the Bible can help people, at least he didn't give any reasons I agreed with.

T: No pills for your particular pain then?

N: (*laughs*) Well, there may be something to that. Nobody over at the hospital reads the Bible. And my mother and father never do either. I'd feel funny if I tried to do it.

T: It isn't part of your own background?

N: No, it isn't. Of course we all went to church once in a while at home, and I went to young people's meetings there too. But gee, the Bible is thousands of years old. What good can it really be to us now?

T: It's problems today we have to face, and the Bible seems pretty old for that?

N: There may be something in it. If what he said tonight is true, a lot of the people in the Bible must have had troubles just like we have today. But I can't see what *I* could get out of it.

T: It's one thing for it to have meaning in general and another to see what meaning it might have for you.

N: Yes. When I came to nursing school, they gave me a Bible with references in the back—you know, what to do when discouraged, when you've lost a loved one, and all that. The only one I tried was for when you're weary, but my feet were just as sore after I'd read it.

T: Maybe you should have read the passages about foot washing at that point. But seriously, I take it you've wondered about this before.

N: Yes, I have. There's one girl at the hospital—she's a student too. She reads the Bible and prays a lot. We kind of respect her, but we all think she's queer. She does all the dirty work anybody will give her, and she's always cheerful, even if she can't throw a wisecrack.

T: You admire her, and yet you wish she weren't such a door mat?

N: That's it. Why, it's just as if she liked to be punished. And maybe some of the supervisors don't take advantage of her! She's got something all right, but I don't want to be like *that*.

T: You wish you could find something for you in the Bible, but still be able to wisecrack and gripe once in a while.

N: Yes. What do you think I should do about it? Once I did start reading it—from the beginning, you know. But when I got to those people who lived for hundreds of years, I just couldn't believe it and quit.

T: If you had some plan that made sense, you'd really like to try it?

N: Yes, I think I would. . . .

Maybe it would not have gone this way—no one can be sure—but the chances seem in favor of something of the sort. Note the differences. Here the student has his eye on the relationship, not just on the ideas, and permits it to develop without forcing it or withdrawing from it. He follows leads, accepts the nurse's negative feelings and questions as facts, and does not try to argue them out of existence. He shows her he understands how she can feel as she does, and he helps her clarify her conflicting feelings. She admires the Bible-reading nurse in one way but pities and dislikes her in another way; with a bit of help from the theological student she sees that there is nothing wrong with having these two feelings. The nurse is, after all, interested in religion and the Bible or she would probably not be at this meeting. The student helps her consolidate her feeling about Bible reading. If she does read the Bible, it will be according to some sensible plan, and it will be on her own initiative. Hence it may mean something, and stick. Furthermore she will not have the feeling that she must avoid all wisecracks and be a door mat in order to be a Bible reader.

Another theological student has reported a similar situation with a college student. The young college student we shall call Bill. Bill is from a small town, and his parents are rather casual church goers. Bill was baptized, but never joined the church. The theological student described him as sensitive and intelligent but poorly integrated and apparently ready to drift. This conversation took place after a social gathering at which both had been present:

BILL: How do you like theological school?

STUDENT: Very well. It's what I've been wanting to do for a long time, but the army stopped me for a while.

BILL: I ought to do something about *my* religion.

S: Should you? What do you mean?

B: Well, shouldn't I join a church or something? But I simply am afraid to go into a church.

S: Do you belong to a church?

B: No, I was baptized, but never joined. When I was older I didn't care much, and now I am always afraid when I go into churches. You know, that's the trouble with a church. You are always made to feel afraid. I mean, the church is so dark and quiet, but so large and everything.

S: Were you really afraid of going into a church?

B: My mother always got something out of it when she went. If she was unhappy, then she'd go to church, and when she came home she was always happier, or at least she felt better. I can't really understand that.

S: But what about your feeling that you ought to join the church or, rather, do something about your religion?

B: Well, I don't know, and I haven't been to church or thought about it much for a long time. But it seems to me that I believe in something that is religious. Maybe I ought to think about it more and decide what religion I belong in (*pause*). But you know, I can't understand so much of the stuff you hear in churches, and I don't think I believe it either. It simply can't be true.

S: What stuff?

B: Oh, you know. All about the Bible. And, well, you don't believe it, do you? You can't possibly believe it.

S: Just precisely what do you mean?

B: Well, for instance, about how the women saw Christ after he was put in the tomb and felt the nail holes in his hands. That's not possible, and I don't believe it at all. Do you think that happened? You couldn't. [Other points of the same kind were mentioned, with the same conclusion.]

S: Well, of course these problems you bring up are related to Christian faith, but are not central to Christian faith. I am not dodging the issue; and since you asked me what I believe, I'll try to tell you in part. But it takes a long time for anyone to find satisfactory answers to some of the questions you have raised. And different people differ as to ultimate conclusions. The question of New Testament criticism and the propositions of theologians are the place you might end up, but they are certainly not the place where you begin to look for final answers. [At this point the student took up the questions seriatim and answered them.] You see, the important point is that the disciples and the early Christians believed that Christ lived, regardless of how he lived. They began with that faith which they could not deny, and they built a Church on it.

B: But so much of all that doesn't seem true.

S: Perhaps not, but the one thing that seems incontrovertible is that fact of faith, of an experience out of which came belief.

B: But that happened a long time ago. And the Church is so bad, or so corrupt, or something.

S: Yes. Our main problem, though, seems to be to discover first of all our relation to God and what he means to us.

B: Do you think God is like the Church says? I mean does he care personally? Why should we have to talk about God anyhow? Things seem to run along by themselves. Oh, I guess I should have been brought up right. I should have been made to go to church, and then I would know what I believed and wouldn't have to worry about it now.

S: I suppose that's true; but after all, the very thing you are thinking about now is the fact that you cannot accept what is so conventionally accepted by so many others.

B: I guess that's right.

S: Now, since you feel you don't have a background of earlier religious training, you can take what are more mature insights, and in working through these things you can come to your religious beliefs with less trouble.

B: Perhaps.

This is really an extraordinary contact. The theological student perspired right down to his shoelaces. Bill began the interview with, "I ought to do something about my religion"; but after this had been discussed, he ended up with, "Perhaps." As the road to evangelism, the student's methods seem to leave something to be desired.

It would seem that the basic difficulty here is that the student unconsciously said to himself, "I'm a theological student. I've studied religion; this is a religious problem; therefore I've got to have the answer." And the more he tried to find it, the farther away he was from helping Bill find *his* answer. Note his inability to accept Bill's feelings as facts. After Bill had reiterated his feeling of fear in relation to churches, the student might have said, "There's something awesome about a church," and accepted that Bill did feel that way. Instead he asked, "Were you really afraid of going into a church?" In other words, "Come, come, my boy, don't tell me you're as childish as all that."

When Bill brought up the various things he could not believe, the student was defensive. He was afraid he could not answer very well, so he made Bill define the question very clearly before he tried. Thus he paid no attention to Bill's feeling, but only to the idea content of what he was saying. Soon he was under compulsion to discourse, which he did for minutes on end. We can see what he was driving at. But Bill could not, and that is what counts here. The focus of the discussion has left Bill long ago, and rests on some ideological stratum midway between Bill and the student but closely related to neither. At the end the student senses this, and thinks to stage a recovery by flattering Bill that it is a good thing to be alert enough to doubt and not merely conform. But by this time Bill can see no point in it, and he says, quite truthfully, "Perhaps." Let us not castigate this student. He is working it through; besides, we have all done much worse than this. The point is not that he did Bill harm but that he failed in an excellent precounseling opportunity.

Let us attempt a partial reconstruction of how it might have gone.

BILL: How do you like theological school?

STUDENT: Very well. It's what I've been wanting to do for a long time, but the army stopped me for a while.

BILL: I ought to do something about *my* religion.

S: Has it been on the 4-F list?

B: That's about it—unfit for service. You know, I'm actually afraid to go into a church.

S: Freeze up inside?

B: Sort of. When I look at a church, it always looks so dark and quiet, but so large and everything. You know, I think that's what's wrong with the church. It always makes you feel afraid.

S: A church looks awesome.

B: Yes, and I don't understand why I should feel quite that way about it. When I think of my mother, she used to go to a church when she got unhappy once in a while, and she always seemed to feel better when she came home. There's something positive in it, I guess, if you could only find it.

S: You'd kind of like to find it?

B: I guess I would, at that. It seems to me I believe in something that is religious, and I ought to think about it more and maybe decide to do something. But you know, I can't understand so much of the stuff you hear in churches, and I don't think I believe it either. It simply can't be true.

S: Some of the theology seems impossible.

B: It really does. Of course you're studying it, so I suppose it makes more sense to you. But I just can't see some of that stuff we're supposed to believe out of the Bible. Why, all that happened hundreds of years ago.

S: If you could get by some of these doubts, you'd like to do something about it.

B: Yes, I would. I don't know. Of course, I haven't been to church for

some time now. Maybe it isn't so hard to understand some of these things as I've thought. Do you think they're all impossible?
S: Well, I'd hardly be studying theology if I thought they were too bad, but I know some of them look mighty peculiar at first.
B: Maybe I ought to give it a try. . . .

Again we may be wrong. But there seems clear evidence that Bill had a reawakened interest in religion; that he needed some understanding of his doubts and perplexities about it; and that if he got a reasonable facsimile thereof, he might safely be left to work out the rest for himself. At any rate, this is the way I would hope the contact might have proceeded. We may leave Bill's predictability to the statisticians, with a probable error of plus or minus one conversion to the Church.

FROM a functional point of view it is probably best to think of the pastor as a group worker with a concern for individuals, and as doing some individual work. He meets people in many kinds of groups, and he meets individuals through the variety of ways in which he carries out pastoral work. If he is to be a true shepherd, he is always alert and sensitive in all of his contacts to the signs that indicate his help may be wanted and needed. His pastoral work is carried out for the sake of what it means to people then and there. At the same time it has always a prospective or anticipatory aspect which has been singled out for consideration in this chapter—pastoral work as precounseling activity.

Not only is there no contradiction between the pastor's counseling and his precounseling work but there is also a dovetailing of one into the other.[6] The fundamental principles of both, as we have tried to show, are the same, but we can run into serious difficulties if we fail to sense the distinctions between them. If we understand both the sense in which their basic principles are the same and the differences in translating these into action, both our pastoral work and our pastoral counseling can be more useful and contribute more to each other.

Both precounseling pastoral work and pastoral counseling itself seek growth on the part of parishioners toward deeper religious insights, greater understanding of life, more capacity to take the slings and arrows, more flexibility to meet changing conditions, and a firmer sense of eternal grounding on which steps may safely be taken. But counseling deals with the people who say, "I want it. I must do something with myself to get there. How can I proceed?" Precounseling deals with the folks who have not reached one of the probably several stages in their lives where they may be able to say this, but whose inner lives or life situations are hammering for growth.

Both want understanding in the relationship between pastor and parishioner. In counseling, the way of achieving that is the demonstration that anything brought up by the parishioner is understood. In precounseling, some anticipation may be necessary to remove probable misconceptions.

Both have no personal ax to grind in the sense that the pastor is emotionally dependent on the outcome. The counseling does not have to be successful in the sense that particular problems are solved in order to demonstrate its value. And in precounseling the test is not necessarily that it leads to counseling—certainly not if the need for what counseling can give is not present.

Both involve defining the relationship and the helping situation implicitly and, as needed, explicitly. In precounseling this definition is likely to have anticipatory elements; for example, the pastor may say, "My function is not to judge your conduct, but . . ." The ways of translating this principle into action differ, but the principle is the same.

Lastly, both counseling and precounseling are eductive. Both leave it up to the parishioner—after certain things are done. By the time counseling has started, it is up to the parishioner (within limits of time, of course) how far he will go, where he wants to arrive, what he wants to talk about and what he does not. In the precounseling situation all these things are up to the parishioner, plus whether or not he wants counseling. In both cases his right to be responsible for, and to run, his own life are held to throughout. The pastor may well know what would be better for him in a general way; that is, if these stubborn facts of the parishioner's emotions and background did not have to be considered. But since they do have to be considered, the pastor does not really know nearly as much as the parishioner does about how far he—the flesh and blood and emotional man—can go up the scale. It *is* up to him. And the pastor bethinks him that he is, after all, not a policeman or a judge or even a guide to Alpine heights, but a pastor, which is to say a shepherd.

The Pastor's Total Work as Preparation

Chapter Seven WE HAVE DISCUSSED PASTORAL COUNSELING IT-self—its aims, its methods, its meaning in a time perspective, its relation to what is done by nonpastoral counselors, and the basic approaches to it. In the previous chapter we have examined the pre-counseling significance of pastoral work; that is, we have seen that all the pastor's contacts with individuals may help prepare the way for pastoral counseling when and if needed. We have suggested that preparation for counseling is not the only valid focus from which to view pastoral work, though it is perhaps as important as any other.

In this chapter our sights will be set still higher as we try to consider briefly the significance of the pastor's total task from the point of view of how it may serve as preparation for counseling. It may be necessary to say here that this is not intended to imply that preaching or evangelism or the other activities of the pastor are meaningful only as they lead to counseling. That would be an imperialistic view indeed. The point is not this, but rather that all the activities—and the total task—of the minister have a significance, for or against, in relation to counseling. They may dispose people to seek counseling if and when it is needed, or they may successfully inoculate them against readiness to take such action. Therefore we have not adequately understood preaching and evangelism and the other activities until we view them from the one focus, among others, of their implication as preparation for counseling.

THE PASTOR'S ROLE AS ONE ROLE

THERE are two views current today concerning the role of the minister, with many shadings in between these views, and all quite apart from theological differences. Let us try to state these two, each in its own terms.

A person advocating the view of a multiple role might argue: "I realize that the pastor as a human being is one unit and not several. But that is more than can be said of his job. When we make a job analysis of the things he is called upon to do and the skills he

must have in order to do them, we may well be shocked at their
breadth and diversity. He is expected to be a shepherd and counselor, and in this role he must be understanding, sympathetic, wise,
and patient. He must also be a religious and ethical educator,
thoughtful, persevering, courageous, and pioneering. In his third
role he is a leader of worship and of that preaching which leads persons already within the Christian fellowship to move farther along
the road. Here he is dynamic and prodding, but also understanding
and encouraging. In his fourth set of garments he is an evangelist,
leader of missions, and preacher to those not within the fellowship
—striking, prophetic, fearless; one who is in, but not of, the world.
Fifth, he is an administrator and group leader—in which role he is
firm but selfless, getting others to work hard and find themselves
in service, showing the wisdom of Solomon and the patience of Job
in working out controversies, organizing with a skill worthy of scientists. Finally, he has a message of action for the world, in social outreach. He must be prophetic, caring not for the princes of this world,
faultless in social wisdom, strong as Hercules, brave as a martyr and
willing to be one. In all conscience, what do we want: man or para-
gon? In his person a minister may integrate these conflicting things.
He can learn when to be tender and sensitive and when to be tough
and resolute. But the reconciliation must be in him, for it is surely
not in his job. Small wonder if ministers occasionally develop a good
case of parochial schizophrenia."

A person advocating the view of one role might reply: "There is a
lot of wisdom in the multiple-role approach. The minister does need
a variety of skills, and he must engage in a variety of activities. The
trouble with that view, though, is that it sees nothing but activities.
In fact, it looks at the minister's role from the point of view of an
outsider. It is true that to an outsider the activities in which the minister must engage look entirely multifarious, because he is unaware
of the context in which they take place.

"As a matter of fact, the minister has one role; he is leader of a
particular section of the Christian community. Though he has many
activities, it is his relation to the Christian community which defines
his role. The role is not only deeper than the activities; the activities
would be quite different in their meaning if they were not based on
the role. As the leader of the Christian community, what does the
minister try to do? In general that is not hard to answer. He is concerned with growth of all within the Christian fellowship and with
growth of the fellowship itself. He is the leader in developing that
growth for children as they come into the Church (religious educa-

tion) and for all members of the fellowship as they come together (worship, preaching, religious education). He is the leader of the Church's outreach to bring others into the fellowship (evangelism, missions, religious education). He guides the Church as it reaches out to help build and rebuild the community (social outreach). He is the leader of the aid and support the fellowship gives to those who are handicapped, who face temporary obstacles, or who find unusual difficulties in the growth process (pastoral work and counseling). And he is the leader in the organization necessary to make all this really work (administration). There are many activities, but one role; many members, but one body. The pastor's task is organic, precisely because it has a variety of functions operating to the same end.

"There is a point to the multiple role in that the diversity of activities has still not received the consideration due it—for example, in the training of ministers. But if we merely followed it, we would either be tempted to commit ecclesiastical suicide, or else we would turn out technicians who could perform many functions but would be unable to serve as leaders of the Christian community. We do need job analysis. But we shall never get it unless we recognize some framework into which it fits. Probably we do need a more specialized ministry, in which one pastor does more counseling; another more education; and a third more evangelism. In an urban society that sounds like sense. But that is merely wise functional division of responsibility, not the refutation of one role."

The multiple-role view has had the field overwhelmingly to itself ever since the great development of modern science and technology began fifty or more years ago. Consider the plight of the seminaries. In a small school a few decades ago a single teacher was handling the entire practical field—preaching, pastoral work, and all the rest. He had to think of them as something of a unity. And if his students left without much of the knowledge we now have—thanks to the development of the social and psychological sciences—they had at least some protection against the idea that their task was to put together a lot of activities that contained no inherent bond of unity. Then came experimental and therapeutic and dynamic psychology, sociology and social psychology, cultural anthropology, psychiatry and psychosomatic medicine, and all the other studies of man as a social and psychological human being based, for the first time in human history, upon systematic observation. The teachers in the practical field were overwhelmed. For a time they declared these new studies out of bounds, having no significance for their job. Then, as it became obviously clear that the studies did have implications for the background of many things the pastor did—for example, the significance of dynamic psychology for pastoral work—our teachers had to change. They began to specialize. One of them became a specialist in sociology with reference to religion; another, a specialist in education with particular reference to religion; and so on. Such specialization was and is essential. But entirely too many teachers forgot there was a fundamental sense in which the minister's task was still one.[1] If the seminary student today has all of his work in the practical field with one professor, even a genius, he will have a very spare meal indeed. But if he gets his practical theological proteins, carbohydrates, and fats, from different people, who are so much more concerned with what makes them different than what makes them one that no sense of unity is communicated, then the student finds his theological body, unlike his physical body, will not do the rest unassisted. The moral of this story is not to throw out the specialists or to make them less expert, but to get them more interested emotionally in why they are all in the practical theology field than they are in their differences.

This may appear to be a digression. But what we are considering in this chapter is the total task of the minister from the focus—one of several possible—of what it means to his task as a counselor. We did not call it, "What the Minister Can Do to Drum Up Counseling Business." If we have only the multiple-role view in mind and fail to see the minister's task as a total task, then "drumming up counseling business" might be a fair charge against us. But if counseling is to be understood as one aspect of a task which has unity because of its very nature, then it is not only unfair but also inaccurate to talk of drumming up business, as if one set of activities existed chiefly to be used by another set. Full acceptance of the one-role idea has far-reaching implications—which work in no way against the proper and necessary specialization in the process of theological education.

The practical implications for our focus of counseling are immediate. For example, if what has been said about basic approach is correct in pastoral counseling, then we should find the other aspects of the minister's activities successful to the degree that they too support the one role which has been defined in previous chapters as we discussed counseling. Or if this volume had been focused around preaching or church administration, we should be able to discover that the fundamental approach and attitude involved would also be applicable to counseling. This is far from saying that they look alike on the surface, or that the details of their methods are the same. The differences in details are so obvious as not to require comment. But either we have been talking about the basic approach and attitude of the minister to his total task from the standpoint of counseling or what has been said is misleading, not only about the total task but about counseling as well.

This may be clarified by an illustration from preaching viewed in the light of the counseling and precounseling principles and approaches that have already been considered.[2] Ministers Arden and Barden are preaching sermons on the same subject, "The Forgiveness of God." Both recognize and include in their sermons such points as forgiveness is given freely by God, not earned by us; we are, in fact, sinful, and we need forgiveness; forgiveness cannot be understood or experienced merely as something we do to ourselves; Christ has made possible both our understanding and experiencing of forgiveness. In other words, if the theologians will concede the point, the Christian theology of these gentlemen is sound, and there is no fundamental difference in their theological ideas.

But if we take a cross section of Minister Arden's sermon, this is what we find:

The world of today does not want forgiveness. It wants pleasure, and prestige, and power. You and I live in this world, and we want those things too. Day after day we strain after them; then on Sunday we come here and try to clear our consciences. Will God forgive that? Suppose you come here today and say, "God, I've been a sinner all week, feeding my sinful pride. Give me a potion so I'll feel all right about it—even though I have to do the same thing all over again next week." My friends, you can't do it and be a Christian. What does your heart say to you this morning?

By this time half the congregation, the conscientious half, is feeling as guilty about something that is an amorphous blur in their minds as the preacher seemingly wants them to feel. The other half is stopping up its ears by rationalizing until the preacher gets to what they are probably calling to themselves "the positive side of his sermon." Here is moralizing and generalizing at work in preaching— and by no means in their crudest form. It seems reasonably clear that Preacher Arden is, before he is finished, going to try to coerce them into admitting something. And what he says will undoubtedly distract them from clarifying meditation upon why they, or man in general, face the conflict and predicament they do. The chances are that the sermon will conclude with a vague section on what we can do about it, while the congregation feels sufficiently browbeaten to get consolation only out of the idea that if they do what the preacher says, it might do someone good, but it is probably a good thing he did not become more specific about what should be done.

What, in the excerpt, does Preacher Arden not do that we have seen in counseling is of basic importance? He does not understand or communicate understanding, that is, help us comprehend why we are in the predicament we are. He does not make it clear that he accepts this as a fact; one moment he flames because it is true, and the next moment he implies that it could not be otherwise with man as he is—like castigating the potential divorcé for considering a divorce and then suggesting it was inevitable, relations between the spouses being what they were. Preacher Arden also fails to clarify the nature of the conflict in which we are caught individually and collectively. He does not show us that there may be some increase in awareness of how our attitudes and feelings may be released in such a way as to move us, individually and collectively, closer to true acceptance of the forgiveness of God.

Preacher Barden, on the other hand, in his sermon spoke like this:

It is impossible for a man even to be interested in the forgiveness of God unless he has faced the fact of sin. And while it is very easy for us in church to admit we are sinners, it is very difficult to confess—even in church—why and in what way we are sinners. And yet if we are to experience again and again the peace and renewal of God's freely offered forgiveness, we need to face how and why we are sinners. Sin is like a net in which we are caught, not like an ice cream cone we have bought despite our parents' order not to buy it.

It seems reasonably clear that Preacher Barden is not going to moralize by trying to force his congregation into feeling they are to blame—as if awareness of blame were the same as confession of sin. He is not going to generalize in such fashion as to let anyone make of sin either a club to hold over his head for an hour, in atonement for past naughtiness and in preparation for similar naughtiness to come, or a kind of spiritual fig leaf to conceal the nudity of his wrong approaches to life. He has no intention of distracting or diverting from the central matter under consideration, and he is not going to tell his people they *must* accept this or that. He is going to describe why we experience the forgiveness of God as little as we do and indicate how to make changes in our attitudes which may help us move toward that experiencing if we wish to do so. He is going to leave it up to us. Preacher Arden, in contrast, seemed to assume it was up to him.

Preacher Barden accepts the fact that life, including man's inner life, is like this. He will describe the fact vividly enough to make it clear, we may hope, but not as if it made him boil that this is so, or gives him backhanded satisfaction that it is so. He understands something of why it is so, and he will attempt to communicate that understanding. He will try to clarify what the essential conflict is, what pulls man two ways at once. He will finally consolidate and talk of what we may do as well as how we may look—but not before there has been preparation. And even then his final implication will not be, "You must . . ." but instead, "If you would, this . . ."

The point is that far from there being a fundamental contradiction between preaching and counseling, these two functions should exhibit the same basic approach; and in so far as they do, each aids the other. Preacher Arden's parishioners would tend to hesitate before approaching him for counseling, since he has revealed in his preaching attitudes which are moralistic, coercive, diverting, nonaccepting, nonunderstanding, and confusing. On the other hand, Preacher Barden's parishioners would sense in him acceptance, understanding, capacity to clarify, and genuine interest, which would tend to create confidence in him as a counselor.

Still we need to recognize that some of Preacher Arden's parishioners, sensing the authoritarian approach he represents, will seek his help, apparently on the basis of wanting to be told what to do. If in counseling he follows, as he is likely to do, the same approach he has shown in the pulpit, he will—perhaps after listening to the story—tell them what to do. They may consider him a wonderful man. But they will not have been helped to grow toward capacity to face their sin and accept the freely offered forgiveness of God and to move, under God, on their own responsibility and under their own steam. In contrast, the parishioners of Preacher Barden who come for help are likely to receive aid of the kind that helps them to help themselves. Such help as they get will make for growth and, under God, movement powered by their own engines.

Were we to imply that there was to be direct transfer of the principles or methods of pastoral counseling to, for example, preaching, we should be talking obvious nonsense. In counseling we listen more than we talk. In preaching we talk. But this is a situational difference, not a fundamental difference of attitude and approach.

We have already seen, in examining pastoral work in relation to pastoral counseling, that the bases are the same, though many very important things are different. We may recall what we stated as basic elements in the approach to precounseling pastoral work as they relate to preaching. The first was that help is offered in such a way that it may as easily be refused as accepted. People cannot be forced into counseling or into finding solutions for their troubles, nor into the kingdom of heaven or the Christian Church. A sermon should so clarify that he who is ready may move closer toward the Christian approach to the matter under consideration and he who is not so ready will be more clearly aware of how it is that he is not. A sermon accepts the fact that some people are choosing hell just as others are choosing heaven. It recognizes that every day is judgment day and that life, or the relationship of the person to God, is the judge.

Our second point in precounseling pastoral work was: The incorrect expectations which the parishioner is reasonably sure to have of the nature of counseling help are, as occasion warrants, explicitly disclaimed. Transferring this to preaching, we know there is a kind of everything-but-the-kitchen-sink preaching, which apparently offers much but which in reality is so self-contradictory that the fulfillment of one thing would automatically make another impossible. Good preaching is explicit in denying what we cannot expect as well as in affirming what we may look for. Good preaching defines a situation, such as God's relation to man. A sermon about eternal life, for example, would be but half good if it attempted to suggest only the "quality of life" idea, or in other ways dealt only with the positive. It should also attempt explicitly to disclaim ideas about immortality which every preacher knows to be current and whose continued existence imperils any fundamentally helpful approach to the question of the meaning of eternity.

The third point was: Once the pastor's role in the situation has been defined to the parishioner as well as possible, the pastor is content to wait. From the standpoint of preaching, this means the preacher is an interpreter or a witness, not a judge, a jury or a policeman. He describes and clarifies. He does not coerce or exhort.

We said also that the pastor is alert to evidences of the desire for help, but he does not exploit them. In preaching terms, the pastor stimulates the desire for growth in the Christian faith—by showing why it is so hard and yet so desirable, and he is guided in some measure by observation of the understanding his parishioners have of his interpretation of the message. But when he finds something helpful, he does not exploit it at the expense of the whole gospel. John Sutherland Bonnell reports that he feels a good sermon should show the preacher there is increasing relaxation of tension as it proceeds.[3] The preacher observes things of this kind, and they condition the way in which the message is presented. Yet he does not become a cultist, emphasizing, for example, the love aspects of the gospel at the expense of the judgment aspects just because more people tell him the sermons on love help them.

The procedure we have been following above runs the danger of seeming forced or mechanical. It could be, and to the detriment of counseling, preaching, administration, and the other activities which are within the framework of the minister's total role. But the danger of mechanical misinterpretation has to be risked even to clarify, much less prove, that the minister has an approach which forms a pattern instead of being merely a collection of various disparate attitudes pulled out from pigeonholes in various situations.[4]

ADMINISTRATION AS PREPARATION FOR COUNSELING

IF it is true that the pastor's role is one role and that the basic attitudes appropriate in one set of functions are also relevant—when properly transferred—to his other functions, then it is clear that a deeper understanding of one function should imply a deeper understanding of the other functions. At the same time, each function has special knowledge and skill connected with it, so that the transfer is far from being simple or automatic. As we have seen that the literal comparison of counseling situations with precounseling pastoral work situations is irrelevant unless the difference in the structure is considered along with the basic principles which are nearly identical, so we may believe that the comparison of counseling and preaching, counseling and administration, counseling and evangelism, and others, would be irrelevant unless the structural differences were considered along with the attitudinal similarities.

To attempt such a task adequately is far beyond the scope of this chapter. Here all that can be done is to suggest how the comparison and contrast can usefully be made. With our focus on counseling, our main concern is to see how the other functions of the minister— all within his unified role—may lead to counseling when and if needed.

In an earlier chapter we have given an illustration from the field of administration which is also relevant at this point.[5] Here is another. A young minister of considerable ability came into a new church, where he soon discovered that the church was really run by three men, two in late middle age and an older man. While there was an

undercurrent of opposition to the domination exercised by the trio, it
had never become active enough to be successful. The men ran the
church not so much because they had a faction behind them as
because they were forceful persons and had always been able to
override potential opposition. As the minister saw the situation,
younger leadership was not being developed in the church but was
actually being discouraged; and because of the set ways of doing
things, a number of programs in the church were running into the
ground when they should be expanding their usefulness.

Seeing that the three men were, for all practical purposes, blocking
the wheels of progress and that the undercurrent of opposition was
beginning to move, the minister knew that the situation was all set
for the development of factions within the parish. A little encouragement from him and the church would be torn in two. If the issue
arose in such form, the trio might gather a considerable number of
members around them. Such a split would do no one any good, at
least unless every other method of handling the matter should fail.
On the other hand, the minister could not either in conscience or in
strategy identify himself with the trio. Nor could he play the
hypocrite, saying Yes to the three men when with them and Yes to
others when with them. Not only would this be false but it would
also be poor strategy—and sure to catch up with him eventually.
Already the situation bears resemblance to counseling. There is a
conflict beginning to rise to the surface. On the basis of the objective
issues the minister has conviction on one side of the possible outcome rather than the other. But if he identifies himself with either
in the sense of agreeing on the issues with one or the other, he loses
his capacity to help.

So he followed the course of democratic approach in leadership,
understanding, and encouraging younger leadership for its own sake
when it could do the job, but listening as patiently and understandingly to the suggestions of the three men as if they represented the
type of leadership he felt would be helpful. Other leadership began
to develop in the church. It came first in the young people's groups.
Here it was educed by the minister to get the job itself done, not as
a means of developing opposition to the dictators. Then came a
change in the church school, from which, strangely enough, the trio
had excluded themselves.

The time came, however, for the annual financial canvass. For
years one of the three had served as chairman of the campaign, and
the results had been a good deal less than general analysis of the
congregation would seem to suggest as possible. The methods had

fallen into a rut, especially on the publicity end. This year, for the first time, the local council of churches was considering a united church canvass in the community, with the great advantage of a community-wide publicity and promotion campaign on a unified basis, thus aiding the actual canvass made by each local church. Naturally the pastor himself saw the advantages. When first proposed and discussed at a board meeting, it was presented by the secretary of the local council of churches. One of the trio, board chairman, then abruptly dismissed the secretary of the council, informing him the board would discuss it and let him know. The chairman then explained he was against the idea and presented reasons which, to the minister, were clearly specious. He called upon his two supporters, and later upon others. The others were all doubtful. They felt the trio must be wrong, but lacked the knowledge and leadership to say so emphatically. Finally the minister was called upon. He attempted to summarize the issues, not as he himself saw them, but as they had emerged in the discussion, concluding that the decision was up to the board. The chairman asked if someone would move against participation. One other member, who had learned something from the minister's analysis of the issues, moved instead that the matter be tabled until the next meeting so there would be time to think it over. This action, despite the chairman's objections, was seconded and carried by the other members of the board.

The three men were on the spot. Next day the chairman of the board came to see the minister, and the following ensued: .

CHAIRMAN: I didn't like that discussion of the canvass last night, and I've come here to talk to you about it.
PASTOR: I'm glad you have, with our final decision coming up next week.
CHAIRMAN: I must say I didn't think much of what you did last night. I know you didn't come out and say you were for the united program, but you know as well as I do that if you had said you were against it at this time—until it had proved itself—we would have decided the question then and there.
PASTOR: Because I didn't explicitly support your suggestion, you feel that I in effect opposed you.
CHAIRMAN: Well, yes. It does strike me that way. And it isn't the first time either. When we brought you here, we were told you were a good man, not wild-eyed with a lot of newfangled ideas. And you have done a good job with the young people.' But we have built up something distinctive in this church, and you don't seem to place much value on it.
PASTOR: In other words, my not seconding your suggestion last night

suggests that I am not following the tradition that has been built up here.

CHAIRMAN: I think it does. I don't think you quite realize the time that Brown and Green and I have put into this church—and you know we're all busy men outside.

PASTOR: I do know you've given the church a great deal of time. And your feeling is that because you have, I should get behind your suggestions?

CHAIRMAN: I don't mean to say you should always agree with me. But I don't think you've thought over the consequences of such a thing as our going into this united canvass. If you had, I think you would have supported me.

PASTOR: What you're saying then is that if I don't support you, I'm against you—and that shows I don't know the real issues involved.

CHAIRMAN: That's a blunt way to put it, but I think that's about the size of it. It's not that I want to run things, you understand, but I have been around here a good while, putting a lot of time in on the church. And I think I know what this church needs.

PASTOR: Well, I think you define the issue clearly enough. You believe that until I've been here at least as long and had as much experience as you and Mr. Brown and Mr. Green have, I should have no ideas or convictions which are in conflict with yours. Do you really think that as a Christian minister I could give any individual or group a blank check like that?

CHAIRMAN: Oh, I'm not talking about your theology or anything like that.

PASTOR: No, so long as my convictions are in a realm where they don't affect the everyday administration of the church, I may have them. But if they touch the day-to-day work, that's a different story. That's a distinction I find it very difficult to make. When I came to this church, a number of people informed me that it was run by you and Brown and Green. As I observed it for myself, I saw that you men had done many fine things for the church. But I saw also that new leadership was not being developed in the church, the young people's program was not in good shape, the religious education program had been neglected. We have done something about those things and will do more, and I know you are for improvement in those fields just as I am. In board meetings and other things here in the church I have viewed my function as a minister to be one of helping, not of telling just what should be done or standing with one group against another. I believe a church should be run democratically. Last night in our discussion, as you yourself have pointed out, I did not take sides on the issue. What I did when you invited me to speak was to clarify the very issues—on both sides—the rest of you had raised. It was not I who made the motion to postpone decision; it was Jones; and all the others except you and Brown and Green immediately supported him. It may be true that if I had supported your suggestion, a negative decision could have been reached last night. But it was not I, but the board, that vetoed you. It seems to me that what you are objecting to is not really me, but the fact that the rest of the board overrode your suggestion.

CHAIRMAN: You could have supported me, and then we wouldn't be where we are now.

PASTOR: I want to make it perfectly clear that I am not against you. Even beyond the fact that you have contributed valuable service to this church, I am your pastor. But if we have a board, then the board itself must exercise the right to decide the questions that come before it; and if the board requests my comments, it has the right to have them.

CHAIRMAN: Of course we could think of getting a new pastor.

PASTOR: If you feel that my presence here threatens you in any way, and if you put that consideration first, then you will probably want to consider that seriously. But I think you realize what that would do to the church.

CHAIRMAN: I'm not saying we are going to do it. I'm just reminding you it's within our power.

PASTOR: And I in turn am defining my position. You are free to be as frank and as angry as you like with me. You may say what you think. But I in turn am free to exercise my function as I understand it.

Subsequently the board voted to enter the united church canvass. The chairman, recalcitrant on the question, tried unsuccessfully for a while to regain the control he had had; eventually he resigned and left the church. So did the second member of the trio. The third man, with whom the pastor also talked, made a readjustment and is still a valuable member of the church.

This shows the difficult kind of administrative situation in which the minister occasionally finds himself and how important his basic approach is in handling such situations. At the proper time the situation had to be defined to the chairman. It had to be made as clear as possible that the pastor did not equate his ideas and his dominance with his self-respect, as the man himself did. He had to be left free to change his mind or not, to try to oust the minister or not, to try to create factions in the church or not. But since he had been given a chance to declare his intentions, the minister had to deny explicitly acceptance of them without giving the impression that this meant he was against the man himself.[6]

The elements we have previously discussed in connection with counseling and precounseling pastoral work are relevant to good administration. Being understanding and not passing judgment, sticking to the point as the parishioner sees it, helping to clarify the situation and the relationship, defining and redefining the relationship as needed—these and other points are also relevant in administration. A further reference to the democratic approach in administration may be in order. One sometimes hears pastors speak of church administration as if it were something they themselves had to do alone. And in contrast some others speak of administration as if there were a coercive trick, concerned with getting other people to do work which otherwise the minister himself would have to do. The real point is not how much any one does but the way in which it is decided what should be done and who should do it. These attitudes are travesties on the eductive approach. It is a clever trick to get people to become active, for example, by flattery. It may work in administration for a longer period than in counseling; but eventually it feeds on and consumes itself.

If administration is carried out consistently by the eductive approach, it is bound to be excellent preparation for counseling. Suppose the board chairman, instead of merely becoming more defensive the more clearly he saw what he was really trying to do, had become more open to the possibility of change, as one of his friends did. Then the situation would have been defined, and there would have been no inconsistency if it moved over into a counseling relationship. In this way administrative relationships can prepare the way for counseling.

One additional illustration may help. In a certain church small sums of money had for some weeks been taken from coats in the coatroom during the Sunday morning service of worship. Finally a guard was set, and he discovered a fifteen-year-old boy, active in the young folks' department, stealing. He took the boy to the minister's study, and following the service the minister came and found him there. Here is what followed:

PASTOR: Sorry I have to see you here under these circumstances, Bob. You must have had some reason for doing this.
BOB: You can't prove I took money just because I was in that coatroom.
PASTOR: The money was found in your pocket by Mr. Weems, wasn't it, Bob? Of course I know it was. And we've got to decide what to do about the situation. What I'm more interested in is why you felt the need to take this money. I'd like to know how you felt about it.
BOB: I don't know. I just felt like doing it. What are you going to do to me?
PASTOR: What we're going to do depends entirely on you. I can't think you did this for no reason at all. You may have done it because you don't get an allowance at home, or because you wanted to treat some-

body, or because things have been going badly for you at home or in school. I'd like to know how you feel about things.

BOB: Oh, I don't know. I suppose I'd better admit I did it. I don't know why. I just felt like doing it. Yeah, I get an allowance at home, but it isn't much. And by the time I get my club dues paid, I look pretty cheap down at Henry's (drugstore). My old man says a dollar a week is enough for someone my age. That makes me pretty sore.

It is clear that from this point on the pastor has something to work with. His first temptation would have been to bawl the boy out, or to say he never expected this from such a fine lad brought up in the church. He resists that. Then his temptation may be to say, "Don't give the money a second thought. That isn't what counts. It's you. You must be unhappy." This would have closed Bob up like a clam. The minister is, whether he likes it or not, in a position where the interests of the group of which he is leader seem to run counter to Bob's interests. But this conflict is only apparent, not real. It might become real, and does so in some situations, as with the board chairman. But even there the pastor had exercised everything he was capable of, not only in the interests of the group but also in the best interest of the chairman himself. In Bob's case it works. A difficult administrative situation handled wisely becomes a counseling situation. The pastor was able to help Bob get at the family relationship situation which was behind the theft. Good administrative handling, even in the most unlikely situations, is not basically different in approach from good counseling, and it may serve as preparation for counseling as needed.[7]

OTHER FUNCTIONS AS PREPARATION FOR COUNSELING

WE have given brief attention to preaching and administration from the standpoint of their serving as preparation for counseling. We might also do the same for evangelism if time permitted, but I have discussed that elsewhere in easily accessible form.[8] There are also implications in religious education, and these too have been discussed elsewhere. We may give merely a paragraph or two about each.

In our own society, and indeed in much of the world today, the task of evangelization is not one of bringing the message in the form of certain ideas, convictions, and practices to people who have never heard such a message presented before. It is rather a matter of helping people to see and accept and act on a message of which they have heard the word but not the tune; of helping them understand why they have previously considered the message to be nonsensical or irrelevant or threatening instead of true and meaningful. To do this the evangelist needs to know not only his message; he needs to understand also what has hitherto prevented its acceptance.[9] He ceases to be a high-pressure salesman out to talk down sales resistance and becomes instead an interpreter of people to themselves in the light of the Christian message, which he makes specifically relevant to the person or group with whom he is dealing. In mission lands there is still ignorance, and that must be met on that basis. But even there missions fail unless they understand the people as well as the Christian message; for if they do not understand the people, they do not understand the relevance of the Christian message to those people. Most missionaries discovered this truth long ago. The main evangelistic battle, outside mission lands perhaps, is with paganism rather than with merely intellectual ignorance. A pagan is a man who has heard the words but has been deaf to the tune. We do not get him to hear the tune by yelling more loudly, but by helping him look into the causes of his tone-deafness. We may condemn paganism, but we try to help pagans.

The religious educators keep pointing out that from one perspective the entire program of the Church is religious education; and if religious education means that which fosters Christian growth, this is true.[10] But in the more formalized sense in which religious education is discussed, meaning groups of children and adults studying together, the potential significance from our focus of preparation for counseling is no less clear. There are two ways in which the basic eductive approach we have discussed in relation to pastoral counseling finds its way into such group work. The first is through person-mindedness, or individual-mindedness.[11] A church-school teacher does not merely run a group program, becoming irritated at anything which retards achievement of group objectives. She is interested in the persons in the group; a retarder is to be understood and helped, not merely condemned.[12] The second way is that in the conduct of the group itself the teacher will apply eductive principles. If Johnny can be helped to state and interpret, if Susie can correct it a little, and if the teacher will then clarify it, it is worth ten times what it would be if the teacher merely told Johnny and Susie the right answer.[13] This is not the method versus content issue, nor even the issue of the extent to which the teacher decides what should be covered and discussed. It has to do with basic approach to the process of helping people comprehend and assimilate the meaning of religious truth.

If the pastor and other leaders of the program of religious education are both person-minded and eductive in their approach to group teaching, then relationships and attitudes are set up which make it relatively easy for counseling to begin, either with teacher or pastor, as need arises. If the basic approach is of a different order, then it has to be discounted when and if help is needed.

It may be well to add a word indicating that teaching from an eductive approach does not mean complete freedom on the one hand or on the other hand cleverly coercing students to do what the teacher has decided on in advance. Contrast the following definitions of the teaching and learning situation, all made in a seminary classroom by three different teachers during the first class session.

FIRST TEACHER: We have no set plan in this course. What we do is entirely up to you. We are supposed to be a class in religious education, but if you want to discuss thus and so, that is all right with me. I believe in the democratic process, and your interests alone will guide this class.

Suppose he really means it just this way, which is unlikely. Then one can imagine that a few of the most aggressive students could so manage the course that others would fail to get what they wanted, and the result would be not democracy but anarchy.

SECOND TEACHER: I always have my classes decide how we are going to take up the subject. We can decide how many topics we want to take up and then how we want to proceed. What we take up and how we do it are up to you.

Strangely enough, however, the class came up with eleven topics for discussion, which with minor changes, turned out to be precisely the eleven topics considered by the class the year before and the year before that. This was shadow of democracy without substance. The teacher knew exactly what he wanted and intended to have. He did not have the confusion that the first teacher had between lack of structure and democratic method, but he had so little faith in real democratic method that all he could do was to use it as a screen for his unrevealed intentions.

THIRD TEACHER: There are some conditions and requirements in this course, and I am going to outline them. That will tell you the framework in which we are working. Within those requirements we shall conduct this class on a democratic basis. You say what you believe and feel, within the limits of decency, and I will do the same. I have no intention of withholding my own views; if I tried to, you'd guess them anyhow. But neither am I going to lay them out in such fashion that you may be made to feel you have to accept them.

If this teacher really follows this—and it can be done—then he is applying the eductive approach to his classroom. And as he hears, understands, and conveys his understanding of the point of view each person may try to express, he is not only serving as an effective teacher but he is also laying good groundwork for counseling when and if needed.[14]

We have now touched on preaching, evangelism, religious education, and administration from the standpoint of their function as preparation for counseling. And in the process we have at least suggested that the basic approach in counseling and pastoral work, if correct, is equally applicable—properly adapted in methods and details—to these other functions. There remains one major function to be mentioned, the social outreach of the Church.

There should be no need for arguing that social outreach into the community is as great a concern of the pastor and the Church as is any other of the functions previously discussed. So we shall assume it, despite the fact that it is the "high-tension" area of the pastor's work and of churchmanship today. From the Christian gospel itself we find clues to the reorganization of life not only within the individual and the Christian fellowship but also within the whole community of mankind—which means the social order.[15] There are considerable differences among different branches of Christendom as to how detailed the clues are from the gospel itself. And there are certainly wide differences on the nature of the approach—as distinguished from details of method—which is believed to be inherent in Christianity. There is almost universal agreement that Christianity has an approach rooted in its essential character—however that be defined—which is relevant to the social order.[16] But because of the wide differences in what that approach is considered to be, it is especially important to see whether or not our eductive plan fits here as it did in relation to the other functions of the pastor.[17]

Programs of social action and outreach tend to be more successful in achieving their legitimate Christian objectives when they are carried out with an eductive viewpoint. We may have specialists who are priests or prophets, to the gain of the Church and community. But no priest can be wholly a minister unless he has some of the prophet in him, and no prophet can be wholly a minister unless he has something of the priest and pastor in him. And before the real dilemmas can be confronted, the false dilemmas must be set aside.

The latter are illustrated by the theological student who said, "I believe Christianity has a revolutionary message to the social order. When I go out to preach next fall, I must in conscience preach the gospel as I understand it. A lot of people aren't going to like that. And then what happens to me and my wife and children?"

A pastor said to him, "Is there something in the idea that we need to earn the right to speak prophetically? Do we need first to understand the people and serve them, so that we will know what the prophetic message will mean not only to us but also to them, and so that the relationship between us will be strong enough to take this aspect of the whole Christian gospel?"

After a few minutes of such discussion the student said, "I've been to a good seminary and have almost finished, but no one ever said anything like this to me before. I begin to see there's a difference in the way of going about the social gospel—looking *with* them at an evil situation we have all tried to avoid instead of batting them over the head with it. I need to be concerned with results, not just having a clear conscience."

A false dilemma had been done away. Let us hope the student continues, however, to see the true dilemma and to act with vigor and courage as well as wisdom.

A pastor in a fairly large northern city bethought him of one way to implement his nonsegregation convictions on racial questions—to hire a qualified Negro, if available, as one of his three secretaries and office workers, since one of his workers had just left. He first called in the other two girls and spoke as follows:

PASTOR: Now that Miss Winters has left, we must get someone else for the office. I am considering something very seriously; but before I act on it, I want to talk it over with you because it concerns you too. You know my feelings about the way in which we treat minority racial groups in this country and this city, especially Negroes. And you know that I don't believe in arbitrary segregation of Negroes just because their skin is black in such matters as housing, employment, and the like. I think you know that I hold these beliefs basically because they seem to me entirely clear implications of the Christian gospel itself. It is not a mere matter of taste or preference, or even a sense of pity for the oppressed. My belief is based on my understanding of the gospel.

You know I've tried to do things here in the community and support things in the nation which seemed to me to help move us a bit closer toward Christian brotherhood in race relations. But we have not been very imaginative as we have come closer to home. Of course we have the exchange of pulpits with Negro ministers twice a year, and the one-Sunday visitation by the young people. These things are good, but we need more. What would our session do if a Negro applied for membership in our church tomorrow? Would he be a Negro first and a Christian second or a Christian first and a Negro second? I don't know what they would do.

But there is one thing we can do right here in this office. We can, I think, find a perfectly competent secretary to work here with us who happens to be a Negro. She must be competent; we cannot afford to have someone who is not. I think we can find one, and I'd like to try.

But you girls are concerned also. I could not make a move like this without talking it over with you. You know you can be frank with me.

FIRST SECRETARY: I think it's a good idea, and I think it would help.

PASTOR: How about you, Miss Jamieson?

SECOND SECRETARY: Well, I'm going to be frank about it. I just wouldn't like it at all. You know I'm interested in justice for Negroes. I know they don't have proper educational chances and can't get lots of jobs even when they are well trained. And I'd like to do all I can for them. But I just can't see it here, in this neighborhood. For instance, what would Mrs. Burley say if she walked into this office and found a Negro working here?

PASTOR: I'm not sure what she'd think at first. But after she had stayed around for ten minutes, I'm inclined to think she'd make just as much or as little fuss about it as you or I were making.

SECOND SECRETARY: Well, maybe. But I just don't know how I could take it. It's not that I dislike—well, I've just never worked or been with any Negro before. Of course we've had Dr. West from Howard here speaking, and that's all right; but that's different. This would be every day, lunch, washroom, everything.

PASTOR: You feel a kind of revulsion about the matter?

SECOND SECRETARY: I guess it is something like that. I don't know why I should. I certainly don't have any race prejudice. But—oh, last night when I was going home on the bus, a big Negro got in and just bumped or pushed me as hard as he could. He just wanted to get through, and he didn't care who was in the way. I don't know. The idea just sort of gets me.

PASTOR: You can see some logic and meaning in this idea, but you have a kind of reaction inside when you think about what it would mean to everyday work here?

SECOND SECRETARY: Yes, I do feel that way. But I do see why you think it would be a good idea too.

PASTOR: Would you like to think it over and talk about it again tomorrow?

SECOND SECRETARY: I guess that would be a good idea.

PASTOR: Let's keep this entirely quiet for the moment. If we do decide to do it, we would want to take it as a matter of routine business and not make a special issue of it. And if we decide against it, then it would be bad if it were known we had made such a decision.

The chances look pretty good that Miss Jamieson will be willing to try the plan. If she does, it will work vastly better than if the pastor had announced his decision as a *fait accompli*. Suppose she moves in the other direction? The pastor can try again—perhaps helping her to see that making a decision in the face of the feeling she has demonstrates more the kind of thing which must be done to solve racial inequities than if she were like the first secretary and had no such feelings. Maybe that will fail. The pastor may decide to keep on working with her or to ignore her feelings and go ahead. She may resign. That would defeat the purpose of the plan, so he would use it only as a last resort. The point is not whether or not he will be successful in helping her, because the two of them already share common Christian convictions. But he must show her how to apply them concretely and voluntarily where before they have been only an abstract issue. He may or may not succeed; we do not know Miss Jamieson well enough to know. However, it is clear that any other method of approach will run the risk of having poor consequences. He is using strategy, but the strategy is not a mere device for getting something. It is inevitable once the eductive principle is applied to the social outreach of the gospel.

This is in no sense to suggest that there are not times when the pastor and the Church need to stand up and be counted. But this is not necessarily every time anyone says, "Now is the time to stand up and be counted." Furthermore, the eductive approach cannot be defined solely in terms of majority votes—as much as we respect majority votes. The criteria, as we understand them from the Christian gospel, may or may not be in accord with the majority. A majority vote on a question shows what the majority believe, not necessarily what the gospel implies. In our democratic approach to Christianity we think some attention must be paid to both.

The adaptation of the eductive approach to the social outreach function of the pastor is perhaps the most complex of all. These comments have been merely suggestive. In any case, our illustration shows one of the ways in which the pastor's function in social outreach may also and at the same time serve as preparation for counseling.

SUMMARY

THE pastor has several functions but one role. He carries out a variety of activities requiring several kinds of knowledge, but he works within one framework. His counseling and pastoral work, evangelism and missions, worship and preaching, religious and ethical education, administration and social action are not indications of fundamentally conflicting roles, but are inherent aspects of his performance of his role. His role is defined as a leader of a segment of the Christian community or fellowship. It is this that defines his total task.

The rest of this book focuses on the pastor's counseling work. The basic approach developed is essential to all effective counseling activity and to pastoral work. This has been distinguished from precounseling pastoral work in details, while at the same time demonstrating the essential identity of the principles. When it is understood that other aspects of the minister's activity and functions have significance as they do or do not prepare people for counseling, it becomes clear that the approach which is basic to counseling and pastoral work is also, if properly adapted, equally important and fundamental for the other functions of the minister.

From this focus—and it is not the only possible one—of counseling the total work of the pastor as well as each of his functions has significance, positively or negatively, as preparation for counseling.

Chapter Eight THE PASTOR HAS TWO REASONS FOR BEING INTER-
ested in the way other counselors prepare for counseling or carry out
their precounseling work. First, he may learn something from what
others do. Second, if what we have said in the chapter on the pastor
and other counselors is true—that all good counselors share some
knowledge and some method and some approach—then we must be
concerned with the means of contact used by all counselors in seeking out those who need aid. What kind of public relations do
counselors have? [1]

Someone has defined a profession as a group of people who talk
to one another in a language no one else can understand and who
make their living out of exhibiting this fact. There is a grain of
truth in this. Generally speaking, understanding among members
of different professional groups that they have interests in common
antedates admission of this same fact to the public. One might say
that public relations tend to be the last stronghold of isolationist
professionalism.

It may be of more help to us if instead of taking up each group of
counselors separately we consider the various representative types of
appeal they—and we—make to the public concerning counseling
activity, the impressions that are given about who needs what help
and when and the degrees of skill with which various media of communication are used to enable the people who need help to get it.
And we shall also suggest the principles or elements in the approach
which might well be common to the precounseling work of all the
counselors, pastoral and otherwise. [2]

TYPES OF APPEAL

NO professional group that does counseling confines the type of
appeal it makes to potential clients, patients or parishioners to any
single one of the appeals mentioned below. Nor is this list intended
to be exhaustive. The following elements, however, can be found

implicitly or explicitly in the type of appeal which the respectable counseling groups—including pastors—make to people.

1. *"Get help the scientific way."* Science is a magic word. The public sees some of the fruits of science in technology and calls them science. Because they are wonderful, anything which can with success identify itself with them carries the prestige of science. This means that the layman's unspoken conception of science tends to be, "Something mysterious that experts carry out, from which come results we can trust because we see they are wonderful." That which can identify itself successfully with science, therefore, carries a prestige and authority, and even a dogmatic loyalty, which in past ages has generally been characteristic only of religion. As in some more ancient societies the priests or experts may know better, but the public does not, else our advertisements would not be so filled with references to "science" that have nothing to do with the methodological exploration and elucidation which characterize science.

Because of the nature of this prestige, and also because our knowledge and methods in counseling have in fact come from application of the true scientific method, hardly any group which does counseling can afford not to mention science if it is to have an appeal. The problem is: Does the appeal say what it means by science? Is it the glamorous appeal, as in the advertisements, of the prestige value involved? Or is it, in however brief a way, an appeal to the authority of experience tested by the nonmysterious methodical application of scientific investigation? "Get help the scientific way" may be the legitimate appeal to the authority of investigated experience, or it may be merely the modern version of appeal to the mysterious. It may be authoritative or authoritarian. The criterion is the extent to which it explains how it arrived at what it knows and does in relation to helping people.

2. *"We reinforce your common sense."* Many people have been burned by previous experience of responding to appeals of mystery and magic, and it is as if they had then said, "A plague on both your houses." In their heads they have the idea that an atom, for instance, exists somewhere; that is, they have not theoretically rejected the authority of the expert in his own field. But any time the expert gets close to their personality, they reject him categorically, making no attempt to distinguish whether his claims are based on demonstrable evidence or on prestige appeal. He is rejected just because he claims to know something or to be able to do something, the processes of which are not immediately apparent. To these folks—and they are many in our society—the appeal to common sense is

powerful. It appears to protect the ego. It implies, "We will do nothing you can't understand at a glance; hence you are completely protected throughout."

Like the appeal to science, the appeal to common sense may mean two things. It may make contact with people who do not respond to any type of "expert" approach. And it may indicate that there is nothing inherently incomprehensible in what occurs during the counseling process, that nothing basically magic or esoteric is involved. If the appeal to common sense is a way of making contact and if this is then followed in counseling, it can be legitimate and important. On the other hand, it can be a trick or device falsely deluding people into believing the human psyche is so simple it can be understood at a glance, like the appeal of the phrenologist against that of the physiologist. It can also be, from the point of view of the counselor, a kind of screen behind which a counselor may hide—just as another counselor may use the screen of "science." Such a counselor cannot study complexity without feeling complex; so to reduce his anxiety in the face of complexity, he resorts to oversimplified, rough and ready methods and calls them common sense. And since almost any method, however bad it is, gets some superficial therapeutic results if there is some interest in the client or patient, enough results are secured here to anchor the counselor more firmly in the theory of oversimplified common sense.

Again the point is what does the appeal to common sense really mean? A legitimate means of contact with those disillusioned by esoteric pseudoexpertness? An assurance that the dice are not loaded? Or an attempt to win power on no more reasonable basis than oversimplification of the realities of psychic life? A defensive device to make the counselor feel comfortable in the face of complexities he cannot understand and whose existence he is prone to deny?

3. *"It's normal to have problems."* Every counselor knows this can have a strong appeal. So deeply do people tend to fear nonconformity that any deviation from "normality" is always assumed to be something bad. Nearly all counselors, in their strategic problem areas, began their work and built up their initial legitimate claims on the basis of pathology, helping people who had troubles and did deviate from statistical averages. Hence the public has some legitimate reason for believing their work is with the sick, the abnormal, the pathological, or the problem cases. Yet all these counselors have found two things: first, that they can help those other than the "abnormal"; and second, that everyone has at least sometimes "problems" in his life, and that handling these by recognizing them and getting

help on them is a mark not of pathology but of superior insight and courage.

The appeal to normality may, therefore, be legitimate or illegitimate. It may mean, "Problems are a part of growth; to recognize them and get help on them as needed is a mark of continued growth. We help people, not put labels on them." Or it may mean, on the other hand, "You are not abnormal. We don't deal with abnormal people. Your problem has nothing to do with *you*. See us and be reassured." The second panders to the common misconception, and in such a way that the expectations of the person coming for counseling will be illegitimate. In the first meaning of the normality appeal, the opposite is true.

4. *"Every problem is different."* Modern clinical medicine began with differential diagnosis based on knowledge of the underlying processes, and this has proved its indispensability in other areas as well. Every person *is* different, from fingerprints to temperament. Over and above the realities of these differences, however, there is, in an increasingly mass-influence society, a reactive tendency to assert and reassert that difference in any respect in which personality is involved, as if individuality were maintained only if each of its component parts was equally individual. The result is misleading. If what the counselor intends to convey is, "I do not treat people like machines, or merely in mass, but as the individuals you all are," then he is quite unlikely to achieve the goal of communication if he merely says, "Every problem is different. Your situation is unlike that of anyone else. I will look at the real you." For what this will be likely to convey to his hearer is, "I can be somebody, at least in the eyes of this fellow, though I know better myself down underneath. Maybe he can convince me I am."

Like the other appeals we have considered, this one may mean two things. On the one hand, it may convey the respect which the counselor actually has for each person as such, his respect for basic individuality, his disclaimer of knowing more about what the other person is capable of than he knows himself. On the other hand, it may be an appeal to a person oppressed with the sense of conformity but willing to take only such measures to overcome it as require no pains of transformation. Instead of receiving help on the proper ways of looking at and cultivating his own individuality, he merely receives the evaluation of someone else, who may value it more highly than he himself does. Therefore he is likely to emerge with higher, but still more illusory, positive self-feelings.

5. *"You must experience it to know."* There is something in every

effective counseling experience which is not foreseen by the person. He gets some insight or transformation which he had not entirely expected. This is like any effective religious experience. There is a sense in which the potential values cannot be entirely communicated in advance to the prospective "consumers." On the other hand, "You must experience it to know" may also be an appeal to the esoteric, a kind of magical promise, a suggestion not only that there are cards up the counselor's sleeve but also that they are all aces. It is important to distinguish these two meanings.

6. *"The cause of your trouble is more respectable than you think."* If a man has gone to five physicians who tell him the basis of the difficulty he is having with a sore leg is not organic but functional, he is quite likely to believe a sixth doctor who tells him the trouble is real. The delusion that only physiological causes are real is widespread, but it is based on something broader—that we do not feel personally threatened if something is wrong with us so long as *we*, what we identify as *ourselves,* are not the cause of our difficulty. The physiological form of this is simply the most common expression.

As a matter of fact, no single case of delinquency can ever be adequately explained as "mere willfulness"; nor is "personal instability" ever a satisfactory process explanation of paralyzing inner conflicts. The delinquent may occasionally have had everything— but love. The neurotic too may have had everything—but understanding. In other words, a true genetic picture of any individual difficulty is always complex, an interweaving of strands. A compulsion to disclaim any responsibility is no more true to the facts than is a preoccupation with assuming complete personal or "self" responsibility for one's difficulty. Good counseling, if sufficiently extended, helps the person to sort these things out. His focus shifts from one of blame—acceptance or rejection—to something more positive.

There is, therefore, a very important sense in which the person's trouble is more understandable, hence less "blameworthy," than he thinks. Whatever can suggest to him that counseling may help him so to alter the focus of the problem that he will not constantly be preoccupied with whether or not it is his fault will lead to desire for counseling and to correct expectations of the help counseling can give. On the other hand, "The cause of your trouble is more respectable than you think" may reinforce the preoccupation with blame, merely shifting its content a bit towards rejection of blame and away from acceptance of blame. This is likely to make counseling harder, if counseling is undertaken; and it is still more likely to keep people away from counseling on this basis of reasoning: "If

I'm less to blame than I thought, then there's no point in trying to get help on my problem by understanding myself. Therefore I'll see if I can talk myself into rejecting blame, and forget about personal responsibility." He is not just giving the wrong answer; he has been led to ask a wrong question.

7. *Other appeals.* We have intended here merely to suggest, not to exhaust, the facts about the types of appeal which counselors make as a conscious or unconscious aspect of their precounseling work. We have seen that the differentiating factor tends not to be the simple idea, or even what is said by the counselor in explanation, but rather what is communicated to the hearer. That means an examination of whether or not the counselor affirms certain things, clearly disclaims other things, and alters his methods of presentation if he finds the distinctions are not being adequately communicated.

We could suggest other types of appeal. There is that seen in, *"You have more creative powers than you know."* That is true. Everyone has. But these are not going to mean anything if the implication is that a psychological shot in the arm will make one into a genius. There is also: *"Get help! Don't be trapped by modern civilization."* Of course modern civilization—war, depression, postwar dislocation, etc.—helps to create problems or to bring them into the open. Life is more complex and baffling. But this can also be a form of preoccupation with blame, attempting to shift it from self to society as the neurotic is eager to shift it from self to physiology. However, it is equally misleading because the preoccupation with blame remains even though its content is changed. *"Neurotics are superior people"* may sum up a very important truth. The normal-average person, as Harry Bone calls him, has probably sunk into a dead level of conformity; he has solved his problems by pulling in his creative horns, denying the tension between life's possibilities and life's achievements.[3] In contrast, the neurotic has refused to give up hope that life is more than it has been for him to date. He has not found a solution, and he has not learned to use tension for creative ends, but at least he still has a chance.

This is very often a true insight, and a fundamental one. But it has sometimes been used as a kind of precounseling suicide, as if to say: "Be glad you're neurotic; that proves you're better than other people. Forget about trying to get help, for then you'd be no better than anyone else." In this form it appeals to people who think being "better" than other people is the same as creative achievement in life—an equation not supported by the facts.

These appeals, the content of the public relations, are found in various forms, from relatively simple or crude to relatively complex and sophisticated. What has been attempted is to suggest to the pastor criteria for examining what other counselors, and he himself, may do in letting people know what they may and may not expect from counseling. Some appeals are better than others. Some appeals reach more deeply than others. But all should define, affirm what deserves affirmation and disclaim what does not, if they are to lead to counseling, and they should define on premises which will help, not hinder, the counseling process, once initiated.

WHO NEEDS COUNSELING AND WHEN

EVERY type of counselor has a difficult time with this question in his precounseling work. In all probability he has begun his study on the assumption that he was preparing to help certain people at certain times with certain techniques. The deeper he goes, the more he sees that his knowledge and skill can help other people at other times, and that he uses methods over and above those he had originally set out to learn. For example, a medical student may have begun the study of medicine on the assumption that he was going to help sick people, the kind depending on whether he would later decide to go into general practice or a specialty, at times when they were sick, by the methods distinctive to medicine, or to a specialty if he decided on that. Later he discovers psychosomatic medicine, learning that pills and penicillin and the scalpel will not help perhaps half his patients. As he looks at methods for helping this other fifty per cent, he enters the field of counseling. But if he then has the psychosomatic approach and the knowledge of psychotherapy, his basic knowledge and methods are applicable not only to a certain group of sick people at certain times in their lives but also to more people at more times. Whether he decides to become a general practitioner, an internist, a surgeon, or a psychiatrist, his view of what people he can help, when, and by what methods, will have expanded considerably over what it was when he began.

Every professional group concerned in any way with counseling has done this same thing. We have already discussed the similarities and differences between various counselors in their actual counseling. In this present chapter our focus is on preparation for counseling, and our question in this section is: Who needs counseling from us, and when?

Generally speaking, the trend in all the groups has been "imperialistic," reflecting the trend in counseling itself. Groups which were once content to be labeled "strategic-problem" deny such compartmentalization vigorously. The psychiatrist opens a speech by saying he does not deal only with psychotic or neurotic or even sick people, the implication being that he has something for almost everyone. The case worker opens by saying she does not deal only with poor people or with financial problems, the implication being she has something for all. All groups, including pastors, have been loath to admit that there are people we could not help (if the conditions were right of course), or times in people's lives when we or what we stand for would not help them, or that there are methods we use in helping which are not entirely distinctive to our group. Our practice of co-operation and mutual understanding on an interprofessional basis has improved, but our public relations are still showing little sign of being guided accordingly.

There are those who tend to imply, "Everyone needs what I've got," believing the widest and most dogmatic imperialism to have the virtue of excluding nobody. Others are content to imply, "Some people need what I've got," leaving the troublesome question of the occasions when others may also need it to take care of itself. A third group implies, "All of your group need what I've got," avoiding the issue of whether other counselors have something equally valuable or more valuable for some members of this group. The only statement that makes entire sense, however, is something like this: "Most people may profit from what I've got, at least on some occasions in their lives; and some people sometimes will find it essential." To this should be added: "Other counselors can help some people better than I can on some occasions." If this is then defined, the public relations or precounseling work are accurate, non-imperialistic, but confident in a justified sense.

MEANS OF COMMUNICATION

THERE are two types of precounseling selection, those in which selection is exercised by the counselor or group and those in which the selection is made by the person himself. In the former there is always an administrative angle. For example, a group test is given, and those whom the scores show to be at the bottom of the scale are offered counseling. There may or may not be coercion involved. There is certainly interpretation of some kind, though such interpretation is not necessarily contradictory to the eductive approach. If it is, "Sit down, son. Your tests are pretty bad. They show you need counseling.

How about it?" then there is interpretation of a kind which counseling, if it is held at all, will have difficulty in overcoming. If it is, on the other hand, "Those tests of yours suggest that you might profit from some counseling, provided, of course, you think it might be helpful to you. Had such an idea occurred to you?" then the precounseling situation contributes toward the proper approach in the counseling situation, if that develops. Thus if methods of selection by the counselor are used not as clubs but as suggestions; if they merely raise the initial question and then leave the decision up to the person, the counseling procedure is still eductive.

We can think of other methods by which selection is made by the counselor: observation of behavior in groups, initial interviews, many kinds of tests including projective tests, general observation of behavior, and the like. It is not our place here to discuss the validity or usefulness of these as preparation for counseling but only to point out that provided they make sense in their own right, they may or may not be used in such a way as to be effective preparation for counseling on an eductive basis. Are they used to start the person thinking about counseling or to club him into it?

Properly used, such selective measures have some actual, and much more potential, significance. If a physician calling on an elderly woman notices a miserably unhappy child in the house, he may raise the question of the guidance clinic. If a vocational counselor finds through his tests a very poor emotional adjustment, he may suggest a depth therapist. If school teachers are sensitive to children's needs, they may observe those who will be likely to profit from special help and get them to the guidance department. If the courts have well-trained probation officers, they will get into the situation when small things are involved instead of waiting until delinquency has reached major proportions. These preventive services of selection by the counselor can be of great importance. They need not conflict in any way with the eductive approach in counseling.

When we turn to the other type of selection—that initiated by the person himself on the basis of what he feels is a need—we are in the field of public interpretation and communication. Here we may distinguish three fields: writings for particular groups; meetings with particular groups; and the media of mass communication—radio, motion pictures, newspapers, and general-circulation magazines.

Most of the professional groups who do counseling—in contrast to the quacks and partly because of the quacks—began by ignoring the communication problem. Let the work speak for itself, or let satisfied customers speak for it. Perhaps the situation may be typified in that the American Medical Association for many years published nothing except what was intended for doctor readers, but in more recent years, a journal and other publications for the laity.[4] That is, it is increasingly recognized that the best protection of a profession is not keeping the public in ignorance of what it does on the ground that misinterpretation is inevitable but rather making the best and most responsible interpretation come from members of the profession itself. This change is in a democratic direction. It involves more trust of the people and requires more study and ingenuity on the part of the profession to make reasonably certain that what is understood and what is intended are the same.

In a general way it would seem that the professions which deal with counseling are barely at the beginning in exploring the most effective ways of carrying out their precounseling work through public communications. Members of some counseling groups have given such long lectures on the values of listening and receptivity that they have left no time for the discussion which was to have followed; others have become suddenly impressed with the value of proper public interpretation and then jumped to the conclusion, which would be abhorrent to their counseling work, that telling a group something and having them understand what it means are the same thing—provided only the intentions are good. Counselors who are concrete and specific and person-centered in their counseling have been known to talk in public without the slightest deviation from an abstract or technical vocabulary which left every one gasping, and consequently achieved no communication. Naturally there are many individual exceptions, and most of the counseling groups contain some who are masters at public interpretation. But even in meeting with groups or in teaching courses, it is astonishing to find such reluctance as often exists to recognize that communication requires special skill and practice of its own which, in some measure, should be part of every counselor's training and equipment and which is no more born in him, eliminating the necessity of training, than is his skill in counseling itself. If the clergy sometimes have an advantage in communication it is because we long ago took the problem seriously and have attempted to study it.

There have been and are among counselors many good writers of books, pamphlets, and articles. But there has often been a reluctance to face the differences between materials intended for some segment of the public and those meant for professional interchange. There is a clinging to technical terms, a preoccupation with definitions, a dull tone on the ground that one's colleagues may suspect him if he diverges from the objective mood of science which lies in the tone, and similar misunderstandings. This is not to suggest that every counselor try out for the *Reader's Digest*. But thoughtful attention to professional correspondence would help. Many letters from excellent and thoughtful counselors have had no relation to their basic approach in counseling. If a correspondent writes the counselor to ask whether, in his judgment, such and such a problem might be helped by the counseling he has to offer, it is ignoring the spirit to write: "Dear Sir: I have your recent letter inquiring about the advisability of coming to me with your type of problem. The answer would seem to me to be entirely up to you. I do not believe in advising people to come or not." This is not a counseling, but a precounseling, situation. The words which might be used to express the eductive approach in a counseling situation once initiated may mean something very stiff, impersonal, or even repulsive when used literally in a letter. What is involved is partly a matter of skill and partly translation instead of transliteration. One may, in reply to such a letter, say something like: "Dear Sir: This will acknowledge your recent letter in which you ask whether someone with the kind of problem you indicate could profit by counseling with me or someone of my training. Naturally I cannot be sure what you feel the issues involved in this question to be. If on the one hand, as your letter seems to suggest, you are most concerned about. . . . If on the other hand, what you feel you should seek is such and such. . . ." The effort to define issues raised in a letter is good experience for the counselor and also a genuine aid to the potential seeker of help— when we recall that this is a precounseling situation, defining what the counseling relationship may and may not mean.

In the several scientific fields there has emerged in recent years the responsible "scientific journalist." [5] He is not a scientific practitioner, but his knowledge of science is such that he cannot be accused of being a "popularizer." He is a specialist in the mass communication of information about science. The announcement of atomic energy gave the competent science writers, who were merely tolerated for a time, a place of deserved prominence in the eyes of both the public and the scientific professions which they had never enjoyed before. It may well be that the counseling professions ought to look at such handwriting on the wall and give more encouragement to writers of talent who might be interested in counseling.

The counseling professions have, for the most part, done little in connection with mass media. And when they have had a chance, for example, at the radio, they have tended to be so much concerned with putting into words a vast amount of information—that the audience, accustomed to getting its information in easy doses, misses most of the important points—quite apart from the question of whether or not these are worth getting. One does not have to be a huckster to communicate something by radio, but neither do dullness nor abstraction nor lack of imagination testify to the soundness of one's knowledge and the impeccability of his practice.

The question may well be asked: Since almost all counselors are busy now, why drum up more business at all? If public relations is merely drumming up more business, then the answer would probably be Don't. But it is not just that, and should not be chiefly that. It is interpretation to a public which, in a democracy, we are supposed to trust, provided it is informed. The better it is informed, the less time any counselor must throw away on people who are not yet psychologically prepared for the help he can give. The clearer the public's understanding of what counseling means, the larger proportion of counseling time is actually devoted to helping. Counseling, by however many professional groups of whatever competence, is not a panacea for the world's ills. If better interpretation results in more persons wanting counseling, having a good idea why they want it, and recognizing with fair accuracy what it can do to help them, we will have still more of a waiting list than we have now. And it would mean that we need more trained counselors. But if the nature of counseling help is properly understood, the utopia is not, as some caricatures would make it, having half the population trained as counselors and the other half supporting them.

There could be, especially in the media of mass communication, much more effective impact in interpreting counseling if the cooperation and increased mutual understanding which is growing among several professions which do counseling should be extended to the point of looking seriously and together at the opportunity and obligation for such interpretation. There have been a few signs in that direction, but they are small as yet.

It might be just as well to remind my own profession, for whom this book is written, that we have been discussing not only those other fellows but also ourselves. Of course we have something distinctive. But so has each of them. Ours may be of a different order of distinctiveness; we think it is. But that does not relieve us of our obligation to co-operate on such lines as have been here suggested— so long as our basic approach and convictions are not done violence to in the process.

PRINCIPLES OF PREPARATION

IN SUMMARIZING, the following may serve as a set of questions for any counselor to use in asking himself about the work he does and contacts he has which are of a precounseling character. This does not mean that he should minimize differences or soft-pedal convictions. But any counselor should know the distinction between disliking a group because one has reason to dislike some of its members and disliking "imperialistic claims" or "mechanistic philosophy" or "mystical preoccupation" when found in some members of this or that group. Tribalism should eventually give way to democratic federation. Here are the principles which would seem applicable to the precounseling work of all counselors, regardless of the importance of other principles distinctive to each group:

1. To what extent am I interested in seeing that people get help as against my interest in their being helped by me or my profession?

2. To what extent am I interested that people get help when they need it as against convincing them they do or may need my help or that of my profession?

3. In interpreting my counseling function to what extent do I define it as broadly as my convictions tell me it is relevant and at the same time acknowledge fairly what the public in part falsely believes it to be?

4. To what extent do I know and acknowledge the differences and similarities between counseling and precounseling work and clarify them fairly to the public?

5. To what extent have I worked through the differences between professional and interprofessional exchange on the one hand and public interpretation on the other, with proper translation but not transliteration of principles?

6. To what extent have I disclaimed what counseling cannot do as clearly as I have affirmed what counseling can do?

7. To what extent have I given thought and study to the ways in which understanding can be attained by those I try to reach, in addition to the thought and attention I have devoted to the content of my interpretation?

8. To what extent have I given a fair interpretation of the work of other counselors, describing differences as well as similarities?

9. To what extent have I followed an eductive approach in my precounseling work as well as in my counseling itself?

10. To what extent have I taken seriously my responsibility for interprofessional co-operation on precounseling work?

PART III: *Resources for Pastoral Counseling*

Religious Resources

Chapter Nine IN CONSIDERING RELIGIOUS RESOURCES IN PASTORAL counseling, we may begin by summarizing the chief things which have already been said in this volume concerning the way in which religion is related to counseling.

In the chapter on "The Pastor's Total Work as Preparation" we attempted to establish the point that the pastor's role is one role—that there is an inherent unity in it despite the diversity of activities because in all activities the minister acts as a leader of a segment of the Christian community or fellowship. The fellowship nurtures its members, aids them to grow. Anything, therefore, which knits the fellowship more closely together around Christian aims makes a Christian contribution. Since the pastor as a leader tries to do this, his total work, including his counseling, performs a Christian growth function, explicitly or not. If the pastor helps, he helps not just a problem or situation but a person who is a member of the fellowship; hence the person is aided to grow in the fellowship. Suppose the counseling has not happened to include prayer, the sacraments, Bible reading, or doctrinal discussion in theological language. Nevertheless if the man says, "Pastor Blank certainly helped me out when I was in a jam. Anyone who says the Church doesn't help people ought to come to our church," then there has been a closer tying of this man to the fellowship and a religious element in the counseling.

We have discussed religion as a "channel of access" the pastor has to personality, thinking of it as his "strategic problem area," where he is considered to be expert and where people therefore frequently begin when they want to talk about their situation in general. Another way of saying this is that since the pastor represents religion to people, he will sometimes find he means to them anything which they happen to believe is religion—whether or not it bears any resemblance to what the pastor believes religion, in a normative sense, to be. The lady who was thinking of a divorce and assumed the pastor would be against it, no matter what, illustrates this. What the parishioner projects onto the pastor from his own idea of religion may or may not coincide with what the pastor believes to be religion; but in any event the pastor deals first with what the parishioner believes and feels, knowing that only so can he help either the person or the person's religion to grow.

We considered a third way in which religion enters the counseling situation—through the pastor's long-time perspective, his concern for human destiny, and the Christian framework in which he therefore sets life situation problems. In the first chapter we gave a brief statement on what this means in terms of the assumptions about human nature and human destiny which lie behind the pastor's aims in counseling and, incidentally, of any other counselors who are committed to the Christian faith and the Christian Church. We were careful not to suggest that the pastor is necessarily the only counselor interested in human destiny or the only one who approaches it from a Christian point of view. But such a viewpoint for the pastor is inevitable if he is to be a minister at all; for others we can tell only by looking at the individual counselor.

We pointed out also that the pastor's inevitable perspective of concern for human destiny does not automatically make him wise in the processes of helping people to approach Christian destiny, that skill and insight as well as good intentions and accurately defined Christian goals are required. And we indicated that the minister's Christian convictions about the directions in which human life ought to move and the ends of that life do not necessarily mean that he "knows what is best for people." Given all the factors influencing an individual person the pastor is no wiser than any other counselor in knowing what step the person ought to take next. He may more readily admit to himself that he believes this is much better than that—if the person is capable of it at this time. But he knows as well as the next counselor that the *if* is a big one. Hence the pastor is no more omniscient than anyone else about what, all things considered, is the best possible course a parishioner should take. On the other hand, the pastor is explicit in pointing out—in public, rarely in the counseling situation itself—that some courses of action bring more enjoyment, growth, stamina, and maturity than do others if people are capable of those courses. If Christian theology has at times been perverted into a narrow moralism, its essence can no more be judged by that than the essence of psychology could be judged by phrenology or tea-party hypnotism.

Having recalled these three major ways in which religion is associated inevitably with pastoral counseling, we may turn to examination of what are sometimes called the "distinctive resources of religion" to see their place in pastoral counseling. To call them "distinctive resources" does not mean they are necessarily the private property of the pastor. Protestantism still stands for the direct relation of man to God, for the priesthood of all believers and not just the priesthood of the clergy. A surgeon may pray; a psychologist may use a Biblical quotation; a social worker need not be ignorant of the Christian view of the meaning of suffering; a nurse may assist in the administration of the sacraments. But for the most part it is the pastor in whose counseling they can appear as special resources. There are no "hands off" signs on most of them, however, for any other Christian counselors who take the trouble to be well enough informed to utilize them relevantly.

PRAYER

REV. James A. Young, of the First Church of Monroe, received a telephone call from one of his members reporting that Ernest T. Hargreaves, local business man and church pillar, had had an attack two or three hours before and had been driven to the hospital in the near-by larger community by his wife and the local physician. Mr. Young immediately telephoned the hospital, learned that Mr. Hargreaves was alive and on a medical rather than a surgical ward, and that Mrs. Hargreaves was still at the hospital. He left a message for Mrs. Hargreaves saying that he would be there himself in about three hours. When Mr. Young arrived at the hospital, he learned from the attending physician that Mr. Hargreaves was expected to live but that his condition was serious. This was likely to mean several weeks in the hospital, after which there would probably be considerably lessened activity. At the suggestion of the physician Mrs. Hargreaves went home with Mr. Young in his car.

On the ride home Mrs. Hargreaves told Mr. Young the circumstances of the attack that morning and then was able to talk about the feeling of being lost which the experience has given her. We shall assume that Mr. Young used the best of approach and method in these circumstances. As the car drove up to the Hargreaves' door, Mrs. Hargreaves said she expected a good friend to arrive to stay with her. As they walked together to the door, she said, "I wonder —would it be asking too much if you could come inside a minute. I'd like—it would help me if we had a prayer together." Mr. Young said, "Of course," and they went inside.

Imagine you are Mr. Young. Give the prayer you would use in this situation, and explain why.

This situation was presented to a group of theological students, who wrote prayers and explained why they would use them. This is a situation in which there can be no question about whether prayer is appropriate. The only question here is what prayer and why. Here is one of the best of the prayers:

Our Father, who art closer to us than breathing, may we know in our hearts that we are supported—in joy and in pain, in sickness and in health—by the constant and never-failing strength of thine everlasting arms. Even when the way seems dark, and the days ahead appear difficult and unaccustomed, grant unto us the sense of thy presence, our refuge and our fortress, the rock on which we may stand. Help us, in days of re-adjustment, to lift up our eyes unto the hills, that the support thou offer-est so freely may be ours. Bless, we pray thee, those near and dear to us. In their pain grant them the sense of thy power which worketh for their restoration and their health. Through Jesus Christ our Lord. Amen.

The explanation given for the use of this particular prayer was as follows:

1. To help Mrs. Hargreaves feel the nearness and supporting presence of God.
2. By recognizing the naturalness of her feeling of tension and disturbance help her to face the pain of the present experience.
3. By emphasizing the inner peace which can come from reliance on God's love, to foster the sense of inner peace and assurance of strength from the Holy Spirit.
4. To help her to feel continued fellowship with her husband instead of isolation, through the presence of God with them both.
5. To help her sense that God wills health and explicitly to avoid the idea that Mr. Hargreaves' suffering is by God's will.

This is a prayer entirely relevant to the needs of the situation so far as the story had shown them to the student, and his explanation indicates that he sensed the probable needs very well. We might sum up the assumptions or convictions the student had about the relevance of prayer in any particular instance.

1. The content of prayer should have a close relationship to the present spiritual need as revealed.
2. In a reactive-emotion situation such as this one, this means chiefly three things: understanding the naturalness of the lost or disturbed feeling; affirmation of the resources which can

eventually bring peace in the face of sorrow or trouble; and dissociation of the resources from the cause of the situation.

3. The degree of formality or informality, of the personal or im- personal tone, should depend upon the tradition and expecta- tions of the parishioner. Had Mrs. Hargreaves been an Episco- palian, a more formal prayer might have been more relevant. Or had she come from a different segment of Christian social culture, the prayer might have properly referred to "this sister," depending on her tradition.

4. The prayer deals with the spiritual needs of the person with whom the prayer is offered, not mainly with concentration on other persons affected; but if the welfare of other persons is naturally a spiritual concern of this parishioner, then it should be explicitly remembered. That is, the prayer should not be entirely about Mr. Hargreaves, regardless of how Mrs. Har- greaves felt about it.

Let us contrast the prayer and explanation of Student A above with that of Student B below.

Help us, O God, not to be ruled by self-pity. Give us the courage to forget our suffering and to be moved by the greater needs of others, those who are starving and dying in other parts of the world. Keep us from being concerned with ourselves. Help Mrs. Hargreaves to have the larger vision and to know that thou dost send sufferings upon us to make us strong in Christian character. If it be thy will, bring peace and the re- covery of health to thy servant Mr. Hargreaves. Through Jesus Christ our Lord. Amen.

The explanation:
1. Mrs. Hargreaves' great danger is self-pity. Help her to look away from her own little needs to something much more im- portant.
2. Try to help her forget herself, to get the broader and more Christian perspective.
3. Show her that it will do no good to complain against God for the suffering of Mr. Hargreaves, but that she should be strong enough to have it make her character grow.
4. Prepare her in case Mr. Hargreaves dies.

Student B has been selected purposely as being at the opposite ex- treme from Student A. Probably most theological students and pas- tors would not be so relevant and helpful as Student A, and few would be so irrelevant and unhelpful as Student B. The errors of Student B are doubtless plain, but interpretation may clarify them.

1. He believes the danger of Mrs. Hargreaves to be self-pity. There are no indications to suggest this in the material given, which means the student is assuming from general experience that this is present even if there is no sign of it. In the midst of a shattering experience such as Mrs. Hargreaves has had, the student's assumption is tantamount to saying, "She will go down the wrong road unless I use my club and tell her not to."

2. In using his club on Mrs. Hargreaves the student uses the "statistical comparison method" in its guilt-producing form; that is, through reference to physical suffering in devastated areas. Suppose he were dealing with a parishioner who had cancer; we might imagine this student thinking in his own mind even if he did not say it in a prayer, "She may live for a year or two yet, shouldn't yield to self-pity. Why, Mrs. Braden down the block hasn't more than a week to live, and look how fine she takes it." Not only is this kind of thing irrelevant to the needs and feelings of this person; it represents a scandalous confusion of God's Holy Spirit with the devil's pitchfork. Screwtape could make something of this one.

3. What "self" is it which Mrs. H. will be better to forget? True, the term is used in our language in a confusing number of senses: selfishness, self-respect, self-preoccupation, various selves, and so on. But the student's assumptions are fairly clear. Any look by Mrs. Hargreaves at her own condition and feelings sug-gests something bad. What she needs is not strength and support to enable her to face her pain and come through it but blinders so she will not be tempted to look at it. This is another way of saying she has no right to feel disturbed. Thus the student wants her to repress feelings which he has judged and found unjustified.

4. The student's interpretation of suffering from the Christian point of view is warped. There are differences concerning the Christian view, but there is general agreement that once suffering has come and man has followed the proper course of fac-ing it, and with God's help done the best he can in overcoming it, the result in terms of growth in grace can be positive and not negative. God permits, but does not send, suffering. Imagine what Mrs. Hargreaves will feel after this prayer. God made her husband sick, and has not decided whether or not to let him get well—or at least we do not know which God wants. What the student is feeling for is something like this, "Help us to take it no matter what." He thinks this is the time

to declare God's judgment—and his view of this too is warped —when to us the failure to declare God's love in such a case violates the elementary human sympathy of civilized society, to say nothing of Christian theology.

5. The student wants to do everything at once, including "prepare her in case Mr. Hargreaves dies." Later on, if Mr. Hargreaves grows worse and death seems possible, his prayer ought to face that possibility. But there is no sense here of appropriateness or of timing. It is like trying to preach the entire gospel in one sermon.

Generally speaking, the following seem to be the general rules for the relevance of prayer in pastoral work and counseling, once it is clear that prayer itself is appropriate.

1. Like all other prayer, it should be addressed to God and thoroughly consistent with that fact. It should not be, from the pastor's point of view, a way of getting out of tight situations, or a way of getting authority behind points he has failed with in the counseling or pastoral work situation.

2. It should recognize before God the essential spiritual need as recognized and understood by the parishioner himself. This is well illustrated in the prayer of Student A. It should not be so general as to avoid all reference to spiritual need on the false ground that prayer should be affirmative only. That is, it should make contact with the need of the parishioner and communicate to the parishioner in the presence of God that the need is understood by the "three." Hence the need is accepted as a fact, a point from which to start, not something to be denied or repressed or about which to feel guilty.

3. To the degree that stress and tension exist, for whatever reason, it should emphasize the free availability from God and his Holy Spirit of the resources of peace, strength, quietness, and fellowship. To do anything else is like pushing into the water a person who is afraid of drowning. After he has gained confidence and learned that the water can support him if he relaxes, one may encourage him to swim and not merely float. But it is brutal to push him in before that. During stress and tension the supportive aspects of the gospel take priority over the prodding aspects; in other situations this may well be reversed. The "Word of God" in Luther's sense is always relevant to the need and situation.

4. The parishioner himself should be helped to pray by clarifying in prayer, as explicitly as may be needed, the Christian attitude

toward trouble and suffering. So widespread is the belief that
God sends suffering to try us, in the sense of throwing the ter-
rified nonswimmer into the water, that this must sometimes be
explicitly disclaimed. If this idea is retained in time of stress,
then prayer can be nothing but a magical attempt to placate
a God at whom one is secretly angry.

5. The form and content of a prayer should be consistent with
the troubled parishioner's tradition and experience in the
Christian life. The form of prayer by a Southern Baptist and
an Episcopalian may be different in the degree of personal or
impersonal references or in the degree of formality without
there being any necessity for basic difference in approach to
God.

Perhaps better than any other contemporary pastor, Russell L.
Dicks has developed through both his parish ministry and hospital
chaplaincy experience the capacity to make prayer relevant to the
spiritual needs found in conditions of stress and tension. Consider,
for example, a prayer which he calls simply "Prayer for Health," designed as a general prayer for use with sick people:

> O God, our Father,
> In quietness and confidence we turn to Thee,
> Thanking Thee for the joys of life and living;
> Eternal Father, we pray for the return of health;
> We rest in Thee: as a ship rests upon the sea.
> As a house rests upon its strong foundation,
> Knowing that Thou dost work to give us health
>   of body, and courage of soul,
> Through the doctor's knowledge, through the
>   nurse's skill,
> Through the minister's quietness and prayer,
> Through the affection of loved ones,
> Through food, and rest, and fresh air of hope;
> We trust Thee, our Father, and we thank Thee
>   for health-giving forces within us.
> And in that trust we are strengthened, in that
>   confidence we are made whole.
> Through Jesus Christ our Lord. Amen.[1]

What Dicks writes about the relation of awareness of God to health
and healing is relevant to all situations of trouble, sorrow, and dis-
tress. In the pamphlet *God and Health* he has been discussing the
"wisdom of the body" and the "wisdom of the mind," the self-regu-
lating capacities of the human organism which work so steadily, so

magnificently, and with such remarkable ingenuity toward the main-tenance and restoration of health.[2] He has been careful to make clear that these have to be guided and helped by human intelligence in the form of doctors and nurses and others. But then he writes:

The problem of health and of regaining health . . . is basically the problem of establishing and maintaining a proper relationship with God —that God who has created us in the very cells and structure of our body, even when our thoughts are far from him. His healing power is at work whether we are serene or full of apprehension, whether we have a sense of fellowship or are sunk in the depths of loneliness, whether we are living creatively or are drifting, whether we have love in our hearts or resentment and bitterness. God's will and his healing power work in us whether we know it or not, whether we pay attention to it or not, whether we co-operate with it or fight against it.

If we do know God's healing power, if we do pay attention to it, a measurable change occurs. Let a man be deeply anxious, or lonely, or despairing, or bitter in his illness. Then let him really experience in his inmost awareness the consciousness that, all the time he has been anxious or lonely or despairing or bitter, the healing power of God has been trying to break through and bring him health and new life. He relaxes, not just on the surface, but deep inside. A power greater than himself, greater than his physician, is fighting, has been fighting, and will go on fighting on his side. Something happens in his body as well as in his soul. The extra and unneeded secretions that his emotions have kicked up and that have held back the process of healing, begin to diminish. Exactly the same thing happens as when the surgeon cuts away offending tissue. The potential healing power was there all the time, but something got in the way and kept it from doing its work.

The consciousness of God's healing power is thus itself an agent or instrument of that healing power, hand in hand with medicine, psychiatry, and all the other arts of healing based on scientific observation.[3]

In his pamphlet *Strength in our Sickness,* designed for selective distribution by the pastor as a supplement to his pastoral ministry to the sick, Everett B. Lesher begins with a meditation, "On Understanding a Bedside Prayer." He writes:

When the doctor comes to our bedside to examine us or give some treatment, we take it for granted that he is trying to help us get well. He looks at the disease in us so that, understanding everything he possibly can about it, he can use every resource in getting rid of it.

Sometimes we do not realize that this is equally true of our minister or chaplain. His visit does not mean we are approaching death. He wants to make sure we are using every possible spiritual resource to speed our recovery.

The bedside prayer is not a magical rite. It is a tested method of helping to bring to our stress and anxiety the quieting influence of the Eternal—of making available to us the spiritual resources from which can come peace of mind and, very often, healing strength for the body.

A bedside prayer can help. But it can help more if we participate in it and make it ours by recalling and meditating upon it. A bedside prayer is a start—not a finish.[4]

This is a positive definition of the function of prayer in dealing with sickness and trouble, but it takes fully into account the fact that wrong expectations must be excluded as explicitly as right expectations are affirmed. From this point on other meditations and prayers have a much better chance of being relevant and genuinely helpful.

Is prayer consistent with the counseling situation? The answer always lies in looking at the further question: What situation and what prayer? Prayer is essential in the case of Mrs. Hargreaves; the only question there is: What prayer? And we have discussed the criteria. In a moment we shall return to the situation, but we may first emphasize the consistency of prayer, properly relevant, to the pastoral counseling situation. In the prayer of Student A with Mrs. Hargreaves there was no moralizing, generalizing, coercion, or distraction. Instead, within the setting of prayer itself and in the awareness of God's presence, there was acceptance, understanding, clarification, affirmation of resources, and consolidation of strength. The eductive approach was properly translated into pastoral prayer. The pastor's role is one role, not a mélange.

When is prayer indicated in pastoral counseling and in precounseling pastoral work? A girl of sixteen had recently moved to a certain city and had joined the young people's group. The pastor noticed that on this particular Sunday she had attended both the Sunday morning services of worship. Following the second service she spoke with the pastor and asked if she might talk personally with him. An appointment was arranged for later the same day. When she came to the study, she looked nervous and embarrassed.

PASTOR: Hello. I see you found your way all right.

MARY: (with a nervous laugh) Yes.

PASTOR: Come in and have a seat.

MARY: (Sits down, fidgets nervously, looks away. There is a moment of silence which the pastor describes as "awkward.") I hardly know where

to begin. I enjoy your sermons so much. I wish our minister at home—
but my mother doesn't go to church, you see, and she doesn't like to
have me go. About once a month I go—go by myself—but she's always
mad, in an awful mood when I get back. So . . . (*she sighs*).

PASTOR: You mean she makes it hard for you?

MARY: Yes. You see, I'm interested in religion. I wish I knew more about
it. But if my mother knew—if it gets back to her that I'm here now—
oh boy!

PASTOR: There's no need for her to know unless you tell her. And I'm glad
you find religion helpful.

MARY: Yes. In your sermon this morning I was thinking—I want to be
like in your preaching (*she hesitates embarrassedly*).

PASTOR: You mean be a Christian?

MARY: Yes (*she looks down and blushes*).

PASTOR: Would you like it if we prayed?

MARY: Let's.

PASTOR: Our Father, help us to find thy truth, to want to be followers of
Christ, and give us courage to follow that way wherever it may lead.
Wilt thou strengthen and encourage us by thy Spirit that we may know
it is thy hand which leads us, thy strength which supports us, and thy
love which enfolds us. Give us peace, we pray thee, through Jesus
Christ our Lord. Amen. (*Silence when prayer is finished. Mary appears
more relaxed.*) Would you like to read a good book I have here? I believe it will help you to think things through.

MARY: Oh yes. I was going to ask if you had something I could read
evenings.

PASTOR: Try this; if you like it, I have some others.

MARY: Thank you (*gets up, takes book, heads toward door, and then stops
a moment*). May I talk to you again some time?

PASTOR: Of course. Any time.

MARY: Tomorrow? (*A date is made for the next day.*)

This story of Mary seems to be a good illustration of the well-
intentioned but misplaced use of prayer in the counseling situation.
It is apparent that Pastor Leland's use of prayer here is consistent
with his entire approach to the situation but inconsistent with what
we have said the counseling relationship should mean. Leland's first
two comments make it appear that he is going to do effective counseling. But in the third, which begins, "There's no need for her to
know," it is clear that the pastor is looking only at what Mary says
and not at her feeling, and that he is going to array himself on the
side of religion against something abstract and, so far as we can see,
meaningless to Mary, not against what Mary feels is against religion.
He follows this up with, "You mean be a Christian?" When Mary
says Yes, he suggests prayer.

Apparently Pastor Leland sees the situation somewhat like this: "This poor child is yearning for religion. What a termagant her mother must be to try to keep her away from it. Better soft-pedal references to the mother—no sense in getting her worked up. Just reinforce her interest in religion. Looks sincere to me, too." In the process he has completely overlooked the conflicting feelings that Mary has. There is no awareness that Mary could be helped if these were accepted, understood, and clarified. The resort to prayer is therefore a resort to obfuscation, to repression of the conflict, to "whipping up the will" with no attempt to understand what is behind the situation.

The nature of the prayer itself shows further the direction of the pastor's thinking. In other circumstances it would be a good prayer. But what he intends by it here is to reinforce her interest in religion, let the chips fall where they may. After all, it is Mary and not he who must deal with her mother. If she makes up her mind strongly enough, he believes, truth must rise victorious. But he forgets Mary may be unnecessarily ground to pieces in the process. He talks about strength, but he does not know how to help Mary find it.

What is the meaning of Mary's relaxation after the prayer? From Mary's point of view external sanction has been given by the prayer to pursuing her religious interest in spite of her mother. She does get a reinforcement to face her mother with something like, "It's bigger than any of us, Mother. You just can't get my goat any more," and to be able then to ignore anything her mother may say. But of what value is that unless some understanding has been achieved? Maybe she can stand up against her mother, and maybe she cannot. If she can, it will be through sheer force of will without insight, always subject to lightning changes. If she cannot, she will feel religion has let her down, and the conflict will be deeper.

The pastor's giving her the book is of the same order as his prayer. He wants to convince her he is *doing* something about the situation. He declares this, and Mary accepts his good intentions and his interest. He has given Mary what she thought she wanted when she came in, and she has a book to prove it. When Mary asks if she can return the next day, it probably means that his interest—and his meeting her expectations on the literal basis of her intention—have created some relationship of trust despite his approach and method. But it also means that Mary, while pleased in one way, feels a vague dissatisfaction in another way. She cannot accept the fact that this is all there is to it. And she knows she still has her problem, even if Pastor Leland has not acknowledged that fact. Mary has seemingly got what she wanted, but what she wanted was really something bigger and deeper than what she got; and even in the vague way in which she senses it, it is sufficient for her not to give up now.

If the eductive approach had been applied in this situation, it might well have been that both prayer and the loan of a book would have been entirely in order. Let us try to reconstruct what might have happened under those circumstances.

PASTOR LELAND: Hello. I see you found your way all right.

MARY: (*with a nervous laugh*) Yes.

PASTOR: Come in and sit down. I take it you wanted to talk over something with me.

MARY: (*fidgets, looks away. Pastor waits but is not embarrassed.*) I hardly know where to begin. I enjoy your sermons so much. I wish our minister at home—but my mother doesn't go to church, you see, and she doesn't like to have me go. About once a month I go—go by myself—but she's always mad, in an awful mood when I get back. So . . . (*she sighs*).

PASTOR: Then it's hard for you to decide what to do about church.

MARY: Yes, it is, awfully hard. If I go to church and tell her about it, she just nags at me all the time. She says I'm disobeying her, that I'm a nasty brat who isn't out of kindergarten yet, and things like that. But I want to go, and I like to go.

PASTOR: You are pulled in both directions.

MARY: Yes. And I feel so much that I want to come to church that, as I said, I've been coming here and not saying anything about it. I suppose I can do that for awhile, but she's sure to find out, and then she'll be after me again.

PASTOR: You'd like to get the whole thing straightened out.

MARY: Yes, I would. Oh, I don't know. I guess there's more to it than church. Mother treats me like a little girl. She orders me around, especially when there are other people around. She tells me to get this and get that, talks about me to other people as if I weren't there. I don't know—it's just as if she didn't like me. She even makes fun of me sometimes to other people when I'm there.

PASTOR: You don't like being treated like a little girl any more.

MARY: No, I don't. I'm sixteen. I think my mother has a right to tell me not to come in too late and things like that. But she makes fun of me and won't let me come to church. That's different. I wish I knew what to do.

PASTOR: It would really help if your mother gave you a reasonable amount of freedom.

MARY: Yes, it would, and I don't think it's right when she doesn't. Oh, I know, my mother's had a hard life. My father left her when I was about six years old, and she's had to work ever since. I guess she had a hard time about what to do with me when I was a little kid. But we seemed to get along fine then. She would kiss and hug me a lot and call me her little girl. It was only—well, just a couple of years ago that she began to get like she is now. And since we moved here so she could get a better job—well, she's worse.

PASTOR: You can see some of the reasons why your mother has resentment, but it's hard to see why this is directed at you.

MARY: Well, of course I'm the one who's around. And another thing, she won't let me have a boy friend. I was invited to a dance which was a very nice affair, and she wouldn't let me go. She stayed home all evening herself to make sure I wouldn't leave the house.

PASTOR: You've been restricted about a lot of things.

MARY: It's just—well, it's just as if she didn't want me to grow up. It's like she was mad because I'm not a little girl any more. Even about the church. She says the church let her down when she needed it, and she's not going to let me get tied up with it the way she used to be. I guess she went quite a bit when she was young and when she first got married.

PASTOR: It looks, then, as if your mother wanted to keep you a certain way even though you have to change as you grow.

MARY: It does look like that. But what can she mean? Doesn't she know I've got to grow up, that I'm partly grown up already?

PASTOR: It's hard for her to face what's really happening.

MARY: I guess that's it. I guess she—she thinks she couldn't trust me if she treated me like I were grown up. I never thought of it that way before. If I were still little, it would be O.K. But if she admits I'm not little, then she'd have to treat me differently. And there must be something about that she doesn't want to do.

PASTOR: She feels your growing up works against her in some way.

MARY: I guess she must. That's the only thing that makes any sense. I certainly see that better now (pause). Do you think people like that can change? I mean, what can I do about it?

PASTOR: You still have to decide what to do under the circumstances.

MARY: Well, yes. I wonder if I could talk over anything like this with her. Do you think that would make things worse? Of course I couldn't accuse her. But could I maybe talk to her so she would know I still love her even if I am growing up?

PASTOR: It's hard to know whether it would do any good or not.

MARY: Yes, but I don't see how it could make things any worse if I did it right. Maybe I'd better try it and see anyhow. Gee, maybe all she sees is that I'm sort of trying to get away from her. Can I see you again, Dr. Leland?

PASTOR: Of course (a date is made). Would you like a prayer before you go, Mary?

MARY: Why, yes, I would. That would be very nice.

PASTOR: Our heavenly Father, we thank thee for thy gracious and continuing care for us all. When we encounter the perplexities of life and its misunderstandings, help us to know that we may turn to thee for guidance and for help. Give us courage to face trouble and misunderstanding, to try to understand it and deal with it as we best know how. Give us, we pray thee, courage and peace. Through Jesus Christ our Lord. Amen.

Always remembering that such reconstructions are guesswork, that we can have no certainty what a parishioner would have done *if*, there seems a good chance that the situation might have gone somewhat as suggested above. Some validity to the reconstruction is given, however, by the fact that in the later interview with the pastor Mary did make some of the same points. The pastor's approach was not different in the second interview from the first; but because of Mary's stress and tension some of these things came out just soon as they had half a chance.

In the reconstruction the prayer is natural. The problem is not a religious problem in the sense that it is nothing but religion or that religion is the only thing on which light is needed. The religious aspect is related to other aspects. The religious element is the presented problem and the channel of access to the whole personality. The prayer, following the rest of the contact and used in this way, would seem to be an experience consolidating the acceptance, understanding, and clarification which emerged previously. There is another thing which prayer can accomplish if the situation and the prayer itself are right, and which in a dynamic psychological sense is a part of defining the counseling relationship. Few people who go to a counselor are not torn between the feeling that they may be helped or they may not, that help is possible or that it is not. The consolidating type of prayer, at the proper time, may very well be an indirect assurance that though the precise ways are not yet clear, the general direction which assures some help is beginning to become clear. Hence there is some clarification of what may be expected from the counseling relationship—which includes the primary point that help can be expected.

A set of rules on when prayer is and is not appropriate in the counseling situation would seem impossible. Some generalizations can be made, and have already been indicated here. Further suggestions, such as those given by Dicks, are useful.[5] But the pastor who keeps the proper criteria in mind will find the decision can usually be made without much difficulty, whereas the pastor who insists on a set of rules will always find the decision difficult no matter which rule he follows. If people ask for prayer or obviously expect it, be-cause of tradition or other reasons, it should always be offered. In other cases we may be guided by appropriateness to the situation as a whole.[6]

THERE can be no question that the pastor will use the Bible in counseling, as he understands it and as it applies to particular situa-tions with which he is dealing, in the sense of using the truths and doctrines revealed there. But this is not the same thing as saying the words "the Bible" or quoting Scripture or telling Biblical stories. In the story of the theological student and Bill in Chapter VII we have already illustrated the first, and in the story of the student and the nurse in the same chapter, the second.

This section will be entirely concerned with the second point—explicit and not merely implicit use of the Bible or texts from it. Ex-perience and reports of army and navy chaplains have made us all more aware than ever before of the widespread factual ignorance of the Bible. How much greater this ignorance is now than in previous times is a question for a historian, not a pastoral theologian. But even the most casual observation suggests that the competition the Bible meets from Superman, Donald Duck, *Gone with the Wind,* Smith's Drugstore, the Ford, and many other phenomena of contemporary civilization has a diverting effect. Before the church school and the public school there were undoubtedly many boys and girls who could not read or write yet who knew every detail of the story of David and Goliath or Noah and the ark or Joseph and his brothers. Such stories may not have been learned in the context of their re-ligious meaning. David and Goliath may at first have been no more religiously meaningful than Popeye and a giant; Joseph, than Dick Tracy; Noah, than Superman. But the stories themselves were part of the common culture. In many circles of American society even the stories are gone.

Where the pastor confronts a situation in which his adolescent and adult parishioners tend to be familiar with the Bible in the sense that they know some of the narratives it relates, have read some of its poetry and can recall a line here and there, can at least recognize some of the great passages of spiritual truth, then the Bible can be a resource in counseling to a degree which is not possible without that background. I am not attempting to assess to what degree the churches, in their programs of education in the church school and pulpit and elsewhere, are giving enough of the Bible but only saying that many pastors will find, if they are alert to it, that not a little of their counseling is with people who do not have the Bible in their background. And whatever the deficiencies of the Church in supplying such background, it is plain that the decrease of biblical elements in the common cultural folklore has much to do with the lack of familiarity with the contents of the Bible.

We may look first at a counseling situation in which there is a good background of biblical knowledge. Erwin F. Arkwright is in his late fifties, is a pillar of the church, and has talked on numerous occasions with the pastor. Arkwright's wife died five years ago, shortly after his third child was married and left home; since then he has been looked after by a housekeeper. He is in a type of business where the temptations to gouge, within the law, are numerous; and he has discussed this matter with the pastor previously. The pastor, he feels, was very helpful to him at the time of his wife's death, and afterward. On this evening he drops in at the pastor's home, and they retire to the study.

ARKWRIGHT: You know, what I want to talk about tonight is the thirty-eighth psalm. I read it last night, and I had the most peculiar reaction to it. Does it make sense or doesn't it? Is it me or isn't it? I'd like very much to go over it with you and see. I think it would help me if we did.

PASTOR WEEMS: How would you like to go at it? Read it over together first?

ARKWRIGHT: Yes. Why don't you read it aloud?

PASTOR: All right.

"O Lord, rebuke me not in thy wrath; neither chasten me in thy hot displeasure.

For thine arrows stick fast in me, and thy hand presseth me sore,

There is no soundness in my flesh because of thine anger; neither is there any rest in my bones because of my sin.

For mine iniquities are gone over mine head: as an heavy burden they are too heavy for me.

My wounds stink and are corrupt because of my foolishness.

I am troubled; I am bowed down greatly; I go mourning all the day long.

For my loins are filled with a loathsome disease: and there is no soundness in my flesh.

I am feeble and sore broken: I have roared by reason of the disquietness of my heart.

Lord, all my desire is before thee; and my groaning is not hid from thee.

My heart panteth, my strength faileth me: as for the light of mine eyes, it also is gone from me.

My lovers and my friends stand aloof from my sore; and my kinsmen
  stand afar off.

They also that seek after my life lay snares for me: and they that seek
  my hurt speak mischievous things, and imagine deceits all the day
  long.

But I, as a deaf man, heard not; and I was as a dumb man that openeth
  not his mouth.

Thus I was as a man that heareth not, and in whose mouth are no
  reproofs.

For in thee, O Lord, do I hope; thou wilt hear, O Lord my God.

For I said, Hear me, lest otherwise they should rejoice over me: when
  my foot slippeth, they magnify themselves against me.

For I am ready to halt, and my sorrow is continually before me.

For I will declare mine iniquity; I will be sorry for my sin.

But mine enemies are lively, and they are strong: and they that hate
  me wrongfully are multiplied.

They also that render evil for good are mine adversaries; because I
  follow the thing that good is.

Forsake me not, O Lord: O my God, be not far from me.

Make haste to help me, O Lord my salvation."

ARKWRIGHT: There, now you can see what I mean. If I understand the
  psalmist, he feels the forces of evil are sneaking up closer to him. It's
  getting harder and harder for him, and he doesn't know what to do
  except call on the Lord to help him out.

PASTOR: You mean he feels as if he were going under for the third time?

ARKWRIGHT: That's about it. And, you know, it's disturbingly how I
  have been feeling sometimes lately. Oh, I don't mean in the sense that
  certain *people* are ganging up on me—I don't have a persecution complex—but it's as if life were ganging up on me. You know what Sara's
  death meant to me; we've been over that, and you've been very helpful. But you know, the loneliness doesn't get any better. It isn't a matter of keeping busy. It makes no difference whether I'm out in the
  evening—at the church or at some friend's home—or not; I still feel
  it the minute I walk in my door. If I didn't read the Bible and pray
  then, I don't know how I could get through at all.

PASTOR: Sometimes it's pretty hard to take.

ARKWRIGHT: Last night I turned to this psalm in the readings I've been
  following. When I read about the Lord's arrows sticking fast in me, it
  touched something; that's the way I felt. I got to feeling worse and
  worse. And when I got to that place about being feeble, that's exactly
  how I felt. And then that bit about speaking mischievous things—I
  got to thinking about business. It's not that those men are evil; but
  some of them do laugh when they talk about my principles. Of course
  they joke about it. Last week I was invited in on a deal—I won't go
  into the details, but I just couldn't do it and look myself in the face.

Some of them kidded with me then, but they couldn't really understand it. Last night I was thinking: Do *I* understand it? What *is* the use? I know better, but that's the way I felt.

PASTOR: The enemies aren't people but something else; and that makes it harder to fight them and harder to know whether it's worth while to fight them.

ARKWRIGHT: I know it's worth while in principle. But that isn't enough to keep you going every day. "Forsake me not, O Lord." I don't seem to have any better reason for asking that than the writer said. We both know that's the right thing, and we're doing it, but we don't really see much in it.

PASTOR: You wish this motivation were alive and not just a kind of routine principle.

ARKWRIGHT: Yes, and I'd also like to be sure I know what this fellow in the psalm really meant.

PASTOR: Well, the first thing I see about it, besides what you have said, is that the writer was really experiencing trouble and isolation and loneliness and a sense of being deserted. It's not just rhetoric; he's going through something. And he says so—a little oratorically perhaps to our ears, but in the accepted style of Hebrew poetry. When you read that first part and felt moved by it, it must have had something to do with a companionship of feelings.

ARKWRIGHT: That's right. It was like coming across a diagnosis in a medical book that fits your case—allowing for the exaggerations you speak of. I thought: This fellow knows. But then I felt sorry for myself. What about that?

PASTOR: Not so strange, perhaps, when you're reading one of the saddest songs ever written. But as I look at this, there's something that strikes me that might get us along. Do you notice the various steps he takes as the psalm proceeds? First he faces the fact of how he feels. He doesn't just say, "I feel bad, but I know I shouldn't; therefore I don't." He admits it. He even tells himself that he had tried to overlook the facts for a long time; he was like a deaf man or a dumb man. He had thought he could get along by being perfect, never letting his foot slip. But that didn't help. So next he realizes there must be something about himself, his own sin. So he tells the Lord he is a sinner. But in the next breath he says his enemies follow evil, while he actually follows good. He asks the Lord not to forsake him. He feels he is a good man, though a sinner, but he still feels alone. What can he do? He doesn't know, except call on God to hurry and help him.

ARKWRIGHT: That's certainly the way it goes all right. I hadn't thought of that. There is a regular series of steps he takes. But he doesn't really get anywhere. He may be courageous in admitting how he feels, but what good does it do? He feels just as bad at the end as he did at the beginning, doesn't he?

PASTOR: There seems to be something missing.

ARKWRIGHT: Yes, he's honest and he has courage. But he doesn't get any-where.

PASTOR: And if we could see why he didn't get anywhere, it might have a message for you.

ARKWRIGHT: It might. What else do you see?

PASTOR: Well, I think I see something missing from his experience, if that's what you mean. One thing is that the psalmist is ready to admit he's a sinner in a general way, and he's quite ready to tell all the differ-ent ways in which he feels bad; but he doesn't tell anything about the ways in which he's a sinner. That is, he doesn't seem ready to make any connection between how he feels and what has happened to him and in him to make him feel that way.

ARKWRIGHT: By keeping it on a general level he just keeps on complaining.

PASTOR: So it seems to me. If he became more specific, then he wouldn't feel so bad in so many different ways.

ARKWRIGHT: I begin to see. Do you see anything else?

PASTOR: There's the way he looks at the Lord and what the Lord can do for him. He turns to the Lord, but he doesn't seem to have any confi-dence in him. If he really felt that the Lord was his salvation, even if he couldn't quite be sure just how, he'd talk as if the resources of God were as much a fact as his terrible feelings. But he doesn't. Therefore he seems to know about God in his head but not in his heart. He doesn't really have faith in God. He seems to turn to God, not with confidence, but because he doesn't know what else to do.

ARKWRIGHT: God is somewhere, but not really related to him?

PASTOR: That's the way I read it.

ARKWRIGHT: Well, I guess it does hit pretty close home. I have been feel-ing sorry for myself, and here I come across a fellow who does the same and admits it. But it's a little disconcerting to find he doesn't get any-where with it. Maybe I'm not specific enough about my sin either.

PASTOR: You think there should be something more besides feeling sorry.

ARKWRIGHT: Yes, something about being specific. Maybe I've been going to the cemetery too often and shying away from anything but casual friendships. Think there might be anything in that?

PASTOR: It's interesting that in the psalm it never occurs to the writer that there's any way out except to go it alone. He says his friends—I suppose he means his former friends—stand aloof. Perhaps those par-ticular friends do, he may be right. But it doesn't occur to him that maybe he seems aloof to potential friends. In other words, he doesn't think that the right road may be through any kind of social channels, association and friendship with other people, but only through isolation and loneliness.

ARKWRIGHT: (after a pause) There's a great deal in that. You know, Weems, I guess there was a reason why I felt confused by this psalm and wanted to talk about it. I've been trying pretty much what he tried—admitting I felt lonely, asking God to stick with me, but holding back on doing anything about it myself. Let me think this over a couple of days and then maybe I can see you again.

PASTOR: Let's have a prayer before you go. Would you like to pray too, or would you like me to pray?

ARKWRIGHT: I'd like to also. Oh God, we thank thee that we can have fellowship together, and that we can read thy Holy Word and understand its meaning in our lives. Bless us and guide us that we may see thy true meaning, and that we may know thou art our real resource. In Christ's name. Amen.

PASTOR: God our Father, thou art our ever-present support, and thine arms are ever beneath us, when our thoughts are close to thee and when they are far from thee. Grant us to sense and feel thy presence, thy companionship which comes to us through prayer, through friendship, and through service to our fellow men. Grant us also to feel thy love, which makes us ever and again new creatures as we turn in faith and confidence to thee. Through Jesus Christ our Lord. Amen.

Is this counseling or education or both? It could be called both, but it is really pastoral counseling. If we had only a mechanical interpretation of the eductive approach, we should consider it to be violated in this contact, for Dr. Weems does some expounding. But, and this is what counts, he does not moralize, generalize, coerce, or divert. Instead he understands, accepts, clarifies, and helps to consolidate. He takes the entire situation into account. Arkwright came to him to ask what the thirty-eighth psalm meant. He might have started in with provenance, declined a Hebrew word here and there, spoken aesthetically of the beautiful repetition of Hebrew poetry, given a few remarks on the difference in the psalm if David did or did not write it, and then proceeded with a commentary in greater or lesser detail on all the different things it might mean. That would have distracted. It might have been educational but not personally helpful to the parishioner.

Or Weems might have proceeded immediately to what it meant to Arkwright by asking questions. "Just what do you mean when you say you felt self-pity?" "Have you got any better answer than the psalmist had?" "Haven't you got Christ, whom the psalmist didn't?" That would have been coercion. Or he might have generalized by saying such things as, "Yes, life is difficult now as it was then. We all have our troubles. And even the sense of isolation—you know, there's a sense in which we are all everlastingly lonely." The last remark may be true, but it shows a poor diagnosis of Mr. Arkwright's dynamics.

We should not forget that the situation was defined in this way:

we will look at the thirty-eighth psalm together to see if Arkwright's feelings about it throw any light on his feelings about life. Consequently after Arkwright has discussed something of how he feels and then says, "And I'd also like to be sure I know what this fellow in the psalm really meant," it would have been a violation of the situation for Weems to say, "You're not quite sure you understand him," or for him to think that some interpretation of the story itself was the equivalent of coercion. Note too that Weems did not say, "Here, this is just like you. Take this. It applies to you." So far as the story was concerned, Arkwright applied some of it to himself and left some out. Quite correct; some applied, and some did not. Weem's exegesis was of the Scripture, not of Arkwright. The distinction is important. Hence the basic eductive approach is followed here— and at a point which is perhaps harder than any other.

Incidentally, at least one man has been reported within the past year or two as having committed suicide after meditating on the thirty-eighth psalm. One of the main virtues of Weems' handling of this may well have been the denial of the validity of its paranoid elements—its intense and circular preoccupation with blame.

The next situation illustrates a different use of the Bible, with a person whose knowledge of it is much less than Mr. Arkwright's. Albert Nicely is a young veteran who has been having a fairly rough time at home since his return. He has come to talk with his pastor about it; and after talking about how his mother does not understand him, he has come to the point of saying he feels torn between staying around and trying to make a go of it and leaving home.

ALBERT: I really think I'd be better off if I left home, even if I had to live in a room somewhere. But I just know mother would raise an awful row, and that might be worse than what things are now.

PASTOR: Kind of like Paul—a war in your members between going and staying.

ALBERT: Is that what that means? You mean, you feel pulled in two directions at the same time?

PASTOR: And you're not sure which one is right for you.

ALBERT: That's it all right. Now, if I leave and take that room I can get at Ernie's house, I'll bet Mom . . .

Clearly this can be dangerous. Unless the reference is crystal clear, it would divert Albert from his own situation to finding out all about why Paul felt that way; and before long Albert would have heard a good sermon but would have gotten no help on his own situation. But the Scriptures *are* relevant. Here Albert is seeing, perhaps for the first time in a long while, that this is so. In this situation he gets an interest in them which he did not have before. Nevertheless this kind of approach should not be mentioned without a suggestion of its dangers, particularly the danger of distraction. The more interested the pastor is in the biblical story or passage, the more likely is the parishioner to conclude that the pastor has taken the first opportunity to get away from considering his situation and onto familiar ground.

A third way of using the Bible in counseling has been ably advocated by John S. Bonnell.[7] When he feels the occasion is appropriate at the conclusion of an interview, he gives a short scriptural text to the parishioner, perhaps first discussing its meaning, giving it sometimes orally and sometimes on a card. The value of fixing it in mind, of meditating upon it and saying it over and over, is pointed out. The theory behind this seems to be twofold. First, people do not tend to learn in large chunks or in abstract terms. The briefer and more concrete a unit of material is, the more likely people are to find its meaning for them. Second, if people can have a kind of personal lodestar when the temptation to drink becomes strong or when self-pity knocks at the door or in other such situations, they have a mental, even a bodily, movement to make, and that tends to break up the mental and physical habit patterns sufficiently to give a chance for the new perspective. Such a text as the following would be a good illustration: "Thou wilt keep him in perfect peace, whose mind is stayed on thee: because he trusteth in thee" (Isa. 26:3).

There seems to be validity in texts used in this way, if handled with discrimination and if used in an eductive and not a coercive or moralistic way. The temptation to use them to induce the feelings we think people ought to have, whether they want such feelings and convictions or not, may be very strong. And over and above that, the reactions people have to the text idea differ very considerably. If given to a person who scorns this idea but is too polite to say so, the likelihood is that the counseling situation has not produced an understanding relationship, and the text will accentuate this rather than make up for it. Properly and sparingly used, this method can be valuable.

This can hardly cover the variety of ways in which the Bible can come helpfully into the counseling situation. If one of our good biblical scholars set his hand to examining these methods of communicating meaning as well as to the discovery of the meaning and applied this in a volume on the use of the Bible in pastoral work, many of us would be in his debt.[8]

RELIGIOUS LITERATURE

THERE are many types of religious literature: scholarly, popular, and in-between books; journals of news, comment, special interest, scholarship, and devotion; pamphlets of all lengths on nearly all subjects, addressed to many kinds of readers; folders for promotion or simplified education. There are materials to be read for the impact on the reader; others to be studied and discussed in a group; comparatively few intended as helps to pastoral ministry.

There are three ways in which religious literature can serve a useful purpose in pastoral counseling. The first is as a specific and discriminating follow-up of counseling or of a particular counseling contact. One of the most clearly useful and relevant devices of this kind is the prayer cards developed independently by Otis R. Rice and Ralph D. Bonacker in their hospital work.[9] Each has developed a number of prayers on the basis of their experience with the needs of sick people. As proper occasion arises, one of these prayers is used with a patient, and afterwards the card containing the prayer is left with him. After two or three prayer cards have been so left, Bonacker leaves a special envelope, thus helping the patient to build up a "prayer book" of special relevance to his own need.

The Federal Council's Commission on Religion and Health publishes a series of short pamphlets especially designed as supplements to counseling with sick people or with people under stress and tension.[10] Pamphlets are not as specific as cards, but they can be more specific, and a good deal cheaper, than books. In selecting such pamphlets the question the pastor must keep in mind throughout is: For what group is this intended? Even the best authors are likely, without reflection, to want to include in a pamphlet intended for fairly general circulation among hospital patients a section on preparing for an operation. For patients in general such a section may well produce anxiety. What is needed instead is a special pamphlet on preparing for an operation. It is hoped eventually that this series may include many pieces to help the pastor's work on specific needs, such as preparation for operation, convalescence, and the like.

There are other books and pamphlets not necessarily religious which are also useful as discriminating follow-up. Russell L. Dicks and I have listed some of these in an article called "The Pastor's Loan Shelf."[11] Suppose that a parishioner has talked with us about the increasing symptoms of psychosis being shown by some member of the family and reported that the family physician fears hospitalization may be in order in the near future. Naturally no amount of literature can take the place of the counseling. But the loan or gift of Edith M. Stern's *Mental Illness: A Guide for the Family* could in most cases be an important help to the counseling, for it is not only informative about the procedures involved in hospitalizing and care of a hospitalized person but also written in a tone calculated to help decrease unnecessary anxiety.[12] Or a pastor counseling with the wife of a heavy drinker might discuss with her how she might get her husband to look over the book *Alcoholics Anonymous* with the best chance of its meaning something—perhaps hiding it under some other books and saying nothing instead of carrying it home and saying, "Here, I want you to read this." [13]

There is much to be said for good pamphlets over against books used in this way. Inexpensive, they can be given, whereas that is usually out of the question with books. if the parishioner can keep something, then the heat is off with regard to reading merely so he can report back to the pastor. If it does not prove to be helpful, or if he is not ready for it, there is less artificial motivation to read it. When materials are loaned, not given, the pastor needs to be especially careful about not demanding or coercing certain types of response.

Religious pamphlets have recently been brought to a new level of usefulness after a period of decline. During the war, journals, especially *The Link* and papers from the home church, performed an important function,[14] but most of the denominations and the United Service Organizations found that pamphlet materials tended to meet a wider need than anything else. The Army and Navy Department of the Y.M.C.A., one of the member agencies of U.S.O., alone distributed about twenty-five million copies of materials—biblical and other religious materials, "personal problems pamphlets," pamphlets on public affairs, and others.[15] Repeated studies showed that a literature rack from which men could take materials as their interest was attracted had the appeal of unconstrained choice, which induced serious attention to pamphlets once picked up. In addition, chaplains, U.S.O. personnel, and others discovered that they could profitably call attention to the religious and personal problems pamphlets on various occasions as they were talking with service men or women. Some very important lessons were learned about pamphlets. Unfortunately. there is less evidence of carryover into the present of the knowledge and skill than would be desirable.

The second way in which religious literature may be used in counseling is to stimulate religious growth in a more general sense. There are various legitimate devices for doing this. An unexceptionable one, for example, is to have one or several pamphlets or maga-

zines—such as *The Upper Room* or *God and Health*—either in
the pastor's waiting room or study in such a place that they can be
seen but so that there is no merit or demerit attached to noting or
taking one.[16] A supply of Dicks' *God and Health* in a physician's
waiting room with a sign "take one" might do as much to stimulate
the proper kind of understanding of and confidence in the physician's
function on the part of his patients as anything else.

In counseling the pastor may find religious ignorance, or confusion
about religious matters in general, or other evidences which suggest
to him that some better knowledge of religion would aid the person
in general and his religious perplexities in particular. The story of
Bill, given in a previous chapter, might be such an instance. Of
course literature could not be a substitute for going over Bill's situation personally, but perhaps at the end throwing out a suggestion of
something Bill might find helpful to read—provided it is something
effective and the counselor is fairly sure will not hurt Bill if he reads
it—might positively help.

Some people feel guilty about not knowing how to pray.[17] They
may have tried a devotional quarterly and found it boring, a mystical book and found it beyond them, something else and lost interest.
So even in helping parishioners to pray, considerable discrimination
is necessary. The more of this exercised in counseling and pastoral
work, the more demand there is likely to be from pastors for differentiated types of devotional materials and the wider variety of
such materials—varied not in theological content but in form and
approach—is likely to be prepared. At present nearly all the de-
nominational devotional quarterlies are prepared for an almost
identical segment of the church public so far as the status and
maturity of their religious development is concerned. It is an
important segment, but I doubt if it constitutes more than a fourth
or a third of the adult church public. The circulation figures suggest
the proportion may be less than that.

The following seems to be an instance in which religious literature might have been used in connection with counseling, not to
meet the immediate need dealt with in the counseling, but for more
general purposes. Sheila is a Roman Catholic by background. With
a friend she attended worship at a Protestant church. After the
service she and her friend lingered, and in greeting her the minister
thought he detected a hint that she would like to talk with him.
He asked if she would like to. She said enthusiastically she would,
and at the appointed time the interview was held. In it she pointed
out that she felt very much attracted by the Protestant worship,

especially by the capacity she felt Protestant ministers had to understand people, which was evident even in the worship. She said it was this lack which had driven her out of active attendance at mass. She felt that she could not believe in Roman Catholicism any more but she feared the reaction of her mother if she became a Protestant. Near the end of the first contact she said, "There is still something else that is causing me great worry that I want you to help me with. I haven't even told it to my mother. There are some things that even parents can't take." The pastor did not probe. Time for the contact was up, so arrangements were made for a later talk. Clearly this was not the time for literature. Here is the second contact, in part.

SHEILA: I know you will feel ashamed of me when I tell you what is on my mind. But I'll just have to tell you or I'll die!

PASTOR: Just try to relax and compose yourself. [Not only awkward but paternalistic, as if he were to say, "Now, now, little girl, I am here, and there's no need to worry."]

SHEILA: (wiping tears) If you were a parent, would you appreciate your child being honest and frank with you about the most intimate personal problems? My older brother—well, he's done pretty badly—he's been in a reformatory, and we don't quite know what he's doing now. My mother has been counting so much on me. I've done well in school, and she's counting heavily on my future. And I don't want to shatter her faith in me. Now, it looks as if I might have to stop school. I think I can stand any punishment I'm sure I deserve, but I just can't hurt my mother after what she's been through—with my brother and with my father's death.

PASTOR: You don't feel your mother would understand. [Mechanical and somewhat coercive, subtly urging her to get on with telling what her trouble is. Centered on mother, not on Sheila. Better to have said, "You don't want to hurt your mother" or "Loyalty to your mother has to come first."]

SHEILA: I don't know whether she would or not. It seems as if she has gotten so far away from me since this thing has happened.

PASTOR: You recognize a change in her attitude toward you? [Again centers on mother rather than Sheila. Better, "You feel removed from her" or "There's a distance."]

SHEILA: No, it's not that. It just seems that I don't know how to approach her. No, she's as nice as ever. She doesn't even know about it. It's me that's all wrong. Mr. Bendix (pause), try not to be shocked, but I'm going to have a child (tears again).

PASTOR: Unless you want to, you don't have to give me the man's name, but I would like to know whether or not he lives here. [He was shocked all right, and demonstrated it by this bit of irrelevance. However, he is not unsympathetic; and her confidence in him is such that short of his pushing her aside by moralizing she will go on with her story. Anything that doesn't call her bad will be interpreted by her as positive. Thus the bad error in method is made up for in part by the relationship that has been established. At this point the best method would have been anything which recognizes the high tension Sheila has and accepts it as natural, as for example, "That does produce a new situation," or "Naturally that's upsetting," or "Well, that does bring something new into the picture," or even "I see" spoken with real sympathy and feeling. But not, be it noted, "Why, that's too bad" spoken with whatever kind of feeling!]

SHEILA: He is in Metropolis (*wipes tears*). I'm not afraid to give his name to you. As a matter of fact I told him I was coming here today. He is a wonderful fellow, and we love each other more than I can say. He wanted to marry me when I first entered secretarial school, but I told him I wanted to finish first. So the pressure of things just led to what has happened. And I hate to confront my mother and on top of that be forced to leave school. I don't know what to do.

PASTOR: You want to marry this man, I presume? [Much better, "The situation is coming to a head," or "The old plans will have to be changed now," or "And now it's puzzling."]

SHEILA: Yes, I do, but I did want to wait until I finished school because that's what my mother wants me to do.

PASTOR: You feel that you would have to stop school if you married? [This concentrates on the externals of the situation, not on Sheila and her approach to it. The pastor doesn't really trust Sheila, as he probably would if he had been able naturally to say here, "For your mother's sake you should finish school," or "You're afraid school is out of the question."]

SHEILA: Do you think I could go on in school after the baby gets to a certain age? [Sheila has now been distracted to the externals.]

PASTOR: Well, I do know of mothers who are attending school very successfully. [By this time the entire interview has shifted and is within the province of the ways and means committee; the committee on insight and understanding has resigned. The pastor has brought this on himself. At this point about the best he could do to recoup his losses would be, "I've heard it has been done," or "It's something to be looked into," or "It would ease your mind if you thought that was possible."]

SHEILA: Maybe I could go to Metropolis with Joe and finish school there, and then I would have done what my mother wants. Joe told me before that if we got married, I could on to school.

PASTOR: I feel that since you love each other, that might be the best thing for you to do. [This is of course the worst error in the entire interview, so much out of character with counseling as discussed here that the reasons for its inappropriateness require no comment. But it is interesting why the pastor, who knew at least something about counseling, should feel compelled to do this. The coming of the baby was inevitable now; he had accepted that fact. The main question then, he seemingly thought, was this matter of schooling. If she could be reassured on that, then the problem is solved. She had been reassured, so the problem is solved. Might as well reinforce it. Tell her she's got it in hand now— make her feel better. Or *will* it work this way?]

SHEILA: Things don't look too bad after all. I'll wire him and tell him I will marry him as soon as possible. Oh, Mr. Bendix, you don't realize how much you've helped me!

PASTOR: Do you feel that you can face your mother with the story now?

SHEILA: I believe I can. I recognize that I have been wrong and done something wrong, and according to the Church I have sinned. But I believe that the personal God you talked about in your sermon will understand and forgive. Incidentally, hearing you preach and talking with you has convinced me that the church for me is the Protestant and not the Catholic.

PASTOR: If you trust the wisdom of God in life's decisions, you won't go wrong. [What this really implies is, "What you've got here through me—only as an instrument of course—is the wisdom of God. Follow me—that is, God through me—and you can't be wrong." Let us hope Joe says yes and can find a place for Sheila to live and has enough to support her and still wants her to finish secretarial school and she can get enrolled in Metropolis and her mother takes it all in her stride and the baby arrives in good health and the Protestant church understands her and a few other things. We *do* hope so, along with Mr. Bendix. But if one or more of them should not work out that way, what then? Sheila has not got much help in dealing with the contingencies.]

SHEILA: Mr. Bendix, before I go, I want you to pray that God will forgive my past mistakes and bless my future.

PASTOR: Of course, Sheila. Our Father, we thank thee that all who believe in thee may come to thee directly in prayer. We remember thy many promises to forgive those who come to thee in true penitence of heart. Hear us now, O Lord, and let the assurance of thy pardon and peace be upon us this day. Guide us in all the days to come by thy mercy. Through Jesus Christ our Lord.

Clearly Sheila's whole personal situation came first. What she might do about joining the Protestant Church should properly come afterwards. But why, at the end of the contact, could not the pastor have asked her whether she would like to read something which would tell her more about what Protestantism means? Not at least considering something of the kind in such circumstances is to imply one of two attitudes on the part of the minister: either, "I

must avoid even the appearance of proselytizing," when dealing with
a direct request is far from being in that category, or, "if her heart
is right, nothing else is needed," which is an encouragement to
entrance into Protestantism without understanding the step. At
any rate, it would seem that there is a pastoral obligation to promote Sheila's growth in knowledge of Protestantism, over and above
what the pastor does to help her with the problem situation and
with her general personal growth. And literature might be a way to
do it.[18]

The third way in which religious literature might be used in
connection with counseling is as informative material not designed
to help meet a particular situation or to promote general spiritual
growth. There are few situations in which religious literature could
be said to have only, or even chiefly, an informative function. For
by its very nature religion stretches the perspective, and that brings
in the feelings. But if it is recognized that the information is for a
purpose in the personality, that it *does* something, then we might
think of utilizing religious literature to induce growth or peace or
something positive in the personality—partly, at least, by providing
information. For example, some of the anxiety that a mother would
naturally have if she just learned her child had epileptic tendencies
could be better handled if she had some real knowledge about epilepsy instead of just suspecting the worst she has ever heard.[19] Or
a parent who is puzzled about sex education for his children may
relax sufficiently to look at it sensibly if he learns about the problems
that confront the professional educator who wants to do something
about sex education.[20] Provided the effect and not merely the
information is kept in mind, there can be an important place in
pastoral counseling for selective distribution of materials which
contain information.[21]

Provided the type of principles and approaches suggested in this
section are followed, there will be complete consistency with the
eductive approach in counseling. Indeed, to ignore the field of written materials entirely would seem to be a thoughtless overlooking
of an important resource.

CHRISTIAN DOCTRINE

OUR discussion of the use of the Bible in counseling has of course
also been a discussion of Christian doctrine in counseling. The story
of Bill and the theological student and several other reports have
also dealt with doctrine. Especially did the interview dealt with at

some length in the chapter on dynamic psychological understanding deal with theological doctrine—at the crucial point of understanding the Christian meaning of suffering. Here we shall assume what has been said previously on this point and attempt a little further clarification and illustration.

Once we get down to cases in dealing with doctrine, we are casuists. The common connotations of that term may serve as a warning to us against mere relativism with regard to the truth and validity of doctrine as well as against using it for ulterior purposes. Our approach does not call for changing or tempering the doctrine, but for two quite different things: (1) dealing with it in such a way that it will be meaningful and relevant to the person or persons with whom we are; and (2) coming into the area of doctrine from whatever point is closely related to interest and need rather than insisting compulsively that it is not doctrine if it is not systematic. *Practical* or *pastoral* theology has been learned only when its essentials—not necessarily all the subtleties—can be discussed in common-sense language and when one does not have to think back mentally to a textbook to decide whether or not what is under discussion is theological in character.

Of course there are differences in understanding and interpretation of theology, and what is said here is not meant to indicate either that the differences do not matter or that the practicing pastor is somehow above the differences. But this is not a theological book in the sense that its purpose is to set forth differences of interpretation with other types of views. The point of view represented throughout this volume probably leads in the direction of certain theological views rather than others, and in that sense a particular theological view is suggested. But we are concerned here chiefly with how Christian doctrine gets legitimately into counseling and contributes to its Christian purposes of aiding growth. Apart from certain extreme positions, therefore, what is said should have relevance for nearly all the Christian theological positions widely held in this country.

It may be well to look first at how *not* to do it. A young assistant pastor of a large church called one evening upon a veteran in his early twenties, who had attended church school at this church in his youth but had not been heard from since he was about fifteen. Pastor Tanner found himself in front of a nice-looking house and rang the bell. Only Edward May was home.

MAY: (*opening door and seeing pastor*) Oh, hello (*his face brightens*).
TANNER: How do you do. Are you Edward May? (*May nods*). My name

is George Tanner, and I'm assistant pastor at the First Church. Our church is having its great campaign for converts this week. I wonder if I might stop in for a few minutes and talk to you about it.

MAY: Well, I was just going out.

TANNER: May I come in for a few minutes?

MAY: Yes, come on in.

TANNER. How did you like the navy?

MAY: I was in the army, and the less said about it the better.

TANNER: In what church do you have your membership, Ed?

MAY: None. I don't believe in going to church.

TANNER: Well, the purpose of my coming tonight is not to get people to come to church or just to get church members. We want to tell people what Christian living means to us and what Christ means in our lives.

MAY: Do you want to sit down? (*They sit.*)

TANNER: You went to Sunday school here some time ago?

MAY: Yes, but I don't see the need of believing in God.

TANNER: You mean that religion has no meaning for you?

MAY: Yes, that's it.

TANNER: Of course, religion is supposed to meet the problems of life. If religion does not meet the problems which come up in everyday life, it isn't worth while. People don't worship just because they think they ought to. People pray because they feel a need for it.

MAY: I don't see how religion can be of any use to me.

TANNER: Religion teaches men how to live together. It helps us get along with other people.

MAY: I can solve that problem just by not living with people.

TANNER: Won't you be rather lonely?

MAY: No.

TANNER: You mean you just like to be alone? Really, in order to live we have to live with others. Don't you find living by yourself is a problem?

MAY: I don't want to be like other people. I want to be different.

TANNER: You don't like to follow the herd.

MAY: That's right.

TANNER: Of course, great scientific discoveries and great works of art were made by people who were different and didn't follow the herd. But that can be a difficult life.

MAY: I like it all right. [Here followed some discussion in the form of questions from Tanner and one-word answers from May about where May works, how he liked the army, etc.]

TANNER: Tell me, did you say you didn't really have any problems?

MAY: I can't think of any.

TANNER: A person doesn't get away from problems by isolating himself in a house away from the world. It's a lonely life.

MAY: Oh, I'm not here very much of the time. I have friends.

TANNER: Mm-mmm. How do you live life without having any problems
in it?

MAY: I think I do.

TANNER: Was there anything in your experience that turned you against
religion?

MAY: I'll tell you. When I was overseas, I had to take up rotting corpses
to have them buried. I've thought about it. How can a God let such
things go on?

TANNER: You feel that because there is evil in the world there is no God?

MAY: Yes, he must be powerless to stop it.

TANNER: But God has given man the ability to be free to do as he wants
to. Man can do evil or not do evil. We can oppose God's will. There is
no answer as to why evil continues on in the world. [More was said
along this line; May said But and then Tanner said But. That is, it
was argument. Entirely apart from the validity of Tanner's theology,
the minute he gets a lead that May wants to discuss, he tries to use
theology to show May how wrong he is. Is that what Tanner really
wants?]

MAY: Some people have written down in a book things they thought
were right. Miracles, for instance. God seems to have been able to have
things his way *then*.

TANNER: And you mean he doesn't seem to now?

MAY: Yes.

TANNER: People had a different idea of miracles then. Now we know that
some of the things in the Bible did not, possibly, take place. But that
doesn't mean that life itself isn't a miracle. [We can see what Tanner
means, but May can't. By this time Tanner is chiefly concerned with
showing what he doesn't believe, not in clarifying what May believes
and does not believe.]

MAY: It doesn't seem to me that just because things are written in a
book it should be followed.

TANNER: Certainly not. But if you are thinking of the Bible, that book
is a record of life. It is an account of how God has solved some problems
in the lives of men.

MAY: But those writers must have put down things they just thought
and didn't really know. If you'd had to pick up rotting bodies the way
I had to . . .

TANNER: (*interrupting*) Then, because God lets these things go on, you
think he is some kind of monster?

MAY: Yes, if God lets such things happen, there must be something wrong
with religion.

TANNER: I know people who have suffered greatly, who are suffering right
now every minute of the day, with a cancer for instance, who still believe in God and find great comfort in religion. How do you account
for that?

MAY: They had training in that. They went to Sunday school. Take a

Catholic, for instance. Nothing can get a Catholic to change his mind because in childhood he's been filled with a certain belief.

TANNER: Religion is just a matter of education then?

This is enough. The interview soon closed. We cannot say it accomplished nothing, for Tanner, in the honest confession of writing it up, learned a great deal. But so far as May was concerned, it turned him farther from looking at Christian truth.

Let us be clear about what is wrong with this. It is not wrong because Tanner wanted or tried to get May interested in the Church or in religion. There is no imposition or coercion in the desire, but there can be coercion in the way it is carried out, in the approach. To May, Tanner was a peddler of pills he did not want. But as May thought it over, despite the coerciveness and argumentativeness of Tanner he did have one religious problem, and it seemed to him important. And therefore we would say it *was* important, regardless of whether it happened to have a similar importance in our religious thinking or not. Tanner felt otherwise. If it was not important for him, it was not important for May. Hence the chances he had to help May understand and clarify May's idea of the theological problem were thrown away. Tanner did not give May even the right to raise a question, much less explore the possible ways of finding an answer. This, then, is the way not to bring Christian doctrine into counseling—regardless of how true the doctrine is.

Pastor Kane lives in a college community. One Sunday evening, just before the young people's group is due to meet, he is walking along the hall in the church and meets Randall Young, college student, regular attendant at young people's meeting and occasional attendant at morning worship. They greet, and Randall says, "You know, sir, there's a question I've been wanting to ask you. Have you got a few minutes now?" The pastor replies Yes, and the two go into the study.

RANDALL: I'm puzzled about something, sir, and maybe you can help me. I've been thinking a lot about this lately, and your sermon this morning made me think more about it. You talked a lot about sin. Back in my home church my pastor never did say much about that. Oh, he said lots of things were wrong—I don't mean that. But he used to say in his sermons all the time that what people needed was to know the love of God, and I reckon I liked that pretty much. It kind of puzzles me what all this sin business is about.

PASTOR: You're not quite sure if it's really necessary.

RANDALL: I suppose that's it. The church and my parents weren't too strict. They didn't see that having a party and dancing in the church was a sin, and of course you think the same way on that here in your church. Lots of people thought things like that were a sin, but I was never taught that. Now take this morning for instance—this is what I mean—you were talking about the sin of pride, not letting God guide our lives. Well, of course if some guy is in the gutter, you can say he has sinned, but what good does that do? And you can say Hitler was a sinner; he sure had lots of pride. But what pride have I got? Gee, I'm not even sure I can pass all my courses.

PASTOR: If we talked about sin as some particular kind of act, then at least you would know what was meant. But when we talk about pride as sin, that doesn't make much sense.

RANDALL: Well, I won't say it doesn't make sense for people like Hitler. But what sense does it make for me? Have I got any pride like that?

PASTOR: You're really bothered about what we mean by pride?

RANDALL: I can't quite see how it applies to me. Now if I were a grind or a football star or something like that, I could see how it would. Those people get a lot of flattery or something, and they can get smug about themselves. But me—well, I'm no B.M.O.C. Of course, I am secretary of my class, and I'm in some groups, but I don't have to hold myself up and tell myself what a fine guy I am all the time. I find that I can get along just by acting natural.

PASTOR: The things you really want come easy to you, then.

RANDALL: You could put it that way all right. I guess they do at that. I didn't lift a finger to win that election, and some of the men did a lot of electioneering and then missed. You don't think there's anything wrong in getting along this way, do you?

PASTOR: Not necessarily, but I take it you've wondered.

RANDALL: Well, I haven't exactly wondered. But take Tink Doyle, for instance. He ran against me for secretary, and he worked hard to get it. He's a swell egg when you really get to know him, but a lot of the guys just don't like him because he pushes himself too hard. I've wondered why a smart fellow and a good guy like that should have to take it in the neck all the time. Now me—I just ride along, and I get elected. I didn't do anything about it. But if I'd known what I know about Tink and what I know about me, I think Tink should have been elected.

PASTOR: You're really asking the question about whether things *should* pop into your lap without any effort on your part.

RANDALL: I guess I am. Why you know, I felt almost guilty when I heard I'd won in that election.

PASTOR: There's a question whether it's right for you to get by on what you did get by on.

RANDALL: Yes, but all that got me by was being myself. You know, maybe what I'm worried about is getting a mite smug about just being myself. I hadn't thought of it that way before. But that's exactly what I've been feeling. I'd think how Tink worked for that and the only reason he didn't get it was because the boys don't like him. And then I'd think: Now me, I'm different. Maybe I shouldn't be so smug about feeling different from Tink.

PASTOR: You don't want to be smug.

RANDALL: Certainly not. I sure don't want to be proud of getting by on my charm.

PASTOR: Keep the pride out, eh?

RANDALL: Pride? My gosh, now I see what it means. I can get smug over getting by my way, and somebody else can be proud of getting by his way—and we've both just got pride, regardless of how it comes out. I see that. Every man has to watch his own.

PASTOR: It does have some meaning, then.

RANDALL: Yes, and it could run a fellow into the ground, too, if he didn't catch on to his own pride. But—if I've got my kind of pride I have to watch out for, why have I been thinking about this and not just going on being proud?

PASTOR: In other words, why weren't you content to overlook this?

RANDALL: Yes. I have been worried about it, and yet I didn't really know. All I knew was I'd never heard this sinful pride business before, and it didn't make sense to me. But I kept thinking about it.

PASTOR: There was something inside you more than just the pride.

RANDALL: In other words, thinking about this meant I wasn't satisfied with it. If I had been nothing but pride, I wouldn't have thought of this. Then I've got something besides sin; is that it?

PASTOR: It would seem so. And we'd all have a harder time if there weren't something in us besides sin.

This is sufficient. The interview closed soon. No specific arrangement was made for another, but we can be reasonably sure that Randall will come to Kane if he needs further help. Randall did not come and say he had a personal problem, and would the pastor help him solve it. He said there was nothing wrong, but he could not make sense of what the minister and others had been saying about sin. Consider the temptation Kane faced. He might have said, "Now look here, Randall. Pride may show itself differently in different people, but at root it's all the same thing—setting ourselves up against our Creator, asserting our ideas of right and wrong or truth and error against his creation." After the preaching of that sermon Randall might conceivably have had a slightly better idea in his head of what the pastor meant by "pride as sin," but it would still have had no meaning in his experience. When the actual contact was finished, the meaning in Randall's experience was real. Not all the subtleties and the breadth of relevance of "pride as sin" had been assimilated by Randall. But that is not the point.

The point is he had started on a fruitful direction. He would still be unable to understand Emil Brunner or Reinhold Niebuhr, but he is moving in a direction which might sometime make that possible.

The pastor talks in language which Randall can understand. Had occasion arisen, he should not have hesitated to explain various concepts of "pride" and "sin" that may have puzzled Randall. Or had it proved necessary to use some additional words to explain it, that would not have been inconsistent with the counseling situation. But there should have been no shoptalk without clarification.

Similarly the pastor, having been successful in helping Randall find himself in one aspect, did not feel under compulsion to set him straight then and there on the whole of theology. There may well be occasions in counseling when the nature of the theological problem of the parishioner is so interwoven and complex that there will be a much more technical discussion than in Randall's case. However complex, there is a difference between trying compulsively to "straighten him out" and helping him to work through those aspects which have his interest and concern. Even in the personal contacts that go along with the more formal teaching of theology perhaps much of what has been said here is relevant though in such cases the initiation of the discussion may not be personal perplexity. Also, the teacher may attempt to clarify larger areas. But general observation of theological schools would suggest that there is little danger of overlooking the latter possibility, and considerable tendency not to believe there is anything theological about the task that has been described in this section. And yet it seems to be the proper place for doctrine to have in the counseling situation.[22]

SACRAMENTS AND RITES

THE sacraments and rites of the Church are not intended to have anything inherent taken away from them by considering the way in which the pastor may utilize them in connection with counseling. The point is rather that we have in all Protestant churches particular acts which may have a meaning deeper than words—not only because of their age but also because they symbolize the relation between fundamental religious truth and the most common acts of life. Baptism is not only ancient; it also symbolizes rebirth in its linkage of earth's most common fluid with spiritual regeneration. The service of marriage is old, but the various symbols connected with it suggest on a level deeper than consciousness both the indissoluble character of the union—seen in the circular ring—and the

social character of marriage—"God and this company." The communion links the commonest of man's daily acts, eating and drinking,
with the most sublime fellowship.

The rites of the Church, however, have common significance not
only to all Christians or to particular groups of Christians. They
have particular significance also for individuals, whether the individuals know what that is or not. Protestant chaplains who went with
our first contingents of air force personnel overseas immediately
found men coming to them to ask for Communion prior to a mission—men who had in some cases never attended Communion
service back in the United States. They may not always have known
why, and they rarely knew the different doctrines associated with
Communion, but they felt that it was something very special and
that they needed it when they got into a very special situation. The
rites, as we know, may or may not be used magically. An illiterate
Central American Indian from the mountains may be far removed
from a church of any kind and may never think of it except on one
occasion—when she has a baby old enough to be baptized. Then
baptism, from our point of view, is magic. I am not so sure as I used
to be that the line can always be drawn with accuracy between magic
and true religion. At any rate we do need to think of what the rite
means to the people with whom we deal and not solely of the inherent meaning of the rite itself. And there is no reason why the interpretation that inevitably takes place in connection with the rites
cannot be done eductively, leading from the concern and interest
and understanding of the parishioner.[23]

Since space permits only brief comments, I shall illustrate what
is meant by this only in reference to marriage.[24] But the same essential principles of how to help interpret should apply, if they are
correct, to Communion, baptism, and the other rites.

It will be noted in what follows that Pastor Brown properly believes that there should be premarital counseling and that this
should make a connection between the actual ceremony and the
life of marriage thereafter. Not in any sense does he overestimate
the value of intellectual understanding of marriage. But he recognizes that the direction of the couple's attitudes as they enter upon
marriage may have fundamental significance in directing the pattern of the marriage itself.

We know that the Communion service, for example, to one who
has partaken of it with deep positive feelings for years means much
more than he can tell. Perhaps he becomes less interested in its
detailed content and more appreciative of it as a fundamental act

of worship. In a sense it is treated more as an integrating experience and less as something to be examined for its meaning. Such a development is wholesome and suggests increasing religious maturity. But even with Communion there are stages when interpretation and consideration of meaning can help the experience to be more worshipful.

Returning to Pastor Brown, he has been approached by Doris Sweet and Robert Low, both twenty-three years of age and college graduates. They have grown up together and belong to the same church. Both are working, and they believe they can make it financially if Doris works for two or three years. We may note that the pastor approaches them neither sentimentally nor oversystematically nor apologetically.

PASTOR BROWN: I'm glad we have a chance to talk about this in leisurely fashion. Let's see, Bob, how long have you been out of the navy now?

BOB: It's almost two years now, sir. Long enough to get to know Doris again.

PASTOR: Kind of hard to do when you're separated.

BOB: Doris can speak about that. But it was hard for both of us. We were engaged before I went away, and we almost got married then. Good thing we didn't, I guess. When I got back—well, if Doris could put up with me then, I guess we're safe in getting married now.

PASTOR: Not too easy to come back to civilian life?

DORIS: He wasn't as bad as he says. But he did have a rough time in the navy, and I'll admit it wasn't all peaches and cream when he first came home. But maybe I wasn't so easy to get along with then, either.

BOB: You were an angel, honey. But I didn't know it at first. When I was out there, I guess I put you on a pedestal; and when I got home and found you didn't have quite Lana Turner's looks and Mrs. Roosevelt's brains—well, I got over it anyhow.

PASTOR: You've talked over this idealizing of each other between you?

DORIS: Yes, and I think we understand it pretty well now. Bob did come back expecting a kind of miracle woman. We both know that now. But I've trimmed his idea down to size, and he says I fit in it.

PASTOR: Good. And important for you to understand that together. I suppose you've thought in the same way about what you want to make of your marriage.

BOB: Yes, we have. You know, our whole crowd has had a lot of bull sessions—maybe this will sound silly—about whether you want to have your honeymoon in a mountain cabin or on an ocean voyage. I thought it was silly too when it first came up. But it's more than that.

PASTOR: Of course. It's a question of your temperament, and also of how much your marriage is just yours and how much it concerns society.

DORIS: That's it. You see what we mean. Bob and I—well, I guess we lean to the mountain cabin at first. But after a week or so we'd like the boat ride. What does that make us?

PASTOR: Sounds as if you wanted to be individual for a while, and then be social.

BOB: There's something about that that still bothers me. What Doris says is right. But what I want to know is how much our marriage belongs to other people. Take this matter of where we live. We can't find any place at all to live except with her parents. We just have to live there. They're fine people—Doris knows I really like them—but living with them is something else, and I just don't know. There are so many stories that it doesn't work out.

PASTOR: It's the only thing you can do, but you're afraid it won't work in spite of the fact that you both understand it.

BOB: I don't say it won't work. But I just hear so often that good kids can't make it work out.

PASTOR: The stories aren't very reassuring.

DORIS: But in our case I think we can make it work. I'm glad Bob has looked at it this way. I'm working out adjustments—it's my parents' house—and maybe I wouldn't have if Bob hadn't brought it into the open.

BOB: I think we can too. A guy feels a kind of comedown when he can't take his wife to their own place. But we'll have one of our own someday.

The interview moves on in this vein and eventually touches helpfully on the things that Bob and Doris are concerned about and which need their attention. There is a further interview, and Doris asks for one alone. The marriage ceremony pleases them both; they agree fairly well on inlaws, sex, finances, and other things. They come to church and keep coming. And when storm clouds gather, they know where they can count on getting help. Pastor Brown had some plan, but here, as in most cases, that took care of itself when he made himself genuinely available.

SUMMARY

AN attempt has been made to suggest the approach and general methods by which the distinctively religious resources find their proper place in counseling. We have considered prayer, the Bible, religious literature, doctrine, and the rites of the Church. We might also have considered Christian ethics, the Church, worship, and other similiar things. Here, perhaps more than in any other area of interest where pastoral counseling is the focus, we need more, and more adequate, reports on actual experience. Further experience, adequately studied and analyzed, can disclose things which we do not now know. May such study come.

Chapter Ten Ｈow can the theological student learn to counsel, and how can the pastor learn to improve his counseling? In this chapter an attempt will be made to answer that question in a sufficiently specific way to suggest that some learning and improvement are possible for any pastor, provided he is interested in taking action, whether he is rich or poor, in city or country, near a seminary or university or far from one, very busy or just busy, and whether he has had much or little background either of knowledge or experience. This sweeping statement is made not because there are magic pills which can make all theological students and pastors into good counselors but because it is the direction that counts. If a man is sufficiently interested to want to improve his counseling and can find a way to get his learning moving in the right direction, then what he learns on the job thereafter will become an increasingly refined and competent body of knowledge, skill, and approach to counseling instead of being what experience so often is—the crystallization of unexamined prejudice. Therefore we are more interested in what a man believes is important to learn about counseling and the way he thinks that learning takes place than in how much he knows, or how much skill he has, or the degree to which his approach is perfect.

Before considering the educational devices or instruments—courses, clinical pastoral training, personal therapy, etc.—which the pastor or student may use to learn counseling, we shall consider the *process* of such learning.[1] But since the process does not take place without some educational device, we run the danger of appearing to tilt the scales in favor of the particular device used in explaining the learning process.

What follows here is a record of a certain theological student's progress in learning counseling. It is given in detail to demonstrate how the element which is common to all effective learning of counseling—supervised experience—actually produces some learning.

227

How useful is the device for learning which is described here in comparison with other devices will be considered later.

The student who has consented to have his experience thus described, of course with the omission and changing of identifying information both in relation to him and to the parishioners with whom he dealt, was in a course of mine on counseling. Beyond reporting that he was an advanced student holding a small church on weekends and was a man of better than average maturity and emotional stability, he need not be described. Such description would be pertinent or even necessary for some purposes, but not for ours at this point. It should, however, be said that the student, whom we shall call Peter Manning, had not had much background in psychology or related fields prior to this course under my supervision.

In the course I explained to the students that our process of learning would be chiefly through "contact reports," the writing up and study of contacts with their parishioners—whether they worked in a parish, a boys' club, a hospital, a young people's group, or what. I defined the situation somewhat as follows:

I realize that few of you are in situations in which people will come to you and say, "I have a problem; help me solve it." But what we intend to study here is how each of you in particular, as well as all of us in general, approaches people. Do you so approach them that if help is needed, the kind of relationship will be established in which there is a chance of some help being given? We can study that, whether you are a pastor, club leader, church-school teacher, or something else, so long as you have some contacts with people. Again you will say, "We are not there as workers with individuals, but as group leaders." Very well, that's correct. The pastor is the parish group leader; that is the central definition of his role. But that doesn't mean you do not have individual contact with individuals.

Suppose you are adult adviser of a boys' club. One night Johnny almost breaks up the meeting, something he has never done before. You have to see him, do something about it. What do you do? You certainly do something. Write up what you did and what Johnny did, what you said and what Johnny said, the way you felt and the way Johnny seemed to feel. Then you can study it, and I can study your recollection of it. Or you may be preparing for the club's annual parents' party, and have to call on two or three parents to get their special help. How do you ask for it? What do you, and they, say and do and feel? Write it up, and then both you and I can study it.

Of course you will say, "But we can't write it up accurately. Our memories aren't as good as all that." That is correct; you can't, and they're not. But if you jot down sketch notes immediately after your contact and write it up fully as soon as possible thereafter, you will find you are remembering more than you thought you could. And suppose you do forget? Suppose even that some things reflect so much discredit on you that you wake up one day to find you're concealing them, excluding them from your write-up and your recollection? I can assure you this will be true. My answer to that is that if you forget it, you're not yet ready to learn it anyhow. And when you have a little more confidence and are better aware of the positive assets you have, then you will begin to remember other things you had previously forgotten. These reports are not to be done as objective research studies but as learning devices. And who knows, I might be able to spot an omission here and there.

After listening to such instructions, Peter Manning made a pastoral call upon Mrs. Tompkins and then wrote it up as soon as he could get to a typewriter. We shall give, along with suitable alterations, the student's contact report, then my written comments to him about it. We shall then examine his next report and my comments on that.

MANNING'S CONTACT REPORT ON MRS. TOMPKINS

A few months previously a member of my congregation had reported that Mr. Tompkins was very ill. The family was not associated with my church; but when my parishioner assured me they were not members of any other church, I decided to make a sick call. In two or three days Mr. Tompkins became suddenly worse and died. I was asked to conduct the funeral service, which I did. I then saw her briefly in a call the day after the funeral. At that time she did not show much sorrow or grief. I thought she was one of those people who could handle the situation well, and I didn't get around to calling on her again. A few days ago the same parishioner who had first told me Mr. Tompkins was ill told me she thought Mrs. Tompkins was beginning to show extreme sorrow. I made a call as soon as I could.

Their house is large and on a big plot of ground, and in the rear they have a one-story wing, which is really a separate apartment. I found Mrs. Tompkins cleaning out the wing, dressed in working clothes and with a mop in her hand. She greeted me apparently gladly. I noticed her eyes looked bloodshot.

MANNING: Hello, Mrs. Tompkins. How are you?
TOMPKINS: Oh, not too good. I haven't been able to shake off this cold, and then I guess I worry too much (*pause*). Gosh, am I dirty! You wouldn't think that this wing could get so dirty just over the winter.
MANNING: Say, you have a nice wing here. I thought it was just part of your house, but it's kind of separated, isn't it? It would be nice just living in the wing in the summer.

TOMPKINS: We like it. It's connected with the house, but we keep that door locked. Some summers we move in here and shut up the rest of the house entirely. Get a better breeeze through here, and it's more like living in a cottage off by itself—and then a little place like this is a lot easier to keep under control.

MANNING: A person could almost live in here the year round.

TOMPKINS: Yes, you can see we have about every convenience out here. My husband liked to design things, though he wasn't much good at building them, and he designed every inch of this himself and supervised everything that went into it. He took more pride in this than in the rest of the house. We built the wing when the children were going to college over at Crescent University. They lived at home and complained that they wanted their own place. So my husband had this wing built. In those days of course we kept the door open between the wing and the house.

MANNING: Did your husband design those compact closets too?

TOMPKINS: Yes.

MANNING: He must have been awfully good as an amateur architect. Some of the men around town were telling me about his fine skill. Now I know. [At this point I paused, went over and looked in one of the closets, and then went around looking at some other things too. Mrs. Tompkins picked up some paper from the floor and put it in a wastebasket. She didn't say anything. So I did.] Do you know, I think it might be nice, if you're going to live in the wing this summer, if you kept the door to the house shut and then rented out the rest of the house. It would help you out financially, and then it would be good company too.

TOMPKINS: You know, I've been thinking just the same thing. With housing as short as it is I think I could get a good price, and, as you say, it might be good company. And that's what I need most. I think I told you once, I came from the Southwest. I've never been able to make many friends around here. My husband and I sort of kept to ourselves. [She paused, and her eyes started to water. She wiped them off, put her arm on a shelf, and looked as if she were going to speak. However, she gave a slight sob instead. After this she didn't try to hold back any longer but put her head down on her arms and began to cry quite hard. During this I kept quiet, waiting for her to speak. I thought she wanted to say something, so I waited. After a half minute or so, she lifted her head.] I'm so lonesome (she sobbed again). My husband was all I had. Oh, it's terrible with him gone. (Then she straightened up a little, wiped her eyes, and continued.) I don't know why I should be like this. I shouldn't let this get me down, but I can't help it.

MANNING: [I looked at her and what I said was said very slow and calm.] It wouldn't be right if you didn't feel this way,[4] Mrs. Tompkins. [I paused; then continued.] You miss your husband. He was a good man. [I paused again.]

TOMPKINS: I must stop this crying. [She wiped her eyes again, this time more thoroughly. I didn't say anything, but looked at her in what I thought was a sympathetic way.] One of the neighbors was in the other day, and I pulled this same stunt. Everybody will be thinking I'm just a big baby.

MANNING: No, Mrs. Tompkins. All of us would feel the same way if we were you [B] (pause).

TOMPKINS: [By this time the tears were nearly gone] See this painting over here? I bought it myself a few years ago in New York. [She went on to tell me about it, and we talked about paintings without any personal references for ten minutes or so.]

MANNING: Mrs. Tompkins, why don't you try to make it out to church next Sunday? I think the church would help you these days. And then, we need you too.

TOMPKINS: Thank you, Mr. Manning. I might do that.

MANNING: Good-bye, Mrs. Tompkins.

TOMPKINS: Good-bye, Mr. Manning, and please come in again.

MANNING: I will.

The whole thing lasted about forty minutes more or less. I went to see Mrs. Tompkins to see if I could help her overcome extreme sorrow over the loss of her husband. Perhaps this purpose was not accomplished. I only brought out another outbreak of emotions. Perhaps the visit was helpful to both of us, however. I was able to offer several suggestions, such as Mrs. Tompkins' taking in renters so that she wouldn't be so lonesome. She was able to unload some tension by confessing her loneliness. Meantime Sunday has passed, and Mrs. Tompkins did not come to church. Perhaps it is an indication that I didn't get down to her basic troubles at all.

TEACHER'S COMMENT TO MANNING ON CONTACT WITH TOMPKINS

It is just as important to know when and why you're doing a good job as well as a poor one. Your comment and evaluation at the end suggest that you value your direct suggestion about rental, and yet you don't value the confidence she felt in you by crying in front of you. This lady seems to be the stiff-upper-lip type, so that even a small display of emotion is very significant and betokens very deep inner stress. For the most part you listened understandingly; it is important that you see what this means as a value in a dynamic relationship and not think of it merely as doing nothing. Even at *A* you are pretty good, though I think it would be better to say, "It *is* tough, isn't it?" At *B* you miss your chance. You disagree, try to reassure. Instead, you might have said, "You wish you didn't have such feelings," or "You think it's weakness to express your feelings." Even so, you were all right; but the grief problem with such a person is in being willing to face it and the emotion connected with it.

Had Mr. Manning been my only student, I would have written more and perhaps been able to talk personally with him each time. A good-sized class compels comments that are not too long and does not permit as many interviews with students as would be desirable.

By this time it seems to me Mr. Manning had revealed himself in several ways. In the first place, he is inclined to take seriously the pastor's job as helping people in the whole community if they need it and he can do anything about it. He went to call on Mr. Tompkins when he heard of the illness, despite the fact that Tompkins was not a member of his church. The impression he made must have been reasonably good at least, for he not only was asked to conduct the funeral but also was seemingly welcomed by Mrs. Tompkins when he appeared again. Another thing we note about Manning is that while he took the initiative in getting around when he felt there might be a need, he was not coercive in his approach. He could permit Mrs. Tompkins to cry without feeling under compulsion to say embarrassedly, "There, there, now don't do that. Everything will be all right." He has a real feeling for other people's feelings. It doesn't make him feel any better, but he is not seriously embarrassed himself. This is important, and is a great asset. It speaks well for his own stability. And despite the errors he made in counseling method, of which the two most important were suggested to him in my comment, it seems clear that he helped Mrs. Tompkins a great deal more than he may have harmed her. He did have some real understanding, and despite some elements of misunderstanding and some gaucheness in going about it Mrs. Tompkins felt this to be a fact.

On the other side of the ledger my comment suggested to him the things he ought to look into. He was not discriminating; did not know much about dynamics; felt as incompetent about the things which showed his virtues as about those where he had erred. He equated listening with passivity, understanding with words of reassurance, and did not appreciate at full value his own points of excellence. On the other hand, he did value his active suggestion about renting the house, which might well have been disastrous. He thought he was good to the degree he was able to think up suggestions of things Mrs. Tompkins might do. He assumed, furthermore, that the geographical presence of people was obviously a good thing for loneliness, when in fact it is often not so.

And yet despite his mistakes and misunderstandings he has a great deal from which to start. The purpose of my comment to him is to encourage his thinking helpfully at those points where self-questionings are likely to be most productive. I try to give him some clues, and the suggestion that such questioning is not only finding one's bad points but also a proper understanding of good points. I hope to help him move toward understanding more discriminating criteria in connection with his relationships to parishioners.

MANNING'S CONTACT REPORT ON MRS. CLOSE

I had not had previous contact with the Closes. But since I haven't been in this community very long, I have been spending some time calling routinely on families which, so far as I have been able to find out, do not belong to any church here. I knocked on Mrs. Close's door, and she came to answer it.

MANNING: Good morning. Mrs. Close? I'm Peter Manning from the Blank Church. I'm calling at a number of the homes here just to meet the folks and learn their names and faces. May I come in for a moment?

CLOSE: Why surely. [As we went inside, we exchanged some social conversation, spelling our names to each other, etc. This must have lasted for about ten minutes. Then she changed the subject.] I'm glad you came, Mr. Manning. I'd like to have you do me a favor. I'd like you to help me try and get my husband out to church sometime. I am a Catholic myself and a poor one at that. Haven't been in church since I was married. My husband was brought up in your church here. He never goes, though. I don't know when he was in that church last. Even though I'm a Catholic, I'd like going to the Protestant church once in a while. The church is handy, and I think we ought to go. Jim—that's my husband—won't have much to do with anything called religion, though. When I ask him about prayer, he only laughs at me and says it's the Catholic coming out in me. He says I've had my religion forced on me, shoved down my throat, and that's the only reason why I pray. [I made no comment but sat listening.] I'd specially like to get him started now. Our children will be school age pretty soon, and children have to be brought up in some kind of religion. I don't care what kind. Just so they believe in God. Don't you think? [I nodded my head.] After all, we all worship the same God. What church we go to isn't the important thing.

MANNING: Were you and your husband married by a priest? *A*

CLOSE: Yes.

MANNING: I suppose you remember what the priest told you then about bringing up your children?

CLOSE: Yes, but I don't agree with everything they say. They try to scare a lot into you. I know that. That's one thing I like about the Protestant church. People go because they want to, not because of fear.

MANNING: The trouble with us Protestants,*B* though, is that we make it too easy. People like your husband soon drift away from the church.

It's really a hard job instilling within the hearts of men and women an inward desire for coming to church. But that's what we try to do. It's not easy. Evidently we have failed in the case of your husband. I'd like to talk to him. [The chat lasted about five minutes more. I said I'd be glad to help Mrs. Close try and get her husband interested, and we arranged a time to meet together.]

I consider the interview was most favorable. I found another family the church should be reaching. I was able to get a frank statement from Mrs. Close on her conception of the Church, while at the same time I was able to bring to her attention the step that she was suggesting. Perhaps this could be considered a success.

Teacher's Comment to Manning on Close Contact Report

I find this very interesting, especially because I remain unconvinced by your own conclusion. It seems to me you just plain missed the real opportunity this contact afforded.

You are fine up to *A*. You've been getting acquainted. She's told a good deal and you've had the good sense to listen to it. But at *A* you start off on a tangent. What is in your mind seems to be, "This is an instance of Protestant-Catholic marriage," and not "Here is what she's really been trying to express." That is, you overlook *her* without the slightest intention of doing so. She then goes on, however, unretarded by your diverting her, to say what she likes about Protestant churches. To which you, because you seem to be thinking, "Protestantism is fair and honest, which is more than can be said . . ." say in effect, "Oh, no, you're wrong; we Protestants have serious faults." You're apologetic at the wrong point. You then go on to say that you'd like a chance to talk to the husband, ignoring the opportunity you've had in your hand and have thrown away.

This woman is expressing 100 per cent Protestant attitudes. She hasn't done anything about Catholicism. She's trying to tell you she would be interested in Protestantism if not pushed too much. You withdraw. It's fine not to push, but you don't have to withdraw to keep from pushing. You count on getting to her husband, who may well make mincemeat of you, whereas probably the wife is the only one who can interest the husband.

Do let us be fair. But let us not interpret fairness as overlooking chances to lead into Protestantism people who want us to do so. At *B* you might have said, "Then you feel yourself attracted by our Protestant churches?" You lose nothing of fairness on that, and you find out how far her thinking has gone.

Manning is here in a quite different type of situation from that of Mrs. Tompkins, and there is little if any carry-over of anything he may have learned from that. We now see that his not coercing people, while it may be better than coercing, also smacks of passivity.

And passivity can mean, "If I don't stick my neck out, it won't be stepped on"—rather different from the approach which is most effective in counseling. Mr. Manning apparently feels he must lean over backwards in assuring people he doesn't want to push them into anything. Certainly this is better than if he had said to Mrs. Close, "Well, then, why don't you join my church next Sunday, and then we can work on your husband together?" She would have withdrawn. But by confusing passivity with understanding he failed to follow the leads, and hence did not really understand Mrs. Close.

What is revealed in both these contacts, therefore, is not progress, but different aspects of Mr. Manning's relationships with people. My comment to him again attempts to point out, on the basis of what the report about Mrs. Close has shown, the additional places at which he may helpfully direct his analysis.

MANNING'S CONTACT REPORT ON MRS. WATSON

I have known Mrs. Watson ever since I took this church a few months ago. About forty, she has one child, a girl about twelve. Despite his age her husband was drafted, and is holding down a desk job in another part of the country. Mrs. Watson is active in my church, and I have talked with her on many occasions, though usually about church affairs. She did say to me once that they had thought of going to where the husband was and live with him, but just then he had been moved, and they had all decided it was better not to try it.

After a meeting at the church one evening Mrs. Watson was the last to go, and she turned to me and said:

WATSON: Mr. Manning, tell me, do you think it's right to tell off your father-in-law when it's necessary? I know the story is usually about the mother-in-law, but I mean the same thing.
MANNING: Well, I don't know, it all depends on . . .
WATSON: (*interrupting*) Maybe I'd better tell the whole story, and then you can tell me what you think. You may remember that my husband's father was here about three weeks ago. I enjoyed having him. I always have. But recently he irritates me more and more. I'm beginning to feel glad that he lives as far away as he does and can't get here too often, even though he's so fond of Grace [the daughter]. When Jerry and I were first married, I enjoyed being with him a lot. Jerry's mother died, you know, when he was in college. In fact I liked the old gentleman better than my own father, and I got along with him better. But he's changed a lot in the last few years. He is getting just like his own mother used to be. Jerry has told me about her. The older she got, the more domineering she became. Right up to her dying day she bossed everybody in the family. Jerry's father gets more like her every

day. I think he is beginning to make up for lost time when his mother bossed him around. Well, anyway, I got a letter from him this morning. In it he tells me all the things that he thinks I'm doing wrong with Grace these days. As if he didn't tell me enough when he was here, he sits down and writes this long letter giving me more of his advice. What really burns me up, though, is that I know he has written a letter to Jerry, telling him he thinks I am doing a miserable job of bringing up Grace while he is away. He mentions in his letter to me that he has written Jerry, and I know he couldn't help saying certain things that are going to make Jerry worry for no reason at all. Why should he be cruel? As if Jerry didn't have enough to worry about already. I feel as if I'd like to sit down and write him a nice, long letter and tell him what I think of him when he acts this way. Friendly advice is one thing and it's O. K. But when he tries to dominate our home, then that is another story, and I'd like to tell him so.

MANNING: You really feel that he is trying to dominate your lives.

WATSON: Feel it? I know it! It's the same way with his other children and their families too. One of them—he lives closer to her—is getting fed up with it too. Another one is in South America, and he can't get at him, I guess. And the fourth one, I happen to know, is getting the same thing, but he isn't married and lives a long distance from his father. There's no reason why their father should insist on butting in all the time. I think that once you leave home, and especially when you set up your own family, you should be allowed to go your own way. We may make mistakes, but that's the way we learn. I've pretty much made up my mind that Grandpa needs to be set in his place and I'm the one to do it.

MANNING: You feel that writing a letter to him would help things?

WATSON: I guess not. He'd probably get good and sore at what I'd say. But somebody has to point out his own faults sometime. As I say, he's becoming more domineering all the time. When Jerry was here, he always gave in to the old man, and I hate to see him boss Jerry around all his life. After all, we have our own lives to live. As for taking care of Grace, you yourself know that I do as well as any mother could under the circumstances.

MANNING: Yes, Mrs. Watson, I personally think you are doing a good job.[4] It's not easy with your husband away, and I doubt if many mothers would do a job as good as you are doing. [I paused but she was silent.] About writing a letter to your father-in-law, though. I don't think that it would help things at this time. It would probably make a lot more confusion. He might write to your husband if he got angry and say a lot of things that just aren't so. If I were you, Mrs. Watson, it seems that writing a frank letter to Jerry would be better. You could tell him of his father's visit here and the various suggestions that he gave you at that time. And then you could also tell him about the letter you received today. Maybe you could tell him why some of his father's sug-

gestions seem foolish to you, if they do. Let him know how you are tackling some of your problems with Grace. I'm sure that he would understand your situation. That's what I would do if I were you . . .
WATSON: (*interrupting*) I suppose you're right. If I write a letter to Father now, I might say a lot of things that I'd be sorry for afterwards. Thanks ever so much. Maybe I could explain things a little better to Jerry.

This is the first time that I have felt I was able to put into practice some of the suggestions of the course. It was a real thrill to be using some of the practical suggestions of the course and at the same time help Mrs. Watson iron out her problem.

I personally feel that the conference was helpful to Mrs. Watson. She was able to state her problem at quite some length. My questions were not misleading, but rather seemed to help her go on with her problem. I am glad I suggested to her that it would not be best to write to her father-in-law while she was all keyed up. Certainly there was nothing wrong in my suggestion that Mrs. Watson share these things more with her husband instead of exploding to Grandpa.

This contact has given me a lot more confidence in myself. Perhaps I *can* learn to be of some help to people after all.

TEACHER'S COMMENT TO MANNING ON WATSON

This is certainly better, up to *A*. Until that point you do reflect your attitude of accepting and understanding. And see how much better her feelings come out and how much more quickly she assumes responsibility for her own conduct.

But at *A* you became worried and reverted to the old approach. You thought it had worked so far—a miracle. But you don't trust it too far. So from here on you told her what to do. And then you failed to note that when she answered, she said, "I suppose you're right"—merely making a concession, not being thoroughly convinced. Of course you'd done well before this point, but here you stepped way off. If understanding people works, why get worried about it? Why not let it go through?

Some real development is revealed. Manning is not merely passive in this contact; he sees that there is some meaning in trying to accept and understand and clarify. But he is in the centipede stage—self-conscious about the legs he has just discovered he has. And he doesn't trust them very far. It seems unnatural to be neither active nor passive, reassuring nor judging, but something else. He reports himself as "thrilled"—but he's afraid he'll get shaking palsy if he keeps on. This may be just as well from a learning point of view. As he studies this report and my comment, he may see how great was the difference between what he did and what he intended to do, and what happened in him. It is not easy to get the approach, and it won't help if he thinks it's easier than it really is. He will eventually see that passivity won't do.

MANNING CONTACT REPORT ON ETHEL FORD

Ethel Ford is about twenty and an active member of my church. She has been going "steady" with Elwyn Olson, about the same age or a little older, who is working and who is also active in the church. After a recent meeting at the church Ethel stayed around until the others had gone —Elwyn was not there—and asked if she could talk with me.

ETHEL: Do you have a few spare moments? I have something I'd like to talk over with you.

MANNING: Well, sure, Ethel.

ETHEL: Well, what I'd like to know is what you think of Elwyn. Tell me, what do you really think of him—what you think his good points are, and his weak points.

MANNING: Well, Ethel, that's not very easy for me to do.[A] I haven't known Elwyn for very long, and it's pretty hard for me to say just what I think of him. You feel that my giving a quick, first-impression opinion of him would help you?

ETHEL: Well, I'm just sort of confused at the moment with my relationship to him, and I thought maybe you could help me decide something.

MANNING: I would be glad to help you clarify your problem.[B]

ETHEL: You see, Elwyn and I have been going steady for about six months. I know that he hasn't dated any of the other girls around, and I haven't had dates with any other fellows. I have grown rather fond of him. He's a swell fellow. I know that he would do almost anything that I might ask of him. My folks have grown to like him a lot too. They have always encouraged his coming to the house and my going out with him. I've always had the feeling, though, that they've done it mostly because it has meant a good opportunity for me to get out with the other young people (pause). Well, anyway, over the six months I'm afraid that Elwyn has become much more serious than I have. Recently it's been getting awfully hard for me to keep him from getting too serious. From the beginning I have always made it quite clear that I intended to go to Metropolis and get a job and that I'd never think of settling down to married life in a town like this.

MANNING: You feel then that Elwyn has recently become too serious in your relationship and that it is making a real problem for you.

ETHEL: That's right. I must confess that our dating hasn't been on the purely Platonic side either, and that doesn't help matters now at all (pause). And then there's still another thing. Even though I have grown to like Elwyn a lot, there is one thing in particular that he does that I just can't stand. He's tremendously jealous of every other fellow who even looks at me. He shows his feelings much too easily to suit me.

MANNING: You feel that you must come to some kind of decision concerning your relationship with him.

ETHEL: Yes, I've pretty much decided that something has just got to be done real soon. I've got to think of some way that will stall him off until I leave to go to work. And believe me, it's not going to be easy. I've just got to figure out some way to make him see my plans. And I've got to do it so I won't hurt him. His feelings are so easily hurt, and I wouldn't hurt him for the world.

MANNING: You feel that it is possible for you to do what you say, stall him off until you leave?

ETHEL: That's the idea. It's not going to be easy, however. I might have to call on you for some more help.

MANNING: You feel that I could help you some more. I'd be glad to talk this over more at any time.

ETHEL: (glancing at her watch) Oh my goodness. I didn't know it was so late. Thanks ever so much, Mr. Manning. You've helped a lot.

I have a feeling that this was a rather successful interview. It was cut off somewhat short, but I think the way was open for future help to Ethel. Here is another pure case in which the parishioner in the beginning wanted the pastor to solve the problem. I feel that I was rather cautious and avoided this error, and was able to get Ethel to see her problem a little more clearly.

TEACHER'S COMMENT TO MANNING ON ETHEL

This shows you are making some real progress. You are beginning to forget that you have to reach a decision, or that you have to decide when to listen and when to talk, and instead you pay attention to what Ethel is trying to communicate. When it comes to the details of how you went about it, you are pretty mechanical. For instance, if the "you feels" were laid end to end, they would reach quite a distance. As you study this over, try to see how you might have made some of your comments without falling into such a pattern of mechanical repetition. At A you start to squirm out; then you get a "you feel" feeling, and strangely enough, mechanical as it is—and it reads still more so than it is in conversation—it returns the situation to Ethel. At B you remember about defining the situation, not letting her have the wrong idea of what to expect. This too, mechanical as it is, leads Ethel right back to her situation. I do feel your method here is so wooden that it won't work for long if it remains on this basis. Understanding and communicating understanding is more than "you feel." But once you get the idea, you can be a little more natural and get over the woodenness of the moment. You're moving in the right direction, but be sure you don't stop here.

Manning is a long distance yet from being a first-class pastoral counselor. But he is moving in the right direction. His stability, courage, real interest in helping people, are all much more important assets than he yet realizes. But he was using them indiscriminatingly, wavering between passivity and getting action. He saw that there was a song somewhere, but all he knew was some of the words. So he started to look for the tune. In the third interview he began to find it, but he gave up singing part way through. In the fourth interview he sang throughout, but he still hasn't found out about pitch; his song is a monotone. But he is on the way, and that counts.

Mr. Manning reported one more interview suggesting that he was beginning to get the idea of pitch, that is, getting over being so wooden about his newly found knowledge and insight. We may expect he will continue to improve. To what point, if he does not have further training or supervision, we cannot be certain. But it seems altogether likely that he will be able to use much more effectively his very real capacities to help people in many kinds of situations than would have been true if he had not had this supervised experience. He could profit from some of the things to be mentioned below. After all, what has happened to him is merely the beginning of learning counseling. But the direction is important.

INTERVIEW MATERIALS

MR. Manning's learning, as we have seen, has come about through the supervised use of interview materials in their simplest form. He remembers and writes out what happened. From a research standpoint this is crude, but from a pedagogical point of view its very simplicity commends it, especially as an initial device. Its further advantage of not forcing one to recall what he is not ready to face is also a point in its favor in introductory learning of counseling. However much may be forgotten, it is vastly more accurate than an interview put into indirect discourse. The remembered and then written interview is far from giving a life history, and its defects are especially apparent in extended counseling. But until one is reasonably sure he can know just what his own basic approach is, it is the most useful and practical device for learning counseling.

Of what value is it without supervision such as I gave Mr. Manning? Perhaps not as much, but still a great deal. When Mr. Manning and I talked together, it was clear to both of us that he had learned at least as much from the inevitable reflections which followed the writing-up process as he had from my comments.

Various ways of utilizing interview material for learning purposes have been tried, with more or less success, in group situations. In Chapter II I referred to the device of putting an interview, minus what the pastor said and did, in a small mimeographed booklet, one unit of material at a time, and letting the members of the group imagine themselves into the interview and write what they would do or say. I have also used "scripts." Such manufactured interviews are a more successful learning device than might be thought at first glance, for they can exaggerate in various degrees and yet leave no sting.

Rollin J. Fairbanks has developed a method of spontaneous interviews, in which he plays the part of a particular parishioner whose experience and feelings he has well in mind while one or more members of the group call upon or interview him.[2] This has much to commend it, for it tends to throw into the open the general approach without wasting attention on methodological details. But it requires a good deal of dramatic ability and work on the part of the teacher, and in the hands of a nonexpert it can be entirely unsuccessful. It is a "gross" device, whereas the others have finer discriminations. But this very quality at times makes it useful.

There is no question that we shall have in the future more interview material than we have now taken down by recording machines from most of the professions that do counseling; and I see no reason why ministers should not be in on this also. For research purposes such recordings ought to speak for themselves. And as recording machines become lower in price and the wide possibilities of their use in a variety of ways become clearer, more training schools and centers will have them. There are many complicated questions having to do with the value, the justification, and the methods of using these machines. Without attempting to discuss these questions, two points seem to be pertinent to our purposes. The first is that there is a clear distinction between learning on the one hand and research on the other, especially if by learning we mean what is meant here— getting started in the right direction on an approach which will be cumulative in its effectiveness. Eventually the two may be closer together. But if in a recorded interview a student learns so much about himself that he does not like that it scares him away from counseling entirely, then the method is bad. Just why advanced professional people seem often unwilling to have interviews recorded, even when the person with whom they are dealing has consented, is something for their own conscience to look at. Carl Rogers seems to me irrefutable in advocating recordings.

The other thing we may say about the possible use of recording machines is that the naturalness of their use varies with different situations.[3] A great deal, as we have seen, of the pastor's counseling is not done in his office. Even when it is, he does not bear as a halo over his head the purple aura of science, as a psychologist could in a university, or a psychiatrist in a clinic. If the university psychologist asks, "May we use this for purposes of research?" either it is really all right with the student who understands about research or he knows that saying anything against research in a university is tantamount to committing the unpardonable sin. If some pastors are to use these machines, it will have to be through imaginative translation of what will have meaning to the parishioner involved. Even so, we need these now for research, though the findings might later prove to be useful for learning and teaching.[4]

The emphasis here and throughout this volume on interview material is because of the vividness it has for purposes of learning. It is our most graphic type of illustration, and yet it is more than illustration, for properly handled it contains that which can eventually correct our interpretations. So in reply to the question of whether in interview material learning relates merely to what one person gets insight into which another person already has, or whether there is a genuinely new element in the learning process, the answer has to be something of both. In the case of Mr. Manning, he learned something new to him. I am reasonably sure I learned something hitherto new to me.

The chief defects of learning counseling through interview material are three, but all are in some measure correctable. The first is one we have already given attention to—the temptation to get the tune without pitch, to get some details of method without understanding or inwardly accepting the presuppositions or approach without which the method is meaningless. Enough on that; we have seen that it can be overcome or transcended.

The second defect of learning through interview material is in the temptations it brings with regard to the treatment of psychological dynamics. We have already devoted a chapter to the relation of such dynamics to pastoral counseling, and need hardly repeat how fundamentally important it is to have a grasp of those if counseling is to be more than some mechanical procedure. There is some temptation when we try to learn through interview material to do one of two things: either to declare psychological dynamics to be irrelevant on the ground that we do not "spring interpretations" on people in counseling or, on the other hand, to develop a theory of dynamics

to go along with the interview material which tends to omit con·
sideration of vitally important factors that cannot be seen in interview material—an illustration of the last being the two concepts of
the pastor's role or roles. Russell L. Dicks began using pastoral interview material for purposes both of research and learning as early
as 1933. Since the linkage of it with dynamics is more difficult than
the relation of dynamics to life histories (long case studies giving
family background, etc.), Dicks's temptation was to neglect dynamic
material and concentrate on practical method and techniques—a
temptation which he has since seen and taken steps to guard against.
On the other hand, Carl Rogers, who approached interview material
with an excellent knowledge of dynamics, was at first inclined to
discount the significance of dynamics when he discovered that something other than such knowledge in his head made the difference
between success and failure in counseling. He has since modified this
position very considerably and has acknowledged it in a measure in
publications.

The third defect of learning through interview material is the
most fundamental and important. It is that it *may* not—we do not
yet know—capture the most important elements in a counseling relationship that is extended in time and scope. Rather it may not do
so without resting on some such theoretical basis of understanding
as that being developed out of experience with long-term therapy by
the progressive psychoanalytic groups. But, fortunately, if this is a
defect, it need not concern pastors at this stage, however relevant
it may be to the counselors who do deep psychological therapy. Most
of our counseling contacts are relatively brief in time, and for learning how to do what can be done in relatively short periods, interview material is unsurpassed.

CLINICAL PASTORAL TRAINING

SO biased am I in favor of clinical pastoral training that I could
hardly write in any other vein than wishing we had more of it.[5] I do
so wish, and I think we shall have. But since I am attempting here
to set forth the various ways—complementary ways and not mutually exclusive ways—in which pastors and theological students may
learn counseling, I shall examine clinical pastoral training within
this setting. It should be remembered also that clinical pastoral
training by no means confines itself to teaching counseling, but
teaches also an approach to other activities of the ministry such as
are indicated in Chapter VII of this book.

It seems that clinical pastoral training, in its essence, is a procedure whereby theological students or ministers are brought face to face with individual people in a situation which is susceptible to supervision from the pastoral point of view and in which, through the use of various participative devices—such as interview material and compilation of case histories—both the dynamics of human conduct and the pastoral ways of dealing with it are learned, and learned together.[6]

In the early days of clinical pastoral training, fifteen years ago, there were long discussions on understanding versus method. Most of us held out for understanding on the ground that method would naturally follow if we had that, but others promoted method on the conviction that we needed a new practice but there was no need to change our theory. Of recent years I have come to believe both groups asked the wrong question. A counselor who knew method but not psychological dynamics would be a dangerous machine. He needs a basic approach, not just in his head, but in the total attitude he has toward his parishioners. On the other hand, the bland assumption that proper method follows as the night the day if we but understand dynamics is disproved by the alarmingly large number of counselors who know what makes people the way they are but can find only coercive or moralistic or diverting or generalizing methods for trying to help them. Clinical training, like practical theology, has to relate theory and practice, objective understanding of what makes people tick and at the same time what happens and can happen in relationship between the counselor and the person. Practical theology has its theoretical side, else it could not apply its resources to the aid of real people. But its theoretical insights are meaningless unless that application itself is studied and evaluated. Clinical pastoral training properly includes both.

To date most clinical pastoral training courses have been held in hospitals. Penal institutions, case work agencies, and certain other centers have also been used. The public continues to misinterpret the reasons for this. It is relatively easy to see that a theological student in a general hospital is not studying medicine as a doctor would, even though he does pick up some knowledge of medicine while he is there. It is harder to see that such a student is not just studying how to minister to sick people, but to people in stress situations. However, that can eventually be grasped. It is more difficult to see the point of such training in the mental hospital, a point discussed in Chapter III. In defending clinical pastoral training centered in institutions as being of great importance and based on sound theory,

I do not wish to imply that clinical pastoral training can be only that which is centered in institutions. Hence my carefully broad definition of such training. Its essence will, I predict, be applied in the future in ways which have as yet only been touched, or have not been touched at all. Mr. Manning's experience, despite its brevity and obvious incompleteness, is itself a proper application of the essential method of clinical pastoral training.

What about clinical pastoral training and field work? [7] Sometimes I think that field work is looked on by the seminaries as the "poor relation"—tolerated as necessary, but a financial nuisance, an administrative headache, and a possible producer of curricular schizophrenia. On the other hand, clinical pastoral training is seen as a turbaned and multicolored horseman on a white steed, brandishing a great key in his hand but giving no clue as to which locks he intends to work on. Therefore it is full of prestige but dangerous in some unknown way. This is fancy but contains some fact. Field work began as a money-earning device for theological students, a placement service in churches or settlement houses—carried on mutually by the seminary and the church or other agency—whereby the student could earn money and pick up a little general experience, and the church be protected as much as possible from unintentional malpractice. It has become vastly more than that in many schools. Supervision is given by both the school and the church; tasks of the student are defined so that he has a job sufficiently small in compass to help him grow in experience, not be overwhelmed by it; hours are set so the student will not unintentionally be exploited by the demands of the church; in short, the financial help involved, although not eliminated, has been made subsidiary to the purpose of field work as supervised training. In some places attention is devoted to the contacts the student has with individuals as well as groups, in a fashion not dissimilar to Mr. Manning. But this last is a rarity as yet.

Theoretically the issue of clinical pastoral training versus field work is a false one. But practically there are still important distinctions. Those who run field-work programs ordinarily have to accept as a premise of their work, "Go where you like, but it must involve financial aid no matter what"; whereas those who run clinical training programs have as a premise of their training, "Go as far as you like, but it must involve supervised contact with individuals no matter what." The fact that these are too often, in practice, contradictory is not a commentary upon any theoretical division between them but upon the economics and politics and mores of theological education.

To come again to practical affairs, what can a pastor or theological student learn about counseling through clinical pastoral training? A great deal, but he will not learn the same amount in all the courses that are given. It may still be true that a student can take certain courses in clinical pastoral training and emerge with little understanding of how to apply his knowledge of psychological dynamics to actually helping people through counseling; while in certain other courses he will have learned some methods and something of the approach to helping people but will not have linked it with a sufficient understanding of dynamics to make possible a self-teaching process from that point on. These points of emphasis still exist, but they are growing more closely together.

By and large, clinical pastoral training is by far the quickest, simplest, most comprehensive, and least expensive way to get a toe hold in learning counseling. And if it develops, as I hope it will in the future, it will be still more effective than it is now.

ACADEMIC COURSES

SINCE we have made the point in several ways that the practical field, including counseling, has a theoretical aspect and that various kinds of background knowledge are required, it is clear that any good work done in the practical field can be important and valuable for counseling. It will not teach counseling as such, nor can it be a substitute for supervised and reflected-upon experience in counseling. But without some of it the scope which can be attained in counseling will be seriously limited.

Provided they are taught with some sense of dynamics and movement and with some element of supervised experience, all the courses dealing with activities of the pastor can be meaningful to the pastor as he views them from the counseling focus. Religious education, evangelism, worship and preaching, administration, and social ethics can contribute much—if the pastor's role is seen as one role. And those academic subjects which are properly to be seen as the theoretical aspects of the entire practical field, particularly psychology and sociology of religion, can be immensely valuable, and some knowledge of them is basic however they are organized in the curriculum. I have taken a hand both at reviewing the past work and suggesting a reshaping of the approach to the psychological understanding of religion.[8] It would appear that some similar process is going on in reference to the sociological study of religion.[9]

At least the larger theological schools make provision for some academic courses along these lines.[10] The student or pastor may find little help in linking his knowledge secured from them with practical application to such things as counseling. He may have to perform that function assisted in various degrees or unassisted. Both the knowledge and the linkage are important, whether the schools have got around to recognizing this or not.

Although some introductory work is possible at most seminaries, very few make any provision for advanced work—especially at a doctoral level—and no one of the existing opportunities can be considered as adequate. It is mentioned here because indirectly it concerns a very large group—the pastors and pastors-to-be who need integrated training in the whole practical field, involving both supervised experience and sound theory, if they are to carry out the one role effectively. When talented and far-sighted theological students and pastors must resort to a dozen kinds of expedients in order to secure academically respectable advanced work, then the theological seminaries need to look more seriously at their obligation or face the risk of permitting all advanced training of a practical theological character to be carried out in effect by secular institutions with a nonpastoral focus of function.[11]

If a pastor wishes to take courses on counseling and the background knowledge of counseling but is unable to find these in a pastoral or theological framework, how much can he get out of secular courses, or courses offered from some professional focus other than that of the pastor? The answer seems to be quite a lot—in proportion to his recognition of precisely what, from his pastoral point of view, will be missing from those courses. If he has that clearly and specifically in mind, then he can learn much which it is then his job to translate and put into practical pastoral counseling terms. If he does not, one of two things will happen: either he will be impressed with the knowledge gained, attribute it exclusively to whatever group he is learning it from, and leave the pastorate, or he will have in his mind two entirely different conceptions of helping people, resting content in the illusion that the Church says he should help people in one way while the other group says something quite different.

Some universities, notably Harvard and Chicago, are developing interdepartmental study opportunities for people who want to become familiar with the "life sciences"—at Chicago, the Committee on Human Development and at Harvard, the Department of Social Relations.[12] This integration across formerly separated departmental lines is both inevitable and significant, and it is certainly more relevant to the pastor's purposes in general background to get a view of human development, including biology, several branches of psychology, counseling, sociology, and cultural anthropology, than to take work merely in one of them and be ignorant of the others.

University teaching in psychology is increasingly taking counseling seriously; and although this is generally confined to one or two courses, except at a few great universities, and clinical opportunities are often small, the trend seems to be all in favor of expanding such training and improving it. Psychiatry courses are generally not open to students other than medical students, but there are occasional exceptions. Among the depth psychologists there has developed an increasing sense of educational responsibility for the nonpsychiatric counselors, notably teachers, social workers, and clergy. Certain courses in the Washington School of Psychiatry are open to ministers. This year special seminars for ministers are being held in New York both by the William A. White Institute of Psychiatry and the Association for the Advancement of Psychoanalysis. The social work schools are now generally so crowded that it is difficult for anyone not following regular work toward a degree to be admitted for courses. A number of clergy have found training in case work to be a valuable preparation for counseling.

This is not intended as a catalogue of opportunities but only as a suggestion that certain courses under secular auspices may, if their deficiencies from the pastor's point of view are understood, prove valuable.

PERSONAL THERAPY FOR THE PASTOR

HOW valuable is a personal therapeutic experience (consultations by the minister with a therapist) as training for counseling? I believe that such consultations are extremely valuable, but at the same time I think the pastor is likely to be under misapprehension if he considers them chiefly as training. They are rather a prerequisite to training, or preparation for the insights of training. From the point of view of his professional work they are background rather than training. Their professional value is great, but it is incidental to their personal value.

Ministers and social workers are the only professional groups to whom a depth therapist can say, "Under ideal conditions people in your profession should all be analyzed" without being criticized for saying it. We are the only groups who are collectively disposed to realize that our personal work involves our personalities as well as those of other people and to take the idea of some personal transformation as an opportunity, not an insult. Collectively we do; individually the story may be quite different. We are not above confessing we are sinners, but we confess only the sin which does not strike close to the organizing center of our personality.

No one can grow up in our society without developing some traits of character which, even if they are relevant and helpful and good in some situations, can nevertheless unconsciously betray him in other situations, provided they are permitted to operate blindly and without insight on his part. The same perseverance which made a boy admired as one who "always finishes what he starts" may later convert him into an alcohol addict. The qualities that make a man successful as a leader in some activities may, if he is unaware of what goes on, cut him off unnecessarily from helping people he wants to help in other situations. Thus personal insight into things of this kind can be of great professional value to the pastor, even if he is as stable and balanced and creative and undivided as it is possible to be in our society.

We all have blind spots. But he who knows his blind spots can avoid cutting himself off from people to whom otherwise he would be a person who "wouldn't understand." Even a relatively brief series of consultations with a good therapist can be valuable to the minister, both personally and professionally. Professionally speaking such personal therapy is important not so much in teaching one how to counsel, as in teaching him what to expect from counseling and therapy.

With an understandable enthusiasm professional therapists have sometimes suggested that personal therapeutic consultations would give a minister all the training he needed for pastoral counseling. This is even less true of the minister than of the psychoanalyst, who must carry on therapy under supervision as well as have personal therapy himself, because the setting in which the pastor does his counseling, and the role in which he does it, require study and special experience. Enough has been said in Chapter V to suggest what a pastor may legitimately expect of a therapist when the pastor himself is to be the patient or client. If the standards are good enough for parishioners, they should be good enough for us.

The idea will persist for a long time that seeking personal therapy is a sign of weakness, especially in one who, like the pastor, professes to be a leader. But this viewpoint seems to have striking similarities to the "nonsense" of suggesting that successful people are not really successful unless they can face the fact of sin in their own lives and seek forgiveness and restoration of a relationship they have broken. He who is too proud ever to admit the need of help may also be too proud to confess the fact of sin.

Of course, the number of therapists is small; it costs money to go to them—though not an excessive amount usually; and they are sometimes ignorant of philosophy and blindly antitheological. We do not say a minister must have such consultations. But if he has the time and means and accessibility and interest, he will get something that profits him both personally and professionally. He will still, however, need training in pastoral counseling.

READING

OBVIOUSLY printed material may have some value in learning counseling. At the same time, reading alone can never be considered sufficient preparation for counseling, however extensive or wise it may be. If some pastor should read this volume, take seriously what is said here, follow some such device as writing up the next pastoral contact he has and studying it, decide that he has learned more from the interview than from reading this book, then he would have got the point. Reading is obviously important, but it is just as obviously insufficient in itself.

The literature on pastoral counseling, and even that on the theological aspects of its background, is still small. The best material in journals that appears regularly is in the pastoral work section of *The Pastor,* in the *Journal of Pastoral Care,* and in the *Journal of Clinical Pastoral Work.*[13] Consequently anyone who wants to read must still go partly to the various secular sources and draw his own parallels and conclusions. The reader who is interested may get some clue as to where he may read most profitably by glancing through the notes of this book. But we may have in the future a more discriminating as well as a more specific and clear-cut literature on pastoral counseling and the background for it than we have had in the past or have in the present.

SUMMARY

THERE are various methods a pastor or theological student may follow if he wants to learn pastoral counseling. None of them is perfect, and none is sufficient by itself. He will be guided by the degree of his interest, his sense of need, his schedule, his location, and his pocketbook. But any minister with interest can take some steps toward improving his understanding and skill.

Notes

Chapter I: AIMS AND ASSUMPTIONS OF PASTORAL COUNSELING

1 Charles S. Kemp, in an informal bulletin of the Iowa Society for Mental Hygiene, winter, 1947.

2 Mark 3:14-15.

3 See Lawrence K. Frank, *Human Conservation* (National Resources Planning Board, 1942). Available from Government Printing Office, Wash. 25, D. C.

4 See my article on suicide, "Spiritual Catastrophe," in *Church Management*, December, 1942. See also Karl A. Menninger, *Man Against Himself* (Harcourt, 1939).

5 See, for example, George Thorman's *Toward Mental Health*, Public Affairs Pamphlet No. 120, Public Affairs Committee, 22 East 38th Street, New York 16, N. Y. Additional literature is available from the National Committee for Mental Hygiene, 1790 Broadway, New York 19, N. Y.; from the National Mental Health Foundation, Box 7574, Philadelphia 1, Pa.; and from the various state and city mental hygiene societies.

6 See *Alcohol, Science, and Society*, twenty-nine lectures with discussions given at the Yale Summer School of Alcohol Studies (*Quarterly Journal of Studies on Alcohol*, Yale University, 1945).

7 Frank, *op. cit.*, p. 14.

8 *Ibid.*

9 See, for example, Clarence C. Little, *The Fight on Cancer*, Public Affairs Pamphlet No. 38; and *What You Should Know about Tuberculosis*, National Tuberculosis Association, 1943. Available free from local societies.

10 Frank, *op. cit.*

11 See note 3 for reference.

12 Unpublished paper, "The Toll of Disease in American Life," presented at Howard University in 1944.

13 For a very brief introduction to psychosomatic interrelationships see Chap. IV of my *Religion and Health* (Macmillan, 1943). For a more adequate summary, also written from the point of view of the religious worker, see Part I of Carroll A. Wise's *Religion in Illness and Health* (Harper, 1942). The best-known technical book-length works on psychosomatic medicine are Flanders Dunbar's *Emotions and Bodily Changes* (Columbia University Press, 1935; revised ed. 1938), *Psychosomatic Diagnosis* (Harper, 1943), *Mind and Body* (Random, 1947); Carl Binger's *The Doctor's Job* (Norton, 1945); and *Psychosomatic Medicine*, by Edward Weiss and O. Spurgeon English. See also the quarterly journal entitled *Psychosomatic Medicine*.

14 Carl G. Jung's much-quoted statement from *Modern Man in Search of a Soul* (Harcourt, 1936) is relevant here. Jung wrote that if all of his patients who had passed beyond the turbulence of youth had possessed what the great religions have tried to give their followers, they would not have fallen sick. Erich Fromm, in oral communication, has made a different point relevant to the same issue, namely, that a large proportion of the people who come to psychotherapists believing that all they need is slight assistance on this or that problem in actuality cannot get better until they are aided to get a new and more adequate concept of and approach to their function and destiny as human beings. His new volume, *Man for Himself* (Rinehart, 1947), deals with this and related questions. It merits further comment but was not published until after my book went to press. Karen Horney's

works, especially *Our Inner Conflicts* (Norton, 1945), indicate clearly that ethical and moral questions (and by implication one's conception of his human meaning and destiny) are not merely peripheral, but are fundamental in the progressive approach to psychoanalysis.

15 See especially the now, unfortunately, almost-forgotten volume by George A. Coe, *The Motives of Men* (Scribner, 1928). This book attempted to deal with all aspects of motivation before this became common practice even among depth psychologists.

16 Perhaps the best books among the more popular group which present a contemporary analysis of the general predicament of man from the Christian theological view, with some enlightenment from psychological studies, are: Lewis J. Sherrill's *Guilt and Redemption* (John Knox Press, 1945); D. Elton Trueblood's *The Predicament of Modern Man* (Harper, 1944); Edwin E. Aubrey's *Present Theological Tendencies* (Harper, 1936) and *Man's Search for Himself* (Abingdon Press, 1940). See also the books of such preachers as Harry Emerson Fosdick, Paul Scherer, and Ralph W. Sockman. "Predicament" is of course the lead-off point for the Continental theologians of recent years, and has influenced the United States measurably, as will be noted later from the focus of its relevance to our subject.

17 Modern thinking along this line began with William Healy's *Mental Conflicts and Misconduct* (Little, Brown, 1917). As a young psychiatrist, Healy became the first psychiatric attaché of a juvenile court in this country. He found that "a remarkable, dynamic quality characterizing certain hidden mental reactions to experience is responsible in some individuals for the production of misconduct." Since that time the viewpoint has been accepted and elaborated, with a more sociological orientation, by all professional students of the subject. Many volumes by Healy, Clifford Shaw, Sanford Bates, and others testify to the insight of Healy's first conclusions. The point could almost be said to have been taken for granted by the Attorney General's conference on delinquency held in 1946.

18 This is illustrated especially in the history of Christian missions. For a brief review of the compassionate outreach of the modern missionary movement in the medical and health fields, Chap. III of my *Religion and Health*. The many ramifications may be studied in the monumental seven-volume *A History of the Expansion of Christianity*, by Kenneth S. Latourette (Harper).

19 The classical biblical illustration is, of course, the story of the Good Samaritan.

20 See, for example, the statement on evangelism adopted by the Federal Council of the Churches of Christ in America at its special meeting in March, 1946. The statement carried this prophetic and particular note in an unusually forceful way.

21 See Charles S. Kemp's interesting historical volume, *Physicians of the Soul* (Macmillan, 1947), for an effective introduction to the history of the care or cure (cure in this sense means care, not therapy) of souls.

22 See Arthur Cushman McGiffert, Jr., in *Christianity and Mental Hygiene* (Federal Council, 1939), for a good, brief discussion of this point. John T. McNeill is expected to publish a history of the cure of souls with special reference to what the Protestant Reformation did about it. There is as yet no thoroughly adequate discussion of the question in print so far as I know.

23 In Chap. V we shall consider the sense in which pastors and other counselors are and are not specialists, are and are not general practitioners.

24 See Kemp's volume, note 21 above. From the perspective of approach to healing in Christian history, see especially Percy Dearmer, *Body and Soul* (Dutton, 1923). Comparatively little attention has been paid to the history of this function by American writers—for fairly obvious reasons. The interested student will find relevant material in both the Anglican and Roman Catholic books on moral and ascetical theology and in the works of the German "pastoral theologians," especially those of the nineteenth century. The most comprehensive volume is J. J. van Oosterzee, *Practical*

Theology (Scribner, 1878) . A more recent one is E. Chr. Achelis, *Lehrbuch der praktischen Theologie* (Leipzig, 1911) . Among the Roman Catholic texts we may note J. A. McHugh and C. J. Callan, *Moral Theology*, 2 vols. (Wagner, 1929) ; A. Koch, *A Handbook of Moral Theology*, trans. from German, 5 vols. (Herder, 1928) ; and T. Slater, *A Manual of Moral Theology*, 2 vols. (Benziger, 1924) . For examples of the interest of the "social gospel" in pastoral theology see Washington Gladden's *The Christian Pastor and the Working Church* (Scribner, 1898) , and Charles E. Jefferson's *The Minister as Shepherd* (Crowell, 1912) .

25 My appreciation and thanks to Harry Bone in connection with the list of assumptions of the counseling situation. He has been of considerable help in my formulation of them.

26 The reader should note that these assumptions relate to the counseling situation, but by no means to all of the pastor's personal work. The chapter on pastoral work as preparation for counseling, Chap. VI, clarifies the similarities and differences.

This appears to be the most effective place to discuss my use of interview material in comparison and contrast with the way such material has been used by other writers. The only extensive use which has been made of such material in print has been by Carl R. Rogers and his associates in the so-called "nondirective" or "client-centered" approach to counseling; by John Sutherland Bonnell in *Pastoral Psychiatry* Harper 1939) ; and by Russell L. Dicks in *And Ye Visited Me* (Harper, 1938) . There has been some publication of interview material by social workers, as in the popular and helpful *Interviewing: Its Principles and Methods*, by Annette Garrett (Family Service Association of America, 1942) ; and by the industrial counselors who will be mentioned in Chap. V. Something close to interview material was used by Charles T. Holman in *Getting Down to Cases* (Macmillan, 1942) ; and there are small scatterings of it in a few books by other pastoral writers, including Leslie D. Weatherhead and Charles R. Zahniser. But Rogers, Dicks, and Bonnell are the only ones who have used such material extensively, and a comment on their use and mine is in order.

In *And Ye Visited Me*, Dicks gave reports of actual interviews of a hospital chaplain and his pastoral students with hospital patients. He did not, however, interpret or comment upon the material or attempt to draw any general theory of approach in connection with the material itself. In *The Art of Ministering to the Sick*, written with Richard C. Cabot (Macmillan, 1936) , and in *Pastoral Work and Personal Counseling* (Macmillan, 1944) , he presented a general approach both to pastoral ministry to the sick and to pastoral work and pastoral counseling in general. But in none of these writings has he demonstrated specifically how the theory and approach follow from study of concrete situations, as demonstrated in interview material. That is, he has a theory, and he has presented interview material, but he has not shown their relationship. Since it is that relationship with which my book is concerned, it is difficult to compare this volume with Dicks' viewpoint in any of his books. From our personal association. I believe our points of view to be very similar but differing in emphasis on two or three points, apart, of course, from matters of detail. I believe I attach much more significance than Dicks does to the meaning and relationship of personality dynamics to pastoral counseling. Second, I believe that I emphasize the need for a fundamental theory more than Dicks, or anyhow that there are certain differences in the nature of our fundamental theories. He seems to me at times to rely upon authority in a sense I cannot bring myself to do in view of my conception of the theory of pastoral counseling. But any such differences are certainly minor compared with our wide agreement on most points.

Pastoral Psychiatry is Bonnell's only work to date using interview material. However, in 1948 his new book entitled *Psychology for Pastor and People* was published by Harper. Unfortunately, it was not possible for me to examine it before writing what follows. In the sense that he attempts to work back and forth between theory and the concrete material, as I do in this book, we are together. We also agree in our conception of the need to define the counseling function of the pastor in relation to that of other specialists and to study and understand specifically how the resources of religion may be used most fruitfully in counseling. Further, as I understand him, I believe we would agree in general on our understanding of the essential nature of the Christian faith. But in our approach to pastoral counseling itself there seem to be some fundamental differences. I have characterized my basic approach in the word "eductive," drawing or leading out. Bonnell's approach, as demonstrated in his reported interviews, seems to be more manipulative, or intromittent, or intropulsive. His approach appears to be authoritative, putting a greater burden upon the pastor's capacity for quick grasp of underlying factors than is possible or likely without risking serious diagnostic errors. On the other hand, he possesses a rare and far-reaching knowledge of personality dynamics; and we certainly agree that such knowledge is of great significance. But unless Bonnell has made alterations in his approach and method since *Pastoral Psychiatry*—and I believe that he has—I am not in agreement with him on those fundamental points.

Carl R. Rogers' major works on counseling are *Counseling and Psychotherapy* (Houghton Mifflin, 1942) and *Counseling with Returned Servicemen*, written with John L. Wallen (McGraw-Hill, 1946). Other books and articles by his colleagues and students have been published, and will be referred to later, as Rogers himself will be in several connections. He has made, and is still making, such an impact even upon his critics that his already large contributions require mention at many points. Here, however, I want to clarify what seem to me the basic similarities and differences between my point of view and his with reference to the use and function of interview material.

As I understand Rogers, he has been much misunderstood. Some have concluded that "nondirective" meant mere passivity, which is absurd. Others—mistakenly I think—have implied that he is not "client-centered" because he concentrates on keeping the counselor out rather than keeping the client in. Still others have said his very use of interview material is misleading, on the ground that the words on paper do not give the full flavor of a contact or relationship. At this point Rogers has admitted the obvious fact involved, but has pointed out—quite properly, in my judgment—that interview material comes closer to giving it all than does a highly abstracted account which mixes fact and interpretation and gives the reader no chance for independent judgment.

Rogers has used interview material for research purposes, to draw up a theory of approach and method in counseling from study of such material. I believe he is on sound ground here, so long as the proper allowances are made for the factors which cannot be demonstrated by interview material—something I have discussed in Chap. IV of this book. It does not seem that Rogers has as yet looked adequately at the limitations of interview material—especially the dynamics of an extended relationship and what I have called the precounseling situation. But this is thoroughly understandable in view of the short time in which he has been at work along these lines. Further, he seems to have an irrefutable case in requesting from other counselors interview material from any point of view from which they work. And he is justified in asserting that mere generalizations and abstractions cannot be compared properly with interview material. Undoubtedly interview material, however accurate, has limitations. But it is hardly fair or scientific to decry it without trial and discuss only its limitations. I am certainly for Rogers here.

I believe, therefore, that I agree with Rogers on the importance of interview material, with these exceptions. First, in this book I make no pretensions about the scientific validity of my concrete material; it has not been recorded in such a way as to make that possible. If my material had been secured like Rogers', it would have been better. Second, I confess that my material has two functions; it is both illustration, a graphic form of illustration, and the raw material out of which I have induced general conclusions. Rogers professes to use it only in the second sense. Third, I do not know what Rogers believes about the relation of psychological dynamics to counseling approach and method. He apparently believes the counselor needs such knowledge, but he has not indicated either how it may be induced from counseling situations or how it may serve a function in the counseling situation. Since Rogers is himself a master of such knowledge, I can only conclude that he has not yet made up his mind about its place, importance, and value. In my thinking it is of great importance, and I have attempted to suggest both how we may learn it through counseling and how we may use it in counseling.

As I use the word "eductive" to give a thumbnail description of my approach, I believe it to be in the same direction as Rogers' "nondirective" or "client-centered" approach. And yet I cannot accept either of the latter terms as properly descriptive of what I am trying to say. And I do not believe the entire distinction is that I am considering pastoral counseling and Rogers, counseling in general. In the application of the eductive principle I feel there must be many variations in specific methodology—and of course I consider these only in the pastor's situation. The methodology must never contradict the approach, but it cannot be induced solely from knowledge of the approach. Rogers appears increasingly to be stressing what I call approach as against details of method in themselves. And yet I am not certain how much we are in agreement at this point. Does Rogers have a method which is now being tested to see how wide is its applicability? In other words, is he like a physician who tests penicillin on many illnesses to see where it is and is not helpful? Or is he, on the other hand, the exponent of a basic approach which, while varied in methodological details of application, is valid in all situations because of its fundamental consistency with the psychological helping process? In other words, is he, on the basis of a consistent eductive approach, nevertheless a differential diagnostician when it comes to detailed methods of application? My own position is that approach is most important, that methodological details are always less important than this, and that other factors have to be considered in deciding details of method. Without my postulates it seems to me difficult or impossible to study the pastor's precounseling work in its true importance.

27 The reason for the "usually" is the existence of what I have called in Chap. V "environmental-resources counseling. "Since I believe the eductive approach should be applied there as elsewhere, the "usually" may be an unnecessary qualification. The reader may decide for himself.

28 Erich Fromm's *Man for Himself* is now, despite its antitheistic position, the most far-reaching discussion of psychotherapy and ethics. An introductory article suggesting the trend of my thinking is "Toward an Ethical Conscience," *Journal of Religion,* January, 1945. The most ambitious attempt in this direction is the William Alanson White lectures given by psychiatrist G. Brock Chisholm, entitled *The Psychiatry of Enduring Peace and Social Progress,* published by the magazine *Psychiatry,* February, 1946. Dr. Chisholm, former Deputy Director of Health of the Dominion of Canada and now executive head of the World Health organization, deserves serious consideration.

Chisholm takes moralism apart. He believes that it is the teaching of moral rigidities which makes it so difficult to help people find their way to a freedom proper in democratic society; that the moralisms must be shown up in all their rigidity and antisocial character if we are to get anywhere. This side of Chisholm's case, while it may in spots suffer from lack of knowledge of what theologians have been saying on this point for some time, is true and important. When it comes to building a new and superior concept of ethics, however, the author has little or nothing to say. The implication is that if the underbrush of moralistic rigidity is cleared away, everything will take care of itself. The inadequacy of this view will be demonstrated in the text. Chisholm's approach is the "inner-release approach," and my comment suggests that it is insufficient to stand by itself.

29 Unfortunately there are some who have attempted to utilize Carl Rogers' insights
as if they were a bag of tricks. Every leader has to be prepared for such misinter-
pretations, and they often become widespread—as the inaccurate and misleading
popularized Freudianism of the 1920's. For a good, brief discussion of the quackery
side of counseling see Harold Seashore's pamphet *All of Us Have Troubles* (Association Press, 1947). For an extended account of the quacks, see Lee Steiner,
Where Do People Take Their Troubles? (Houghton Mifflin, 1945).

The difficulty with such books as those of Dale Carnegie, it seems to me, is not
that they are inaccurate or do not work but that the techniques described tend to
be manipulative. They indicate what to do to be liked—on the assumption that
being oneself would not let one be liked—getting someone to buy something—on
the ground that he would not buy it for its own sake—etc. In this sense they are a
bag of tricks; that is, they can be used for or against purposes of growth in the individual concerned. Their popularity attests the widespread assumption that what
people really want and what we want them to have are entirely different things. In
pastoral counseling we categorically reject such a view.

30 Administrative situations involving counseling are considered more fully in
Chap. VII.

31 This is not "nondirective counseling" but the worst kind of mechanical and wooden
misunderstanding thereof!

32 This may be called "definition of the situation." Rogers calls it "structuring the
situation." It can be achieved in effective and imaginative or in mechanical and
wooden fashion, as various illustrations in this book suggest. But it is of real
importance always, whether it needs to be explicit or not. The degree of clarity of
the definition is one of the distinguishing marks between counseling and precounseling pastoral work. Here is a record of a minister to whom the wife of an alcoholic made an appeal. The pastor wrote, "Drinking became worse. His wife left
him once, but came back. He was remorseful. Finally got worse so that his job
was threatened. He borrowed money and gave notes to several persons, lied about
why he wanted the money. Finally his wife came to me. I went to the home. He
broke down. I spent several hours talking with him." The several hours, as the
pastor later realized, while they seemed a good idea at the time, did no one any
good. Somehow or other a proper definition of the situation or relationship, beginning with the pastor's having it clear in his own mind, should have been made.
In that event the abortive results in this particular case might not have occurred.

33 I suspect that in general lip service is paid to this principle, but in practice it is
violated on every side. Some of the talk about "healthy-mindedness" is in direct
contradiction to it. A counselor who believes he believes it, then acts as if the people who come to him for help are thereby inferior people, violates it. More of the
practical implications of it need to be emphasized.

34 Merely as a note, and not a separate book, I want to comment on what seem to
me the relevant approaches to current differing Christian theological views from
the focus of pastoral counseling. Looking at the theological views as if they were
within the hub of a wheel, we may slide down several spokes successively in order
to get closer to the real hub.

First, we may look at the views as overtones of optimism or pessimism, at different
levels of sophistication, understanding, realism, and hope. The pessimists, who tend
to think of any optimism as easy, then become preoccupied with shattering any
optimism because, whether in an obvious way or not, it is assumed to be easy. If
it is punctured, then the person will be driven further back; and when he reaches
the point of realizing that only a radical solution can be any solution at all, then
he may be tendered the olive branch of hope. There is great truth in this. That
truth may be seen analogously in the alcoholic, who must admit he is an alcoholic,
that alcoholism is a disease and is therefore inexorable, and that no amount of
wishing on his part will get him well, before he has a chance to get well.

The difficulty with this pessimistic bias in the alcoholic is that recognition of the seriousness of his condition may just as well mean suicide unless at the same time there is somehow present the hope that something can be done. Just as Christians have sometimes, as a kind of safety chronology, put the conviction of sin before the hope of salvation, so Alcoholics Anonymous puts conviction of alcoholism before hope of release. But what is the real chronology? I am inclined to think it is, in a sense, the reverse of this view—that the hope of freedom from bondage to alcohol, coming from contact with those who have been in such bondage and know all about it, yet who are clearly no longer under its power, is sensed or registered before there is capacity to face the fact of alcoholism. This is an instance of prevenient grace.

The pessimistic bias, regardless of its content or depth of perception, therefore seems to gloss over a vital therapeutic truth. It is not true that once people realize how bad things are, they will take radical steps to try to improve them. Marxism holds such an hypothesis, but not Christianity. Christian pessimists may suggest that there is no other way than this, but they overlook the fact that the sequence of conviction of sin before hope of salvation is false to the actual process. Such views were formulated before we had knowledge of the degrees of awareness or unawareness, in a day when it would have had no meaning to say that one could sense or register something if it were not a part of his conscious knowledge. Now we can see that this chronological view is based on the all-inclusiveness of consciousness, no longer an adequate view. Hence the pessimists are in part lacking in realism in so far as they rely upon seeing the worst as if the better would then appear or, if it does not appear, nothing else could make it appear.

On the other hand the optimists—and they too must be seen at different levels of realism, sophistication, understanding, and hope—tend to become preoccupied with shattering any pessimism because "it's bad for morale." The silver lining is stressed. At the moment, the pessimists are in the ascendancy, but it is likely they will go no higher. Look at the consequences in our friend the alcoholic. Repeated assurances that he can get well do him no good until he admits he is sick. It is quite impossible for him to get well the way he wants to do it—learn to drink in a fashion he can control. Hence all reassuring and optimistic attempts which are preoccupied with showing him he can do it are doomed to failure unless they realize there is no substitute for the suffering of change, of surrender, of facing up to the fact of alcoholism. The implications are obvious.

The pessimistic view might be put in the slogan, "No matter what, we must recognize how deep the bad goes." And the optimistic, "We are not sure, but we must try." Theology twenty years or so ago went through an optimistic period. It has recently been going through a pessimistic period. Whether we shall have a swing to optimism or to a superior synthesis seems to me to depend in part upon whether the theologians absorb sufficient knowledge of psychological dynamics to be aware of the inner as well as the outer motivations of mood, so that one-sided moods go out of fashion. And it might be just as well to point out that a sermon which uses twenty-nine minutes to tell how awful things are, and one minute to say there is hope, is pessimistic; but the reverse sermon would be optimistic. Of course Christianity needs both. But do we understand the dynamic meaning sufficiently to stand up against our own, or our period's temperamental biases? To understand the relevance of Christianity we must not only know Christianity but also be aware of the particular warping tendencies which our temperament or our times tend to put before us in interpreting it.

The pessimism-optimism understanding is important for counseling. Freud was a pessimist; he was fruitful, as pessimists frequently are. But what seemed to be facts as Freud saw them often turned out on examination to be interpretations. Freud's basic facts were correct, but the bias had conditioned what he observed. Jung is an optimist, and reverse conclusions have been drawn by him. We have all varieties and all degrees among theologians. The "psychological facts" do not, of course, tell precisely what is really so in a metaphysical sense; but they seem of great importance as criteria for testing the mood of a theological view, which is sometimes as important as its truth.

A counselor who believes it is nothing but uphill work, who always keeps his finger in the dike, is not a realist but a pessimist. A counselor who thinks counseling can solve almost anything once we get enough knowledge is not a realist but an optimist. What we need is a view which is more realistic, which can take fully into account the dark and evil and even self-defeating aspects and potentialities in human nature, and which at the same time places full value upon the tremendous powers for creativity, for socially useful self-direction, and for responsible and free productivity.

The second theological spoke down which we may slide toward the hub of theological differences is that of the naturalistic versus the supernaturalistic. The realism which has been characteristic of recent theology was brought in mainly by the latter group, which has of course tended to stake out proprietary claims on realism. The naturalistic group now contends that it can and does deal with the same realities, but within a different framework. Plainly there are different degrees of insight and depth among the theologians in their understanding of the issue; and just because I believe the issue to be important, I will not here attempt to consider it from the point of view of truth or validity. But there is one unintended consequence of the controversy which vitally affects pastoral counseling. It is concerned with the relevance accorded to dynamic psychological material. The supernaturalist group has tended to minimize the relevance of the material, as illustrated, for example, in Reinhold Niebuhr's dismissal of Karen Horney's views on anxiety in a footnote. As naturalistic theology now attempts to demonstrate that it is as deep and far-reaching as supernaturalistic, it runs the danger of according an equal irrelevance to psychological dynamics. I do not believe the psychological insights lead necessarily either to naturalism or supernaturalism, but they tend to modify certain aspects of either view if taken seriously. It would be unfortunate if the idea took hold that counseling, because it deals empirically and uses material gained empirically, had to have a naturalistic metaphysic to support it. This is a misunderstanding of the issues. And it would be especially detrimental at a time when naturalistic theology appears to be preparing to face deeper issues than it has faced before.

A third spoke which leads to the hub of current theological views of human nature is preoccupation with the ultimate or theoretical, or with the operational or practical. It includes concentration on the philosophic or the pragmatic; a high degree of rigidity or dogmatism, regardless of content; and a large or amorphous amount of flexibility. This entire volume should make it clear that no single side of these opposites is sufficient, and it may be inferred that in my own constructive theology I would move back and forth from the most concrete material I had to the most fundamental theoretical understanding of which I were capable. Some theologians, with varying points of view, succeed in doing this. For some others the tension is too great, and there is a break for the tension-reducing, but illusory, clarity of choosing one against the other. A flexibility so tolerant as to be nearly without convictions can be as successful in reducing tension, and as dogmatic, as a rigid and unvarying adherence to a dogma or point of view—and equally false to reality.

The temptation of pastoral counseling, or indeed of any who work in the practical theological field, is to be operational at the expense of relating the operational to the theoretical, to be pragmatic at the expense of relating the pragmatic to the philosophical, to be flexible at the expense of relating casuistry to fundamental principle. This is the temptation, just as the theologian confronts the opposite danger. The resistance to the temptation would seem to come not from the concept of balance or of compromise but from that of consistent viewing of the framework in which the particular focus lies, and from which it does its viewing.

For the pastoral counselor this means a particular effort not to overvalue the pragmatic at the expense of objective truth; not to be preoccupied with the methods of operation at the cost of overlooking the aims of the operation; not to conclude from the fact that different people learn to comprehend truth in different ways that there is no problem of truth.

The fourth and last spoke I shall mention is, as far as I am concerned, a matter of white versus black. Is the theological theory of human nature, whatever the content, used eductively or coercively? The good news of the gospel may be either the good news of salvation or the good news of damnation, or both. But which interests the theologian more? Is his theory used to attempt to push people toward something they would not be interested in without the prod? Or is it used to lead them toward one thing and away from another, which is what the most basic and "essential self" in them wants? The latter may be defined as the operation of the Holy Spirit or the grace of God. But the issue here is: What is the emotionally preconditioned motivation of the theologian? Does he want to push or to lead out? There is a real ideological question involved, and it is important. I am trying to separate it from the pseudoideological, emotional bias which, in practice, seems so much more decisive in determining which direction the particular theologian shall take. Naturally I am for the eductive approach and against the coercive in any form or degree.

So far as I can see, the outcome of this issue may be in either direction, with the same or at least similar ideas and convictions. For example, the doctrine of original sin can, with obvious ease, be used as a club, an attempt to induce the conviction of hopelessness—with, of course, the silver lining that hope may then come if the nadir is not avoided. But, less obviously, the same doctrine may also be used in an eductive way. If, because of the basic conditions of human life, social as well as biological, man is bound to find tendencies within himself which predispose toward sin, then a recognition of the depth and reality of those predispositions is a prerequisite to freedom from their obsessive power.

The implication in pastoral counseling is that deciding upon our fundamental theological idea about human nature still leaves us the task of deciding upon our motivating interest in the enunciation and propagation of that particular idea. If the answer is of a coercive nature, involving fundamental distrust of God's ability to move in a transforming way within human character and human society, then it would seem that counseling is a hopeless enterprise. If, on the other hand, in far-reaching knowledge of the evil depths of human potentiality we can nevertheless emotionally affirm God's movement for positive transformation in human life, we are eductive, and counseling has point and meaning.

There is great need for work on the relationship of dynamic psychology and psychotherapy to Christian theology. David E. Roberts has published two articles which, while brief, are far-reaching in their promise of shedding light on the issues: "Psychotherapy and the Christian Ministry," *Religion in Life*, Spring, 1945; and "Theological and Psychiatric Interpretations of Human Nature," *Christianity and Crisis*, February 3, 1947. The Columbia University graduate seminar on religion and health is making contributions. Four of its studies have appeared in the *Review of Religion*, May, 1946, and the two by Paul Tillich and Gotthard Booth are especially important. A new pamphlet by Albert C. Outler, *A Christian Context for Counseling*, Hazen Foundation, 1947, is popular in approach but of great value.

Among the theological books which have inspired my comments are:
Edwin E. Aubrey, *Present Theological Tendencies* (Harper, 1936) and *Man's Search for Himself* (Abingdon Press, 1940)
John C. Bennett, *Christianity—and Our World* (Association Press, 1936) ; *Social Salvation* (Scribner, 1935) ; and *Christian Realism* (Scribner, 1941)
Edgar S. Brightman, *The Finding of God* (Abingdon, 1931)
Nels Ferré, *Return to Christianity* (Harper, 1943)

Walter M. Horton, *A Psychological Approach to Theology* (Harper, 1931);
Contemporary Continental Theology (Harper, 1938); *The Growth of Religion,*
with H. N. Wieman (Willett & Clark, 1938)

A. Graham Ikin, *Religion and Psychotherapy* (S.C.M., 1935) —deals with theory
only

Hendrik Kraemer, *The Christian Message in a Non-Christian World* (Harper,
1938)

Eugene W. Lyman, *The Meaning and Truth of Religion* (Scribner, 1933)

John Macmurray, *The Clue to History* (Harper, 1939)

Reinhold Niebuhr, *The Nature and Destiny of Man,* 2 vols. (Scribner, 1941, 1943);
The Children of Light and the Children of Darkness (Scribner, 1944)

G. B. Smith, *Current Christian Thinking* (University of Chicago, 1928); *Guide
to the Study of the Christian Religion* (University of Chicago, 1916)

Paul Tillich, *The Religious Situation* (Holt, 1932)

D. Elton Trueblood, *The Predicament of Modern Man* (Harper, 1944)

Henry P. Van Dusen and David E. Roberts, *Liberal Theology, an Appraisal*
(Scribner, 1942)

Henry Nelson Wieman, *Religious Experience and Scientific Method* (Macmillan,
1926); *The Wrestle of Religion with Truth* (Macmillan, 1927); *Normative
Psychology of Religion,* with R. W. Wieman (Crowell, 1935); *The Source of
Human Good* (University of Chicago, 1946)

Such reading as I have done in the philosophy of religion confirms the relevance
of the questions I have raised, but I suspect some of the religious philosophers
deal more with my questions than my discussion may have suggested.

35 In referring to the United States I do not mean to imply that some other basic
approach in pastoral counseling would be better in Scotland or Germany. But if
this book were to be as relevant for pastors in those countries as I hope it may be
in the U. S. A., certain secondary but important factors ought to be altered. Some
of the extroverted familiarity which is a part of our American culture, and natural
here, would be an unnatural mode of using the eductive approach in, for example,
the Netherlands. The closer we come to interview material, the more American
material might appear strange to pastors in other countries. Yet if I were familiar
with such a culture as that of the Netherlands, I believe many of the details would
be different but no essential principles would be changed. If any pastor reader
is in a non-American culture, I can hope he will attempt to adapt the principle to
the natural forms of his culture.

36 So wide has been the influence of depth psychology, and consequently of the
inner-release approach, that few views are still untouched by it. But the dominant
social-adjustment approach, slightly attenuated, may be found in most of the writings
of the American school of psychiatry, centering at Johns Hopkins under the
leadership of Adolf Meyer. Such works as Esther Loring Richards, *Behavior
Aspects of Child Conduct* (Macmillan, 1933), and Edward A. Strecker and Franklin
G. Ebaugh, *Practical Clinical Psychiatry,* are examples. It is still taken for granted
in most of the articles in the *American Journal of Psychiatry.* On the psychological
side a good illustration is L. F. Shaffer's *The Psychology of Adjustment* (Houghton
Mifflin, 1936). Leland E. Hinsie, in *Concepts and Problems of Psychotherapy*
(Columbia University, 1937), combines this view with some appreciation of the
depth psychology contribution and consequent correction. Actually the extreme
of the social-adjustment view is rarely found any longer. It tends to persist rather
in the studied ignoring by some workers of the findings of depth psychology and
the refusal to face the question of therapeutic aims at any level other than the
purely pragmatic.

37 The potential contribution of cultural anthropology to our understanding of
things like this is very great. Increasingly this study has been looking at any par-

ticular culture in an integrated sense, that is, seeing how the assumptions and behavior forms of all kinds dovetail into an integrated, meaningful totality. Therefore the mistake of the early anthropologists, who assumed a particular act always meant the same thing in any culture, has been avoided. Studying the cultural patterns of any society is, therefore, no mere amassing of information about what its people do, after the *National Geographic Magazine* fashion. It is studying the dynamics of a culture—what the forces are which really control it—as we study the dynamics of an individual person. The best brief introduction to the subject is probably Ruth Benedict's *Patterns of Culture,* first published in 1934 and now available in the inexpensive Penguin Pocket Book edition. Increasingly the cultural anthropologists are utilizing the methods developed in looking at relatively primitive peoples to the understanding of nations and cultures like our own. Hence Benedict's *The Chrysanthemum and the Sword: Patterns of Japanese Culture* (Houghton Mifflin, 1946). Other valuable books by the anthropologists which are nontechnical enough for pastors are: Margaret Mead, *Coming of Age in Samoa* (Morrow, 1928), *Growing Up in New Guinea* (Morrow, 1930), *Sex and Temperament* (Morrow, 1935); Ralph Linton, *Cultural Background of Personality* (Appleton, 1945); and Abram Kardiner, *The Individual and His Society* (Columbia University, 1939). A volume on German culture, *Post-War Germans,* by David Rodnick, giving the first such view of German society, was published by Yale University Press in 1948.

38 The most accessible writings of Sigmund Freud are to be found in *New Introductory Lectures on Psychoanalysis* (Norton, 1933) and in *The Basic Writings of Sigmund Freud* (Modern Library, 1938), which includes five major works in one volume. A complete works of Freud at a popular price is very much needed. There seem to be a few points which will help the American pastor, in reading Freud, to grasp the revolutionary significance of his work. First, the later works, such as *Moses and Monotheism* (Knopf, 1939), are not generally considered comparable to his earlier writings. Second, his clinical writings and those which deal with psychoanalysis in theory or practice are much more valuable than his cultural and philosophic treatises, such as *The Future of an Illusion* (Liveright, 1928) or *Civilization and Its Discontents* (R. O. Ballou, 1930). Third, Freud lived in a culture remarkably different from our own, and in a day when the materialism and mechanism of science were held to in a dogmatic way which is now rapidly being modified. Fourth, Freud was a prolific writer, and not a systematic one in the ordinary sense; consequently a flat and dogmatic statement may be found in one place, and later Freud, in discussing the question more fully, considerably modifies what appeared earlier to be dogmatism. Fifth, Freud altered many views, even fundamental ones, as his experience suggested more adequate hypotheses. The changes were not kaleidoscopic, but there are at least three or four fairly definite periods in his thinking. To be strictly accurate on many points one would have to ask: Which period of Freud?

In assessing the permanent contributions of Freud, I am most indebted to Karen Horney, *New Ways in Psychoanalysis* (Norton, 1939), and to Karl A. Menninger, *Love Against Hate* (Harcourt, 1942).

39 See Erich Fromm's brilliant *Escape from Freedom* (Farrar Rinehart, 1941). Without holding him in any way responsible for my conclusions, I want to express appreciation to Erich Fromm for discussions which have greatly aided me in formulating the four views mentioned in this section.

40 See the recent reports of the Yale studies, especially Arnold Gesell and Others, *Infant and Child in the Culture of Today* (Harper, 1943) and *The Child from Five to Ten* (Harper 1946).

41 The classic volume on the social nature of personality is George Herbert Mead's *Mind, Self, and Society* (Univ. of Chicago, 1935). See also the monumental *Personality: A Psychological Interpretation,* by Gordon W. Allport (Holt, 1937); James S. Plant, *Personality and the Cultural Pattern* (Commonwealth Fund, 1938);

Gardner Murphy's *Personality* (Harper, 1947); and most books by the social psychologists. See especially John Dewey's *Human Nature and Conduct* (Modern Library, 1930).

42 I am not familiar with any printed references on this point which, to be authoritative, would have to come from the cultural anthropologists. However, I have so understood Ruth Benedict in a lecture.

43 The general trend of Carl G. Jung's thought may be secured from his *Modern Man in Search of a Soul* (Harcourt, 1933), *Psychology and Religion* (Yale University, 1938), and *The Integration of the Personality* (Farrar & Rinehart, 1939). His major works are, however, *Psychology of the Unconscious* (Dodd, 1916), *Psychological Types* (Harcourt, 1923), and *Two Essays in Analytical Psychology* (Harcourt, 1928). Jung's best American interpreter is Frances G. Wickes, in *The Inner World of Childhood* (Appleton, 1927) and *The Inner World of Man* (Farrar, 1938). Fritz Künkel's volume, *In Search of Maturity* (Scribner, 1943), is also oriented to Jung's point of view.

Karen Horney criticizes Jung's point described in the text, with what seems to me justice: "Indeed he was so impressed with the contradictions at work in the individual that he took it to be a general law that the presence of any element would of necessity indicate the presence also of its opposite. . . . To him the neurotic is a person who has been stranded in a one-sided development. . . . Now I, too, recognize that the opposing tendencies contain complementary elements neither of which can be dispensed with in an integrated personality. But in my opinion these are already outgrowths of neurotic conflicts and are so tenaciously adhered to because they represent attempts at solution. If, for instance, we regard a tendency toward being introspective, withdrawn, more concerned with one's own feelings, thoughts, or imagination than with other persons' as an authentic inclination—that is, constitutionally established and reinforced by experience—then Jung's reasoning would be correct. The effective therapeutic procedure would be to show the person his hidden 'extravert' tendencies, to point out the dangers of one-sidedness in either direction, and encourage him to accept and live out both tendencies. If, however, we look upon introversion (or, as I prefer to call it, neurotic detachment) as a means of evading conflicts that arise in close contact with others, the task is not to encourage more extraversion but to analyze the underlying conflicts. The goal of wholeheartedness can be approximated only after these have been resolved."— Reprinted from *Our Inner Conflicts*, by Karen Horney, pp. 39-40, by permission of W. W. Norton & Co., Inc. Copyright 1945 by the publishers.

44 See especially Otto Rank's *Will Therapy* (Knopf, 1936). His *Modern Education* (Knopf, 1932) and *Truth and Reality* (Knopf, 1936) are also pertinent. All are translations. Rank's writing tended to be unsystematic and hard to understand. This fact, plus his attempt to avoid creating a school, have been influential factors in retarding the proper assessment of his influence. Originally an associate of Freud, he finally found it necessary to leave the orthodox group in the 1920's.

It is interesting to note that Franz Alexander, in writing recently on therapy, says of the Chicago Institute for Psychoanalysis, "Our work is a continuation and realization of ideas first proposed by Ferenczi and Rank."—*Psychoanalytic Therapy*, with Thomas M. French and staff members of the Institute (Ronald, 1946), p. 23.

Though careful to cite Rank's work while he was still a Freudian—S. Ferenczi and O. Rank, *The Development of Psychoanalysis* (Nervous and Mental Diseases Publishing Co., 1925)—Alexander suggests that even the orthodox Freudian group acknowledges some debt to Rank. Rank was the first of the Freudians to attempt significant variations in the analytic method developed by Freud, including briefer methods. His writings show, however, that after leaving Freud he developed his methods within an approach which was increasingly eductive—in partial contrast to the therapy described by Alexander and French in the work cited above. One of Rank's students, Jessie Taft, published *The Dynamics of Therapy in a Controlled*

Relationship (Macmillan, 1933), a report on therapeutic contacts with children. This was influential in the thirties, especially in social-work circles, and had much to do with the controversy about "active" and "passive" during this period. Taft wrote, "Either the case worker should prepare herself to do individual therapy responsibly and proclaim it as a function to the client, or she should learn to differentiate social case work with a practical goal from case work with a therapeutic function and to value it for itself." She felt the case worker was doing therapy and ought not to come into it by a back door.

Frederick H. Allen—*Psychotherapy with Children* (Norton, 1942)—was much influenced by Rank. Indeed, one may say that on both the theoretical and practical side it was Rank's work which made possible the development of Carl Rogers' approach to counseling and psychotherapy.

45 Karen Horney has published four major books, all issued by Norton: *The Neurotic Personality of our Time*, 1937; *New Ways in Psychoanalysis*, 1939, *Self-Analysis*, 1942; and *Our Inner Conflicts*, 1945.

Views of the Washington School of Psychiatry may be found in the useful journal *Psychiatry; Journal of the Biology and Pathology of Interpersonal Relations*, published by the William Alanson White Foundation, 1711 Rhode Island Avenue, Washington 6, D. C. The most significant theoretical work with implications for therapy to come out of this group is Harry Stack Sullivan's *Conceptions of Modern Psychiatry*, published in February, 1940, in this magazine and available as a monograph.

The most significant publication of the Chicago Institute for Psychoanalysis is *Psychoanalytic Therapy* (Ronald, 1946). Note 26 discusses the nondirective school of psychotherapy.

46 At least in a general way, this view has been increasingly recognized in most of the recent pastoral books, such as Charles T. Holman's *Getting Down to Cases* (Macmillan, 1942) and his *The Cure of Souls* (University of Chicago, 1932); Russell L. Dicks' *Pastoral Work and Personal Counseling* (Macmillan, 1944); Rollo May's *The Art of Counseling* (Abingdon Press, 1939); H. S. and G. L. Elliott's *Solving Personal Problems* (Holt, 1936); Leslie Weatherhead's *Psychology and Life* (Abingdon Press, 1935); L. Dewar and C. E. Hudson's *Manual of Pastoral Psychology* (London, 1935); C. R. Zahniser's *The Soul Doctor* (Round Table, 1938; J. G. McKenzie's *Souls in the Making* (Macmillan, 1929); and others. These authors usually begin by pointing out that advice-giving does not work. The above books qualify this point in varying degrees, none of them appearing to me to follow the eductive principle to the extent I believe necessary.

47 See the important article, "Selfishness and Self-Love," by Erich Fromm, in *Psychiatry*, November, 1939. He points out that within the dynamics of personality true self-love in the sense of self-respect is concomitant and concurrent with love for other people, and not in opposition. Thus self-love is the opposite of selfishness, which is a preoccupation with a kind of safety-self, not the essential self, which shuts one off equally from one's own self and the relations of mutuality with the selves of others.

48 At the present time the literature on the self suffers from lack of understanding that the subject is of equal importance to psychological studies on the one hand and to philosophical and theological studies on the other. An integration of the present knowledge of each is much needed. A suggestive manuscript on the self by Carl R. Rogers is in preparation.

49 See Ruth Benedict, *Patterns of Culture*, note 37.

50 See J. A. C. Murray, *An Introduction to a Christian Psycho-Therapy* (Scribner, 1938). While suggestive, this volume has a rather narrow interpretation of what a Christian point of view should mean in psychotherapy.

51 Russell L. Dicks' *Pastoral Work and Personal Counseling* gives a good description of the setting.

Chapter II: Discovering Approach and Method

1 This is the method followed in most volumes on counseling, pastoral or otherwise. It has been used with particular skill by Rollo May in *The Art of Counseling* (Abingdon Press, 1938) and *Springs of Creative Living* (Abingdon Press, 1940). The psychiatric literature abounds with such material. See especially Karl A. Menninger's *The Human Mind,* revised ed. (Knopf, 1937). Cases are also treated in this way in Alexander and French's *Psychoanalytic Therapy* (Ronald, 1946). The life history approach has been the general pattern for some years, and its usefulness is certainly great. Interview material which does not take into account the time dimension, which is a feature of the life history, is of course inadequate to that extent.

2 I am in debt to Rogers for his formulation of the concepts of simple acceptance, understanding, and clarification, in *Counseling and Psychotherapy,* (Houghton Mifflin, 1942) and elsewhere. But I am impressed with these as methodological aspects of an approach and with the basic intention of the approach as being more significant than these points in themselves. Hence technical misunderstanding or failure to help clarify, for example, can take place without seriously impeding the helping process, provided something more fundamental has been established and is still present.

3 Anton T. Boisen's *The Exploration of the Inner World* (Willett & Clark, 1936) sheds a flood of light upon the real meaning of the sense of isolation. Karen Horney's *Our Inner Conflicts* is also valuable in understanding the dynamics of the sense of isolation. Some years ago, when I was a clinical pastoral-training student in a mental hospital and had opportunity to see the bizarre forms of thinking frequently found in persons with a schizophrenic type of psychosis, it was illuminating to get interpretations of such thought and behavior from Anton T. Boisen, Lewis B. Hill, Donald C. Beatty, Carroll A. Wise, and others. It was the "reality" of schizophrenic thinking and feeling rather than its bizarre nature which soon impressed me. And when I found, in a paper by Harry Stack Sullivan, that such thought and feeling had some kind of backing in the world of reality—albeit the creative world of inner reality, but thereby no less real—I felt I had come closer to understanding the reality of such phenomena as the desperate sense of isolation and withdrawal which leads to schizophrenia. I was also aided on this point by C. Macfie Campbell's *Delusion and Belief* (Harvard, 1926) and his *Human Personality and the Environment* (Macmillan, 1934).

4 Rogers calls this procedure "reflection of feeling," for the laudable purpose of suggesting the difference between being alert to the feelings the person is trying to convey and following only the idea content involved, and also to suggest that we deal with his feelings, not ours. Unfortunately "reflection of feeling" can be interpreted in mechanical, mirror fashion. I believe that communication of understanding of an essential feeling which has been expressed can usually best be achieved by putting it into one's own words and restating it after the fashion, "In other words, you mean . . ." But the dynamics of this process seem to me far from the mirror analogy. If this is not held clearly in mind, the result is likely to be a confusion between acting as a passive mirror and building a relationship through communicative understanding of feeling.

5 This is the kind of point at which personality differences among counselors become obvious, and where studying approach to the counseling relationship needs to be supplemented by study by the counselor of himself in counseling. The real pastor, in dealing with Miss Smith, had insight into the general approach in counseling. So long as large issues seemed to be at stake, he was understanding. But once it appeared that something had been achieved, he did not feel safe in dealing with anything which looked like backsliding. Therefore his own particular immaturity—and we do not know exactly what it is—compelled him to desert the

approach in which he firmly believed, without any knowledge in a conscious sense that he was deserting it. In one way or another all of us have at least some such immaturities or insecurities; and to the degree that we have them, it is more difficult to follow through on the eductive approach, even when we are convinced of its relevance and value. Personal consultations for the pastor, discussed in Chap. X, can be of great help in getting insight into our own particular blind spots, hence preventing us from unintentional desertion of the eductive approach, as in the Miss Smith interview.

6 See Erich Fromm, *Escape from Freedom*, for a discussion of the psychology of Nazism.

7 On this point there seems to be increasing agreement among counselors. The differences now lie in the extent to which it is felt such concentration of attention has to be deviated from. Rogers says Never. Alexander and French say, "Most of the time." Provided the basic approach is differentiated from details of method, and the precounseling situation so important for pastors is differentiated from the counseling situation itself, I am inclined to say rarely, if ever.

8 What has been said in the note above is also true of the first part of this statement. On the second part there are many differences not only on how understanding is to be communicated but also on how important it is to give attention directly to the communication of understanding. Only Rogers thus far has discussed this publicly in methodological terms.

9 The alternatives to this are (1) concentrating on action at the expense of feeling; (2) concentrating on genetic or historical factors rather than on the contemporary; and (3) moralizing, coercing, etc. Few if any counselors will any longer admit their belief in these alternatives, though they are still widely used in practice.

10 On the principle itself there is general agreement, but there are some differences in interpretation of the specific nature of the freedom and limitations. For instance, directions to the patient concerning many aspects of his daily life are considered by Alexander and French to be consistent with and helpful to therapy, if properly done; whereas I understand the Washington School of Psychiatry believes such directive procedures to be detrimental to the progress of therapy. Pastoral counselors have similar differences in interpretation of the meaning of this principle.

11 Rogers has tended, naturally enough, to group all the views which are inconsistent with his own together and call them "directive psychotherapy," thus putting together many individuals and groups who are sometimes as far apart from one another as anyone of them is from Rogers. On this point Rogers has become sharper in his conviction, not more conciliatory, as evidenced in a recent and still unpublished paper entitled "Current Trends in Psychotherapy." While pointing out the increasing emergence of similarities among counselors, he nevertheless says, "There is an increasingly well defined difference, evidently based upon differing clinical experience, between those who believe the client should be subtly guided toward an independence which is to some degree defined by the therapist, and those who believe that growth forces are present in the client and that, if they are released, the client will himself move toward a self-defined independence."

12 As I understand all the psychoanalytic groups, they have given attention to this point. Rogers appears to consider it merely as one item in the clarification process, therefore not requiring special mention.

Chapter III: DYNAMIC PSYCHOLOGICAL UNDERSTANDING

1 See such works as the following: Gordon W. Allport, *Personality: A Psychological Interpretation* (Holt, 1937); Henry A. Murray, *Explorations in Personality* (Oxford, 1938); Gardner Murphy and F. Jensen, *Approaches to Personality* (Coward-

McCann, 1932) ; Karl A. Menninger, *The Human Mind* (Knopf, 1937) ; Kurt Lewin, *Dynamic Theory of Personality* (McGraw-Hill, 1935) ; Harry Stack Sullivan, "Conceptions of Modern Psychiatry," *Psychiatry*, February, 1940; Gardner Murphy, *Personality* (Harper, 1947) ; and the writings of Freud, Horney, Jung, Rank, and others previously mentioned.

It is important to realize that many of these have eventual significance for personality. For example, Jules Masserman's experiments with cats have helped to clarify some factors in the general development of psychoneurosis—reported in *Behavior and Neurosis* (University of Chicago, 1943) . E. G. Boring's *History of Experimental Psychology* (Century, 1929) gives a detailed history of such work for the special student. But Gardner Murphy's *An Historical Introduction to Modern Psychology* (Harcourt, 1929) is perhaps still the best general historical volume.

3 See Russell L. Dicks' helpful treatment of stress both in *Pastoral Work and Personal Counseling* and in the pamphlet *The Ministry of Listening* (Federal Council, 1943) .

4 Thus, beyond any of the negative values of repression, there is the important fact that under certain conditions they cease to work. For example the psychiatrist Harry M. Tiebout reports that an alcoholic who goes without drinking on New Year's Day is likely to feel so noble the day afterwards that he feels frustrated over receiving no reward for his nobility, and gets drunk. The stimuli of stress arising from repression are to be understood as subtle and individual, but the dynamic process involved is becoming increasingly clear.

5 This seems to illustrate the difference between the contemporary and the genetic foci in understanding dynamics. The former begins with the feeling, deals mainly with it, and uses history only as an aid. The genetic would go immediately to the procedure of finding out what is behind it, at the expense of understanding the contemporary nature of the conflict.

6 Psychological and psychiatric study has shown that the variations are enormous, almost beyond the belief of the ordinary person.

7 "Authoritarian" must be distinguished sharply from "authoritative." The former is based on an assumed authority of status, profession, age, or anything except demonstrable competence in relation to the matter at hand. The latter is based on demonstrable competence.

8 It is interesting that so many theologians, while recognizing the full import of this in society in general, have failed to sense its full significance in the lives of individuals in Western society. The cultural patterns making for walls around individual personality, for a sense of estrangement and isolation and insecurity, are very great; but this is not the same as considering that man has as a part of his nature or as something innate an inexorable diathesis toward these things. To make a metaphysical dogma out of an undoubtedly cultural fact may cut off opportunities to influence both the individual and the culture which has made him walled-off and insecure. The more clearly we understand the factors producing this sense of nonacceptance in individuals, the more we may be able to admit the fact and try to do something constructive about it. The "aloneness" about which the mystics talk, and which is certainly necessary in all individual life, cannot only be endured but can also become of great value—provided the sense of nonacceptance is not so overwhelming as to make it merely a stimulus to increased anxiety.

9 "Perspective," "vision," "new dimension," are words and ideas as important in preaching as in counseling. Mrs. Finch's story may be useful in suggesting helpful or unhelpful ways of discussing the nature, meaning, and processes of approaching the new dimension.

10 See note 43 in Chap. I. Horney's criticism of Jung's point seems to suggest the deficiencies of the geographical type of metaphor—without, within, one-side, levels, layers, etc. It is difficult to discuss without using them at all, and yet the ease with

which we come to treat them as more than metaphors makes their use dangerous. The difficulties which theologians and psychologists sometimes have in getting along with each other seem to come in part from the preferential use by each semantics can help us get together. See, for instance, Wendell Johnson's very useful *People in Quandaries: The Semantics of Personal Adjustment* (Harper, 1946).

11 See note 38, Chap. I.

suggests how the research and learning interest may sometimes work against the therapeutic interest. Franz Alexander writes, "From the point of view of genetic of different aspects of the geographical metaphors; and to that extent at least research, it might be advisable to encourage the patient to wander way back into the Garden of Eden of his early youth; therapeutically, however, such a retreat is valuable only insofar as it sheds light upon the present."—*Psychoanalytic Therapy*, p. 34.

13 See note 1. Among the more popular volumes on psychological dynamics are the

12 G. Canby Robinson, in *The Patient as a Person* (Commonwealth Fund, 1939), following. Joshua Loth Liebman, *Peace of Mind* (Simon & Shuster, 1945) has led the nonfiction best-seller lists for many months. Eminently readable, psychologically wise, it leaves some things to be desired from the theological point of view. Harry Emerson Fosdick, *On Being a Real Person* (Harper, 1943) is excellent, but apparently not suitable for those below the college level of education. Larry Freeman and Edith M. Stern, *Mastering Your Nerves* (Harper, 1946) is a good popular volume. David Harold Fink, *Release from Nervous Tension* (Simon & Shuster, 1943), contains some good material, but in its physiological bias it is misleading. Many have found the books of David Seabury helpful; they are always interesting, unsystematic, paradoxical. There are at least a dozen.

14 See *Clinical Pastoral Training*, ed. by Seward Hiltner (Federal Council, 1945).

15 See Anton T. Boisen's *The Exploration of the Inner World* (Willett & Clark, 1936).

16 A good introduction for the nontechnical reader to the facts about psychosis may be found in George H. Preston, *Psychiatry for the Curious* (Farrar & Rinehart, 1940).

17 Karen Horney, *The Neurotic Personality of Our Time.*

18 *Ibid.*

19 This may go along with a philosophic determinism, but it need not do so. It is a practical determinism; i.e., the situation will be certain to move in such and such a direction unless something else takes place. The point is that an aversion to philosophic determinism cannot gainsay this practical determinism and that the practical determinism does not necessarily imply philosophic determinism.

20 It is difficult to state this idea without resort to geographic or topographic metaphors. Professional counselors of all kinds increasingly accept the reality and relevance of the phenomena. But since counselors are no less human than anyone else, and we all tend to protect our safety patterns, even counselors may find themselves resistive to acceptance of the point. From the point of view of ego-protection, the implications have an absurdity about them which common sense tends to reject. The fact that such formulations can be used for obscurantist purposes as well as for legitimate aims should not be a valid reason for denying their truth or relevance. And while objectivity is a valid goal, it should not be used as a rejection of the fundamental phenomena which the empirical and clinical studies have revealed in striking clarity.

21 The books of Karl A. Menninger are especially fruitful: *The Human Mind, Man Against Himself,* and *Love Against Hate.*

22 There would be general agreement with this statement, but differences and qualifications in its interpretation. To what extent must the depth and rigidity of

neurotic or psychotic conflict be considered as different from conflict in the ordinary person? To what extent does any counseling procedure encourage the bringing out of conflict, and under what conditions? What really happens in helping people to deal with inner conflict? How helpful is catharsis? Is reflection of feeling the key? Or is the key found in helping people to get insight into personality patterns? Or is it in the exploration of the therapeutic relationship? These are further questions in the theoretical field, to which my proposition is a prolegomenon.

23 It hardly needs reminder that this position does not necessarily lead to metaphysical relativism.

24 See Arnold Gesell and Frances G. Ilg, *Infant and Child in the Culture of Today* (Harper, 1943).

25 This is a descriptive statement, not the expression of a moral judgment—as if one could decide to want one rather than the other and get it by wishing hard enough.

26 The term "rigid-normal" is from Harry Bone.

27 See Rollo May's discussion of the "good news of sin," in *Springs of Creative Living* (Abingdon Press, 1940).

28 See note 43, Chap. I. See also the following works of Fritz Künkel: *In Search of Maturity* (Scribner, 1943); *Conquer Yourself* Washburn, 1936); and *How Character Develops*, with Roy E. Dickerson (Scribner, 1940).

29 See Anton T. Boisen, *The Exploration of the Inner World* (Willett & Clark, 1936), and *Problems in Religion and Life* (Abingdon Press, 1946).

30 The implications of Erich Fromm's *Escape from Freedom* are pertinent here.

31 So-called "projective tests" have been built on this hypothesis that one perceives what he is inwardly prepared to perceive. The two most widely used—and these of value only in the hands of specially trained experts—are the Thematic Apperception Test and the Rorschach test. For the former see Henry A. Murray, *Explorations in Personality* (Oxford, 1938). For the latter see S. J. Beck, *Rorschach's Test*, 2 vols. (Grune & Stratton, 1944); H. Rorschach, *Psychodiagnostics* (Grune & Stratton, 1942); and Bruno Klopfer, *Rorschach Technique* (World Book, 1942). All are technical works.

32 The works previously mentioned by Alexander, Horney, and Rogers all agree on this point. In contrast, the Jungian approach seems to have barely begun to accept it. I would interpret this as partly due to the particular Jungian mythology in general and to the collective unconscious idea in particular, which were in themselves a form of protest against geneticism.

Chapter IV: The Pastoral Counseling Process

1 Most of the work reported by Rogers thus far is also, compared with depth therapy, relatively brief, as are a good many of the abstracted reports by Alexander and French.

2 Training for pastoral counseling is discussed normatively in Chap. X. The present situation is described briefly in "Pastoral Theology in the Schools," which was printed in *Clinical Pastoral Training* (Federal Council, 1945).

3 For example, Carroll A. Wise, at the Hennepin Avenue Methodist Church in Minneapolis, and Alexander D. Dodd, of the Toledo Council of Churches—to mention only two who work under parish church and church council auspices. A number of other local parish clergy, and several hospital chaplains, also meet these qualifications.

4 The term "supportive" or "supportiveness" is used by Rogers along with "advice," "persuasion," and "suggestion" to suggest a "counselor-centered" attitude. It ought

to be noted that my use of the phrase "supportive counseling" means something different. I write of a temporary quality of relationship, in a reactive-emotion situation. It may well be that a pastor will, with someone incapable of or unready for insight and growth, maintain something of a supportive relationship over a period of time. This would not be counseling, but it could be a part of precounseling pastoral work. But even this need not be directive in Rogers' sense of "supportiveness."

5 In general, my observation of pastors all over the country has increasingly suggested that they—at least those who have graduated from theological school—tend as often to do too little as too much. I have been one of those suggesting that since the human soul is complex, we should not invade it without some assurance that we know what we are about. We have sometimes been so successful in suggesting these cautions as to leave a general residue of intimidation, which was not intended. The difficulty, of course, is that the people who nod their heads when reading words of caution are probably those who could profit by trying a bit more; while those who do not read such words at all are likely to be the needers. The decision should be made by each man in the light of his own particular time, training, and skill.

6 In this sense it seems that positive improvement, on the basis of whatever standards, is not the only criterion of counseling success in a given situation.

7 However, I believe this pastor was overcautious.

8 I have not had the training for extended counseling in any sense which approaches depth therapy. But there seem to be some significant differences between it and brief counseling, as there are also similarities. How deep are these differences?

Alexander gives a definition of psychoanalysis based on what he calls "more essential criteria" than those of daily interviews, lying on a couch, uninterrupted free association, and the like. He writes that psychoanalysis is "any therapy based on psychodynamic principles which attempts to bring the patient into a more satisfactory adjustment to his environment and to assist the harmonious development of his capacities." He adds, "All forms of therapy, however flexible, having this basis and this goal, may be considered psychoanalytic"—*Psychoanalytic Therapy*, p. 27.

I suspect that Alexander also includes the unstated assumptions that only a physician performs "therapy," is able to use "psychodynamic principles" therapeutically, and deals with "patients." It would be understandable if, in correcting the earlier Freudian therapeutic rigidity, Alexander's statement should overstate what he intends to convey. For the knowledge of psychodynamics is not confined to physicians, great as is the debt of the rest of us to them for discovering many of the principles. And "patient" merely means "sufferer." While if therapy itself is what Alexander's statement says, then in the psychological realm it can hardly be automatically confined to physicians.

9 Horney's *Self-Analysis* and *Our Inner Conflicts* are illuminating in setting forth the meaning of patterns. So is Sullivan's *Conceptions of Modern Psychiatry*. See note 45, Chap. I.

10 As I understand them, Rogers says Never and the orthodox Freudians and Jungians say Usually, though for different reasons. The progressive psychoanalytic groups say usually No, but Yes when the relationship can stand it.

11 E. M. Jellinek tells a useful parable. Behind the shell, he says, there is likely to be a nut. If the shell is cracked, the nut will be injured. If, however, the shell is sloughed off carefully, a seed will be found inside which has only been awaiting its freedom in order to grow.

12 Is the "transference situation" something inherent in extended therapy, or is it something produced by a particular approach on the part of the therapist? French, in contrast to previous orthodox Freudian views, seems to suggest that it may or

may not be helpful in the original sense of repeating "the patient's reactions to a person who has, at some previous time, played an important role in the patient's life."—*Psychoanalytic Therapy*, p. 71.

Once the geneticist point of view is renounced except as instrumental, there is inevitable modification of the old transference idea as desirable or essential, regardless of other factors, and apparently some change in the frequency with which it becomes important in the counseling relationship. Rogers contends that the transference situation in this same sense is unnecessary, and entirely the product of a wrong approach on the part of the therapist.

13 For an effective summary of the Anglo-Catholic approach to counseling, confession, and spiritual direction see Henry Balmforth and Others, *An Introduction to Pastoral Theology* (Macmillan, 1937). Believing that "the traditional science and art of the pastoral care of individuals . . . [may] be profitably combined with knowledge derived from modern scientific study of human nature," they give a summary of the essential elements in moral theology, then discuss the priest's ministry to the individual with special reference to formal confession. Their concluding section on "treatment of special cases" is less helpful.

14 T. W. Pym, *Spiritual Direction* (Morehouse, 1929).

15 *Ibid.*, Chap. 4.

Chapter V: Pastoral Counseling and Other Counseling

1 See S. R. Slavson, *An Introduction to Group Therapy* (Commonwealth Fund, 1943) and Virginia Axline, *Play Therapy* (Houghton Mifflin, 1947). The former is now the standard treatise on group therapy, and the latter is a new volume applying the principles of Carl Rogers to the group therapeutic situation with children. Undoubtedly group therapy will become more important in the future, because it is based on sounder principles having to do with group life instead of being, as it has been in some earlier attempts, merely the application of individual principles to a group situation. See the very useful *So You Want to Help People*, by R. Wittenberg (Association Press, 1947).

2 The derivation of the word from the Latin *consulere* implies rendering an opinion or giving advice. The eductive approach must, therefore, fly in the face of etymology. While unfortunate, this seems better than a neologism, and its increasing acceptance promises to facilitate better understanding of similarities and differences among different groups.

3 Broadly speaking, it was not until the publication of Mary E. Richmond's *Social Diagnosis* (Russell Sage Foundation, 1917) and *What Is Social Case Work?* (Russell Sage Foundation 1922) that social case work may be said to have had a theory. The distance it has since traveled may be seen in the excellent *The Field of Social Work*, by Arthur E. Fink (Holt, 1942) and in the article, "Social Case Work," by Charlotte Towle, in the 1947 *Social Work Year Book*.

4 For a description of the early point of view see J. B. Davis, *Vocational and Moral Guidance* (Ginn, 1914) or J. M. Brewer, *The Vocational Guidance Movement* (Macmillan, 1918).
For the contemporary view see Donald E. Super, *The Dynamics of Vocational Adjustment* (Harper, 1942).
For a suggestion of the extent to which eductive principles have found their way even into the governmental employment services, see John G. Darley's *The Interview in Counseling*, Retraining and Re-employment Administration, Department of Labor, 1946.

5 I am not familiar with the literature on the industrial field, but the most useful volumes are reported to be F. J. Roethlisberger and W. J. Dickson, *Management and the Worker* (Harvard, 1939) and Elton Mayo, *The Social Problems of an In-*

dustrial Civilization (Harvard Graduate School of Business Administration, 1945) .

6 In connection with mental hospitals, see Albert Deutsch, *The Mentally Ill in America* (Doubleday, 1937) . For penal institutions see Sanford Bates, *Prisons and Beyond* (Macmillan, 1936) .

7 Despite his eminence as the leader of the American school of psychiatry Meyer has published no books, only scattered articles.

8 This came about in the 1920's largely through the influence of Freud and Rank, and was formulated with some clarity by the publication of *A Changing Psychology in Social Case Work,* by Virginia M. Robinson (University of North Carolina, 1930) .

9 See note 4.

10 See, for example, C. Anderson Aldrich and M. M. Aldrich, *Babies are Human Beings* (Macmillan, 1938) ; Milton J. E. Senn, *All About Feeding Children* (Doubleday, 1944) ; and Benjamin Spock, *Baby and Child Care* (Pocket Books, 1945) .

11 Eloquent testimony to this fact is given by the existence of the American Orthopsychiatric Association and its publication, *The American Journal of Orthopsychiatry.* The word might be roughly translated as "normative psychiatry." Psychiatrists, psychologists, and social workers are accepted into membership. A joint committee of the American Psychiatric Association and the American Psychological Association has been established. While the proprietary feelings still generally exceed the ecumenical, the latter has grown much more than I had thought possible a few years ago. The war experience and the increased consciousness of tremendous need has accentuated this trend. The 1948 International Congress on Mental Health is being planned on a multiprofessional basis.

12 The British Medical Association so declared in the 1920's. However, there is great flexibility in the use of the term—nearly all depth therapists referring to themselves as "analysts" if not as "psychoanalysts." The orthodox psychoanalytic viewpoint on therapy can be found in Lawrence Kubie's *Practical Aspects of Psychoanalysis* (Norton, 1936) , written to inform prospective patients. The distinction between psychoanalysis and other forms of psychotherapy, he says, "is not concerned primarily with matters of theory at all, but with the problems of technique."

13 Now known as the Association for the Advancement of Psychoanalysis, with headquarters in New York City.

14 This group maintains headquarters both in Washington and New York. In addition to the special training it gives for practitioners, it offers certain courses for members of other professional groups, such as general physicians and social workers. Pastors may take some of these courses if their individual background has properly prepared them. The leader of the New York section is Clara Thompson. The man after whom the William Alanson White Psychiatric Foundation was named was—along with Adolf Meyer and Thomas W. Salmon, both of whom wrote very little—probably the greatest leader to date in American psychiatry. White was originally an American-school-of-psychiatry man, later incorporating many dynamic findings into his point of view. He wrote well and prolifically—for example, *Twentieth Century Psychiatry* (Norton, 1936) .

15 See Kubie's volume, note 12.

16 Alexander and French, *Psychoanalytic Therapy.*

17 See note 43, Chap. I.

18 The publication of her *New Ways in Psychoanalysis* (Norton, 1939) was followed by severe criticism from some of her psychoanalytic colleagues.

19 For example, there is the eclectic group, the Association for the Advancement of Psychotherapy, of which Emil Guttheil is secretary.

20 A striking British novel dealing with a lay analyst is *Mine Own Executioner,* by N. Balchin (Houghton Mifflin, 1946) .

21 Some shift in medical thinking has taken place on this point, as demonstrated, for example, in the existence of the joint committee of the American Psychiatric and American Psychological Associations; the enlarged therapeutic function being given qualified psychologists in some guidance clinics; and the increasing number of referrals back and forth from psychiatrists to clinical psychologists. Naturally such activities will have to gain much more momentum before being recognized by the American Medical Association. Whether its influence will be thrown towards protection of the legitimate interest of the medical profession in the patient—as in the great work the A. M. A. has done in medical education—or merely against anyone but doctors being permitted to help the human psyche—as in the anything but great work of the A. M. A. on medical economics—remains to be seen. The recent conference and report, *Training in Clinical Psychology,* by the Josiah Macy, Jr., Foundation, is a forward step.

22 See, for example, Flanders Dunbar, *Emotions and Bodily Changes* (Columbia University, 1935).

23 Provided, of course, the clinical psychologist can demonstrate that he has had the training to do what is needed. The clinical psychologists now have a "proposed program of professional training in clinical psychology"—see *Journal of Consulting Psychology,* January, 1943.

24 The *Journal of Consulting Psychology, Journal of Clinical Psychology,* and several other psychological journals include material of this kind. Psychologists at such universities as Chicago, Pennsylvania, Southern California, Harvard, and Minnesota are giving special attention to this.

25 See Gordon W. Allport, *Personality: A Psychological Interpretation* (Holt, 1937); Henry A. Murray, *Explorations in Personality* (Oxford, 1938); Kurt Lewin, *Studies in Topological and Vector Psychology* (University of Iowa, 1944) for representative reports on personality study. For reports of psychological research on counseling see Rogers, *Counseling and Psychotherapy;* Charles A. Curran, *Personality Factors in Counseling* (Grune & Stratton, 1945); George Muench, *An Evaluation of Nondirective Psychotherapy by Means of the Rorschach and Other Tests* (Stanford University, 1947). Muench's volume has not yet appeared at this time of writing. Curran is a Roman Catholic priest and student of Rogers. There has as yet been little research study of counseling by psychologists with any variations from Rogers' point of view.

26 A series of events and statements appearing during the first half of 1947 has raised the question whether psychoanalysis and religion are compatible. Following her conversion to Roman Catholicism, Clare Booth Luce published three articles entitled "The Real Reason" in *McCall's.* While asserting that she does not wish to attack the helpfulness of psychoanalysis, the tone of her attack on it may be gathered from this sentence: "Above all, the profoundest mischief of the analyst is the notion he has spread abroad that God is a cowardly concept man invented to keep from giving himself that final pull at his bootstraps which will land him in the millenium."

During Lent, Fulton J. Sheen, preaching at St. Patrick's Cathedral, was reported in the *New York Times* and *New York Herald-Tribune* as having attacked psychoanalysis on religious and moral grounds. Apparently the text of the sermon was not released to the press. Numerous protests were made by psychoanalysts and psychiatrists, and by at least one group of Protestant clergy in New York. Subsequently a group of more than a hundred psychiatrists have signed a statement indicating that in their judgment the implications of psychiatry and psychoanalysis are not antithetical to religion.

In June, *Cosmopolitan* published two articles on psychoanalysis and religion. That by Gretta Palmer said psychiatry was all right, but psychoanalysis was against God. The other article, by Howard Whitman, stated that there is no basic contradiction of any kind, and quoted many Protestant leaders to that effect. The Palmer article relied heavily on quotations from Rudolf Allers, Roman Catholic psychiatrist. Soon after the publication of this series the magazine's publicity department sent the Palmer article, minus the author's name, to a considerable number of Protestant clergy, asking for comment. The reasons for this, for the omission of the author's name, for the noninclusion of the excellent Whitman article are still obscure at this date of writing.

Rudolf Allers has long been an attacker of psychoanalysis, most comprehensively in *The Successful Error* (Sheed & Ward, 1940). Allers not only condemns Freudian theory from beginning to end but also believes that practice and therapeutic method are so intimately bound to theory that they are equally dangerous. Karen Horney is mentioned by Allers not unfavorably, but he apparently considers her claim to being a psychoanalyst as ridiculous, since she made alterations in Freudian theory and practice. Allers is well versed in the literature of analysis and is also skillful in scholastic dialectics. Further, his claim that there tends to be a consistency between theory and practice ought to be conceded. But the essential claim that psychoanalysis is antithetical, inherently and unchangeably, to religion is preposterous. Most orthodox psychoanalysts in this country, whether publicly admitting it or not, have made alterations both in theory and practice. Some undoubtedly are active disbelievers in religion. Others—for there are bunglers in every profession—certainly have a naïve philosophy, a mechanical conception of therapeutic method, and barbaric convictions about morality. But the general conclusion that psychoanalysis in theory and practice is against religion is contradicted in a thousand ways. See, for example, the section on religion and the minister in the revised edition of Karl A. Menninger's *The Human Mind*. And Menninger has been perhaps the most influential spokesman of the more orthodox psychoanalytic groups in this country.

In July Sheen made a public statement on the matter, making substantially the points Miss Palmer had made in *Cosmopolitan*. He said he was misquoted before, that he had not criticized psychiatry but only Freudianism (*New York Herald-Tribune*, July 21, 1947). He wrote, "I did not make any criticism of psychiatry or of the psychoanalytic method in general," the latter statement being quite different from the previous report or from the Palmer article. Jung, Adler, and Allers are mentioned favorably. But anything acknowledging indebtedness to Freud is considered something else again.

The issues involved are complex. Freud was himself a pessimist about human nature, convinced that any idea of God was merely a projection and that group religion was an evidence of collective immaturity which should eventually be outgrown. And, while disclaiming philosophy, he was himself a philosopher, and in some respects an anti-Christian one. Drawing such a judgment, however, is a very different thing from asserting that psychoanalysis is antireligious. If some psychoanalysts have made a philosophy and religion as well as a therapy out of their analysis, that is unfortunate; but it is that fact which should be attacked, not psychoanalysis in general. And the implication that if it grows, develops, or changes, it cannot be Freudian psychoanalysis is patently absurd, though more understandable in representatives of a religious institution which asserts that dogma never changes than in those who distinguish between essential revelation and change in dogma. Psychologically speaking, therefore, the Roman Catholic attack on psychoanalysis is similar to the feelings of Catholicism about Protestantism. What is most disturbing is not the fact that there is a different dogma but that there can be change, even reinterpretation of dogma. It is the dynamic element in psychology of which, with some justice, alert Roman Catholics like Sheen and Allers are suspicious.

It is interesting that Charles A. Curran, a Roman Catholic priest and student of Carl Rogers, has published *Personality Factors in Counseling*. Is is assumed—correctly, I believe—that Curran, as a psychologist, can be nondirective in counseling without this having any effect in the realm of faith and morals. The democratic and antiauthoritarian implications of the nondirective approach, and of my eductive approach, cannot, it seems to me, be set aside so easily—permitting counseling to remain in a watertight compartment of its own. More than twenty years ago T. V. Moore, Roman Catholic psychiatrist, published *Dynamic Psychology* (Lippincott, 1924), which was useful and dynamic for its time. His subsequent work has, however, demonstrated little evidence of keeping up with the dynamic developments. We can only speculate on the future of nondirective counseling among Roman Catholic priests.

27 There are many factors involved in this tendency, including a religious-sounding psychological terminology; a sense of separateness from most other therapeutic workers; the interpretation of the one-sided concept of personal difficulty (see note 43, Chap. I); Jung's sympathetic understanding of the function of religion long before other therapists were prepared to try to understand it; Jung's wide study of religious and other symbolism and extensive use of his knowledge both in writing and therapy; and his engaging personality and "affirmative" theory, attracting many religiously minded persons too tender-minded to work their way through the early antireligious Freudianism. Jung seems to have intended to put forth a psychology, not a philosophy or a religion, and the most competent Jungians appear to recognize this and be explicit about it. The fact remains that for some others, including some therapists and patients, Jungianism has tended to be as totally preoccupying as Alcoholics Anonymous tends to be for recovered alcoholics.

28 See, for example, the *American Journal of Psychiatry* or any standard textbook on psychiatry, such as D. K. Henderson and R. D. Gillespie, *A Text-Book of Psychiatry* (Oxford, 1927). Or see the popular *Psychiatry for the Curious*, by George H. Preston (Farrar & Rinehart, 1940).

In March, 1947, a conference of Protestant clergy and psychiatrists—including depth therapists of several persuasions—was held at the College of Preachers, Washington, D. C., under the auspices of the Federal Council's Commission on Religion and Health, the National Committee for Mental Hygiene, the Council for Clinical Training, and the Institute of Pastoral Care. The findings, clarifying the focus of function of psychiatrists and clergy in relation to each other, are expected to be available in some published form.

29 See note 4, Chap. V. There is a National Vocational Guidance Association, which in its meetings has increasingly emphasized the vocational counselor's concern for personality as a whole.

30 Among the most widely used books on guidance and counseling in an educational framework and setting are the following:

Helping Teachers Understand Children (American Council on Education, 1945) — for background

New Directions for Measurement and Guidance: A Symposium (American Council on Education, 1944)

J. G. Darley, *Testing and Counseling in the High-School Guidance Program* (Science Research Associates, 1943)

Lois B. Murphy, *Emotional Factors in Learning* (Columbia University, 1944) —for background

New York State Counselors' Association, *Practical Handbook for Counselors* (Science Research Associates, 1945)

Daniel A. Prescott, *Emotion and the Educative Process* (American Council on Education, 1938) —for background

A. Y. Reed, *Guidance and Personnel Services in Education* (Cornell University, 1944)

Caroline B. Zachry, *Emotion and Conduct in Adolescence* (Appleton-Century, 1940) —for background

A variety of viewpoints is represented in these volumes. Special reference should be made to the excellent *Religious Counseling of College Students,* by Thornton W. Merriam (American Council on Education, Series 6, Student Personnel Work, No. 4, 1943).

31 See Chap. VIII for suggestions.

32 See notes 13 and 40, Chap. I, and notes 10 and 22, Chap. V. Increasingly the medical journals, even the *Journal of the American Medical Association,* give evidence of some understanding of psychosomatics. The development has probably been greatest in connection with pediatrics, and it is in on the ground floor in the development of geriatrics, but it is increasingly recognized in internal medicine, gynecology, dermatology, and other specialties, including surgery. However, the recognition of psychological aspects in the etiology of disorder and the development of relevant therapeutic methods for approaching those aspects are not necessarily the same thing. The traditional mode of approach on the part of the medical profession has been, "We stand aside, study you, make a differential diagnosis, and then treat you." Psychological treatment is like neither pills nor surgery. Hence, while the increasing psychosomatic sensitivity in the field of causation is fundamental, it will have to be followed also by attention to the approach in psychological therapy if it is effectively to help patients and not remain merely in the doctor's head. There is no effective equivalent of a scalpel or hypodermic needle; one has to begin from a different set of assumptions.

33 See note 5, Chap. V. See also N. Cantor, *Employee Counseling* (McGraw-Hill, 1945).

34 For example, see Evelyn M. Duvall and Reuben W. Hill, *When You Marry* (Association Press, 1945); Ernest R. Groves, *Marriage* (Holt, 1933) and *Christianity and the Family* (Macmillan, 1942); A. S. Nash, *Education for Christian Marriage* (S. C. M., 1939); R. G. Foster, *Marriage and Family Relationships* (Macmillan, 1944); and Sidney E. Goldstein, *Marriage and Family Counseling* (McGraw-Hill, 1945). Some other notable names in the field are Hanna and Abraham Stone, Paul Popenoe, Noel Keys, Emily Mudd, L. Foster Wood, Edgar H. Schmiedler. There is an American Association of Marriage Counselors, containing persons from more than one professional group. Robert W. Laidlaw, M. D., is secretary.

35 See note 3, Chap. V.

36 See the monthly publication *Counseling,* issued by the Committee on Counseling of the Y. M. C. A.'s National Council. See also Tirzah W. Anderson's pamphlet, *Counseling in the Y.W.C.A.* (The Woman's Press, 1946).

37 The lawyers with whom I have talked about this have all said, "We try to help people all right, but I don't know anything that's been written about it." I have so far found nothing but anecdotal material. A brief description of the important work of the aid societies may be found in J. S. Bradway's *Work of Legal Aid Committees of Bar Associations* (American Bar Association, 1938).

38 See note 3, Chap. V.

39 See our pamphlet *Community Help on Pastoral Problems* (Federal Council, 1948). See also my chapter on "Pastoral Work and Community Resources" in *Religion and Health* (Macmillan, 1943).

40 See *Directory of Psychiatric Clinics in the United States,* National Committee for Mental Hygiene, 1790 Broadway, New York 19. The most recent year available is 1946. A free bibliography of the available literature can also be secured from the National Committee. A number of the excellent book publications of The Commonwealth Fund deal with guidance clinics.

41 Examples of these are the Association for Family Living, Chicago; the Marriage Counseling Center, Philadelphia; Paul Popenoe's center in Los Angeles, and the centers Ernest R. Groves has initiated in North Carolina. Many family service societies also give similar service.

42 See, for example, the Federal Prison Service Study Courses, of which a new series on selected subjects is issued each year. These serve as the basis for continuing in-service training of all employees.

43 In the armed forces psychologists were at first assigned inferior and highly restricted roles, while social workers were not at first used as social workers at all. Later there were very considerable alterations in this. In addition, a group of lay assistants were trained and used by some psychiatrists, some of these persons becoming skilled counselors. The present outline of duties of psychologists in the services is vastly broader and more attractive than was true at the beginning of the war. Since there was a great shortage of psychiatrists in the armed services, many physicians received brief psychiatric training; and while this seldom included much that could be called training in psychotherapy itself, the net effect has been to sensitize a large number of young American physicians to the psychological forces involved in illness. This is an important step ahead.

44 The most obvious way in which a pastor works on a team is in institutional chaplaincy service. For information on various aspects of such chaplaincy see the following publications of the Federal Council: *Religious Work in Protestant Hospitals* (with the American Protestant Hospital Association) ; *Protestant Religious Work in Mental Hospitals; The Future of Chaplaincy Service; Improving Protestant Worship in Mental Hospitals; The Functions of the Prison Chaplain* (joint statement with the National Conference of Catholic Charities).

The Art of Ministering to the Sick, by Richard C. Cabot and Russell L. Dicks (Macmillan, 1936), discusses the pastor's place in the hospital team. *Religion and Health in the Local Community* (Federal Council, 1942) discusses doctor-clergy relationships. A study by Harold P. Schultz, *Clergy-Physician Relationships in Protestant Hospitals* (American Protestant Hospital Association, 1942), is of interest.

45 See note 6, Chap. I, especially the article by Otis R. Rice on pastoral counseling. See also *Alcoholics Anonymous* (Works Publishing Co., 1939) and the *Quarterly Journal of Studies on Alcohol* (Yale University).

46 Information may be secured from the National Committee for Education on Alcoholism, 2 East 103 Street, New York 29, N. Y.

47 An excellent development of the past few years has been the employment by city councils of churches of persons—usually ministers with social-work training—to act as liaison agents between the social and welfare agencies of the community and the churches, and to do educational work both ways. The following cities now have such service: Washington, Chicago, Hartford, Detroit, Cleveland, Buffalo, Los Angeles, Pittsburgh, Baltimore.

48 For the phrase "focus of function" I am indebted to George S. Stevenson, in oral communication.

49 The best discussion of the Protestant view of Christian vocation is still to be found in Robert L. Calhoun's *God and the Common Life* (Scribner, 1935).

Chapter VI: PASTORAL WORK AS PREPARATION

1 To the best of my knowledge, formulation of the systematic comparison of pre-counseling pastoral work with counseling in this chapter is original. Counseling and pastoral work have frequently been considered together, and I have profited from many such discussions, especially in books cited previously by Russell L. Dicks, Charles T. Holman, John Sutherland Bonnell, Leslie Weatherhead, and others. E. S. Waterhouse's *Psychology and Pastoral Work* (Abingdon Press, 1940) is helpful in a broad way. So is *Our Personal Ministry,* by T. W. Pym (S. C. M., 1935). But I found myself unable from suggestions in these or other publications to find a satisfactory theoretical and practical accommodation of pastoral work and pastoral counseling until doing this chapter.

2 The first sentence in 1, 2, etc., repeats the tentative conclusions on approach and method enunciated in the latter half of Chap. II. The sentences which follow consider the relevance of these counseling principles to the precounseling pastoral-work situation.

3 The report of research is taken from Erich Lindemann, "Symptomatology and Management of Acute Grief," *American Journal of Psychiatry*, Vol. 101, 1944, supplemented by notes on two addresses given by Lindemann, one before the Federal Council's Commission on Religion and Health in 1946 and the other before the clergy-psychiatrist conference in Washington, March, 1947. One of Lindemann's associates, Ina M. Greer, gave a brief popular report of the findings, "Grief Must Be Faced," in *The Christian Century*, February 28, 1945.

The Federal Council's Department of Pastoral Services expects to publish a pamphlet to be prepared by Erich Lindemann and Rollin J. Fairbanks, Protestant Chaplain at the Massachusetts General Hospital and Director of the Institute of Pastoral Care, reporting on the grief research and suggesting its implications for the pastor.

4 While pointing out that some requests for information are attempts to have the counselor make decisions for him, that others are never satisfied with any amount of given information, and that in still others the request for information is a manifestation of anxiety, Carl Rogers nevertheless writes, "It is true that some clients need only certain very specific information."—*Counseling with Returned Servicemen* (McGraw-Hill, 1946), p. 103. This latter point is true, and the qualifications are important; but it seems greatly to clarify the information-giving function of the pastor to see it as falling within the realm of precounseling pastoral work. Then, as in any other pastoral work, the pastor is alert to what may be behind the request, if it is anything more than the simple desire for information, and leave the way open to counseling if something of that nature does exist.

5 If the essential point made here is valid, it would seem there are many implications, to say nothing of corrections, which it would be profitable for theologians to work out as one of the practical aspects of their task of communicating theological truth.

6 This is discussed further in the following chapter.

Chapter VII: THE PASTOR'S TOTAL WORK AS PREPARATION

1 For assistance in clarifying this concept I am indebted to the Cabinet of the Federated Theological Faculty of the University of Chicago, and especially to W. Barnett Blakemore—though the views expressed here are, of course, my own.

It seems to me that the problem the seminaries have faced in the practical field is very difficult. On the one hand they have been bombarded with suggestions to have courses in counseling, radio, public relations, religious drama, race relations, world peace, mental hygiene, alcohol, and a hundred other specific things which are important in the pastor's work—with most of the proponents assuming that the way to teach a student about race relations, for example, is to have a new course on race relations. On the other hand, the theological educators have known that even if budgets were not limited as they are, there is a point of diminishing returns so far as adding courses is concerned. Most of them have, understandably enough, straddled the issue—adding some new courses, revamping some old ones, maintaining the conviction that somehow or other they fit together within the student if not within themselves. It seems to me that consistent acceptance of the central suggestion of this chapter would provide a base upon which the seminaries could, realistically and with educational soundness, proceed toward the creation of integrated teaching in practical theology.

2 I know that some teachers of preaching make use of methods like this in their teaching. But if any of the books on preaching discuss it in this fashion, they have

escaped my notice. Nearly all books on preaching are assumed, without mention of any other possibility, to concern themselves with the content of the message or with details of sermon preparation, both important, of course. Where preaching as a medium of communication to people, therefore a study in relationship, is considered at all, it appears to have been done only by way of general suggestions. I believe it possible to develop, on the basis of the kind of material given illustratively here, a theory of relationship in preaching which would stand midway between consideration of content and consideration of detailed methodology.

Examination of such works on preaching as the following confirms this point: P. B. Bull, *Preaching and Sermon Construction* (Macmillan, 1922); Charles R. Brown, *The Art of Preaching* (Macmillan, 1922); George A. Buttrick, *Jesus Came Preaching* (Scribner, 1931); Albert E. Day, *Jesus and Human Personality* (Abingdon, 1934); and Carl S. Patton, *The Preparation and Delivery of Sermons* (Willett and Clark, 1938). Ezra Rhoades' *Case Work in Preaching* (Revell, 1942) is merely anecdotal. John N. Booth, in *The Quest for Preaching Power* (Macmillan, 1943), has a chapter on "the psychology of influential preaching," but it is brief, anecdotal, and not far-reaching. E. S. Waterhouse's *Psychology of Pastoral Work* (Abingdon Press, 1940) comes as close as anything. H. C. Miller's *The New Psychology and the Preacher* (Boni, 1924) is old. Karl R. Stolz's chapter, "The Therapeutic Function of Preaching," in *The Church and Psychotherapy* (Abingdon Press, 1943) —the book is inaccurately named—is disappointing in its generality.

In oral communication.

Probably the majority of seminary teachers in the practical field have been recruited from the parish ministry. The theory has been: This man has demonstrated an aptitude in doing this of a high order; therefore he can teach it with equal skill. Sometimes it has worked out this way. But some such men, who have in reality done an excellent job in the local church with worship, administration, counseling or something else, have not succeeded in being nearly so effective in their seminary teaching. This seems to me to be a result of our multiple-role concept of the pastor's task, our failure to realize that there is a fundamental theory involved in practical theology just as there is in theology itself, though its content is of a different order. Lacking such a theory, some of the pastors converted into teachers have resorted to teaching by anecdotal reminiscence, supplemented by comparison with the writings of other anecdotalists, without looking at the basic nature and purpose and approach to the educational task now undertaken. It is not enough to develop a philosophy, or even a philosophy of education. What is needed is a constant interplay between the concrete material of the task at hand and the fundamental, operational theory of practical theology. Of course, a movement to the other extreme, concentration on theory at the expense of operation and approach and methods, would take the teacher out of the practical field, whether admittedly or not, and make him a competitor or colleague of the theologians. Recognition of this point in itself should go some distance in improving practical field teaching, whether my formulation of its purposes and integration is accepted or not.

Confirmation of the above point has come to me in observing what happens to successful parish ministers upon assuming general administrative positions in denominations, councils of churches, and other ecclesiastical organizations. Many, of course, do an excellent job. But clear proof that an excellent job has been done in some aspect of the parish ministry is not a certain indicator that it can be repeated at another level of administration. The reason again seems to lie in whether there is sufficient clarity in fundamental thinking about the essentials of the job in the parish, as distinguished from successful manipulation of details, to enable the man to translate these over into the new framework and structure in which they are now to be applied. For details cannot be so translated. Operational theory, if sound, can be translated, and becomes fundamental then in the building of new details of method. Transliterative attempts indicate lack of sureness or clarity in operational theory, and are therefore as likely to be unsuccessful as they are to be successful.

5 See the interview with the father of the sixteen-year-old girl in Chap. I.

6 While administration cannot succeed if it is unsuccessful in organizing or inept in dealing with structures, it is more likely to succeed or fail on the basis of personal relationships than on either of the first two points. This is by no means the same as saying the good fellow is the successful administrator, for the good fellow may say Yes and No at the wrong times, and with the wrong motives in the sense that he does not define the situation and the relationships in terms of a consistent operational theory of what he is trying to accomplish. Of course this is not, on the other hand, a defense of the "bad fellow." Church administration as a field of study has generally confined itself so closely to technical details of method, or tactics of arousing enthusiasm, securing participation, and the like—all important of course—that it has not developed an integrated approach or operational theory. Attempts in that direction, whether modifying my eductive approach or not, would seem to be worth in the long run more than mere additional anecdotal material about successful programs in particular situations. I call most such material "anecdotal" because it generally omits reference to specifics of personality and relationship, an understanding of which is vital to objective analysis of the factors operating in the administrative situation. We could well use concrete material which included such factors.

Among the general books on church administration, a recent volume deserves special mention: O. L. Shelton's *The Modern Church Functioning Effectively* (Bethany, 1947). Other general books are C. E. Lemmon, *The Art of Church Management* (Bethany, 1933); Don Frank Fenn, *Parish Administration* (Morehouse, 1938); and William L. Leach, *Church Administration* (Doran, 1926).

7 As yet there have been no reports from the Rogers group concerning the use of the "client-centered" approach in administrative counseling, potentially a fruitful field. Such research might help to clarify the difference between the basic approach and the methods seen in conversation, and would thereby aid in defining the essentials of Rogers' approach in counseling itself.

8 *How to Make an Evangelistic Call*, an aid to workers in home visitation evangelism (Department of Evangelism, Federal Council, 1946).

9 See the prominence of this realistic note in the Federal Council's statement on evangelism, March, 1946, and in the British document *Towards the Conversion of England*, Church of England, 1945.

10 It seems to me that the professional religious educators were the first to sense the potential significance of what I am now calling the eductive approach. But some years ago they tended to do with it two things which violated its basic nature, and were therefore unsuccessful.

First, in seeing that religious education could not satisfactorily be placed in a watertight compartment of methods as against content, but that if what they had was true, it had relevance to the whole program of the church, they proceeded to suggest that religious education was the pivot and all other aspects of church work should center around it. This was confusion of imperialistic application of a basic insight—the eductive approach—with attempted adaptation of the eductive approach to different situations, necessarily modifying methods, and reworking them.

Second, when their unintended but undoubted imperialism was challenged, they retreated from an exploration of operational theory (basic approach) in their own everyday field of work in favor of development of a general philosophy of religious education which tended to set up an operational*ism*. This was, naturally enough, rejected by others. Neither of these consequences had been intended; yet they had resulted from the failure to distinguish between the fundamental insight and the fact that it could only be translated, not transliterated, into terms of the other functions of the practical field. Hence it was a failure to distinguish a basic operational insight or approach from methodological details of application and from basic theory in the theological field.

I hope that pastoral counseling has profited from study of this experience of religious education. My book is not an attempt to apply pastoral counseling to preaching, administration, etc. But in addition to discussing counseling itself, through which I have become convinced about the eductive approach, it suggests that the same approach (operational theory) could be induced from the other practical functions of the ministry and would be probably of equal relevance.

Tensions between religious educators on the one hand and general church administrators or pastors on the other hand continue to exist. The first group tends to say, "We are not specialists in the same sense as is a man concerned with race relations or worship. We and our activities parallel the whole gamut of church activity. Therefore we belong in all such activities as a parallel group at every point."

The church administrators tend to say, "Of course you're different. Every specialist group is different. Your work in action does touch everything. But your specialty is a kind of program. Act like such a specialist, and you'll help everyone."

It seems to me that both are partly right and partly wrong. Religious education is one of several major practical functions of the church, each of which is related to all the others—the whole being an integrated unity, not a hodgepodge. The center of that unity is not religious education or pastoral counseling, but the Christian fellowship. If religious education merely insists that it is different, it becomes an obstacle to the very integration which its insights should make it want to seek. On the other hand, in sensing that the whole program of the church will be injured if its elements are considered only as specialties, more or less unrelated to one another in any inherent way, religious education refuses to accept a fragmented and multiple-role concept of the church's work, and here it is right. An understanding of this issue might help in making the current tension count for general improvement all around.

11 See R. H. Edwards, *A Person-Minded Ministry* (Abingdon Press, 1940) .

12 See *Religion and Health* Chap. VI. See also my article "Why Do They Behave That Way?" *International Journal of Religious Education,* September, 1945.

13 If I understand Harrison S. Elliott in *Can Religious Education Be Christian?* (Macmillan, 1940) , I would be in accord with him on the importance of this point. But inferences from this point are not of necessity a sufficient point of departure, or even the central point in terms of content, in relation to approaching theological truth. Elliott's position on this point is not clear.

On the other hand, in his attempt to make religious education Christian by beginning with theological content, H. Shelton Smith, in *Faith and Nurture* (Scribner, 1941) , seems to have minimized the operational importance of the eductive approach.

14 See the interesting attempt to apply the principles gained from "client-centered" counseling to the more or less formal educational situation, in N. Cantor's *The Dynamics of Learning* (Foster and Stewart, 1946) .

15 See F. Ernest Johnson's *The Social Gospel Re-Examined* (Harper, 1940) for a discriminating discussion both of the present and of the recent past.

16 There has been a marked change, during and since the war, in the attitude of the European churches and churchmen on this point. This is demonstrated to us perhaps most graphically in such men as Hendrik Kraemer, of the Netherlands, whose operational conception of the role of the church in society now seems very different from what was set forth in his *The Christian Message in a Non-Christian World* (Harper, 1938) .

17 Because of the diversification and complexity of this field, the tendency is for discussions on operations to center around but one issue and for the more general

volumes to be basic philosophies without much reference to operations. This is the question of middle axioms, lying between gospel and action. The nature of what seems to be needed—while in no way denying the value of what we now have —appears overwhelming; and yet it is so important that someone should make a try at it.

Chapter VIII: PRECOUNSELING METHODS OF COUNSELORS

1 This is not a discussion of the quack healers and counselors. See, for that, Harold Seashore, *All of Us Have Troubles* (Association Press, 1947) and Lee Steiner, *Where Do People Take Their Troubles?* (Houghton Mifflin, 1945).

2 Comparatively few volumes are written specifically to tell prospective patients, clients, or parishioners what may be expected in counseling or psychotherapy. Most of the books addressed to the public by counselors or therapists make some reference to this. The authors count on having the help given by reading the book itself serve as a stimulus to getting counseling if needed. A recent book by Karen Horney does attempt explicitly to define psychoanalysis for prospective patients—*Are You Considering Psychoanalysis?* (Norton, 1946). Lawrence Kubie's *Practical Aspects of Psychoanalysis* (Norton, 1936) also attempted to do this. But there are many pamphlets, folders, and local pieces of all kinds; and I have had many of these in mind in writing this chapter.

Clearly the greatest amount of "public relations" is indirect, a by-product. The motion picture *Going My Way,* for example, would tend to produce the conclusion: "Roman Catholic priests are human and can understand; therefore they are able to help people." In contrast, *One Foot in Heaven* would tend to result in: "Protestant ministers are so human that they tend to be preoccupied with their own troubles; therefore there is doubt whether they could understand others."

See note 13, Chap. III, for books intended for popular consumption and which have by-product value in the public relations of counseling. The very titles of many books give an impression along this line, whether so intended or not, as for example: *Faith is the Answer,* by Smiley Blanton and Norman Vincent Peale (Abingdon Press, 1940); *The Self You Have to Live With,* by Winfred Rhoades (Lippincott, 1938); *Be Glad You're Neurotic,* by Louis E. Bisch (McGraw, 1946).

3 Harry Bone, in oral communication.

4 The monthly *Hygeia.*

5 Those who, in their writing, have come closest to counseling or the fields of knowledge underlying it include George W. Gray, Edith M. Stern, and Howard Whitman. Other well-known general science writers include such persons as William L. Laurence, Waldemar Kaempfaert, Paul De Kruif, and the editors of *Science News Letter.*

Chapter IX: RELIGIOUS RESOURCES

1 From Russell L. Dicks, *Who Is My Patient: A Religious Manual for Nurses.* Copyright 1941 by The Macmillan Co.; used with their permission.

2 *God and Health,* pamphlet (Federal Council, 1947).

3 *Ibid.*

4 Everett B. Lesher, *Strength in Our Sickness,* pamphlet (Federal Council, 1947).

5 See Dicks, *The Art of Ministering to the Sick,* with Richard Cabot (Macmillan, 1936); *Pastoral Work and Personal Counseling* (Macmillan, 1944); and *Thy Health Shall Spring Forth* (Macmillan, 1945). The last is an excellent collection of prayers for use with persons in stress situations. *Comfort Ye My People* (Macmillan, 1947) is a collection of prayers for use in various pastoral work situations. Another valuable source book of such prayers is *On Wings of Healing,* by John W. Doberstein (Muhlenberg, 1942).

6 Some mention is made of prayer in nearly all the books dealing with pastoral counseling, pastoral work, or pastoral theology, although none with which I am familiar takes it up from the point of view expressed in this section. A few of the fundamental books dealing with the basic meaning of prayer in general are: George A. Buttrick, *Prayer* (Abingdon Press, 1942); Friedrich Heiler, *Prayer* (Oxford, 1932); B. H. Streeter, *Concerning Prayer* (Macmillan, 1934); Evelyn Underhill, *Mysticism,* revised ed. (Dutton, 1930); Friedrich von Hügel, *Life of Prayer* (Dutton, 1929) and Georgia Harkness, *Prayer and the Common Life* (Abingdon Press, 1947).

Although there are many excellent collections of prayers, such as John Baillie's *Diary of Private Prayer* (Scribner, 1936); Walter Russell Bowie's *Lift Up Your Hearts* (Macmillan, 1939); and Harry Emerson Fosdick's *The Meaning of Prayer* (Association Press, 1915), none of the ones I know, except those by Dicks and Doberstein, have been prepared from the focus of pastoral use with individuals in stress situations.

7 See John Sutherland Bonnell, *Pastoral Psychiatry* (Harper, 1939).

8 The usual mode of treatment of the Bible in pastoral work is illustrated in the six pages devoted to this by Andrew W. Blackwood in *Pastoral Work* (Westminster, 1945). His discussion is general and anecdotal. Previously cited books by Dicks, Bonnell, and others are more specific, but their discussion is also very brief. If there are extended discussions of this, I have been unable to find them.

9 Ralph D. Bonacker's cards are published by the Cloister Press, Louisville, Ky. Otis R. Rice's cards have not yet been published.

10 Those available now: *A Road to Recovery,* by Robert Rasche; *God and Health,* by Russell L. Dicks; and *Strength in Our Sickness,* by Everett B. Lesher (all 1947).

11 Russell L. Dicks and Seward Hiltner, "The Pastor's Loan Shelf," *The Pastor,* July, 1946. Reprint available from Federal Council.

12 Edith M. Stern, *Mental Illness: A Guide for the Family* (Commonwealth Fund, 1942).

13 *Alcoholics Anonymous* (Works Publishing Co., 1939).

14 *The Link* is published monthly by the General Commission on Chaplains, Woodward Bldg., Washington, D. C.

15 A few of the titles of the personal-problems pamphlets were: *Shall I Marry Now?* (war marriage); *How Much Do You Know about Alcohol?* (alcohol); *Tired?* (fatigue); *Be It Ever So Jumbled* (maintaining family relationships); *What About Girls?* (prostitution); *At Ease* (mental health); *Time on Your Hands* (hobby occupations).

16 *The Upper Room* is the Methodist devotional quarterly. The Presbyterians have *Today;* the Northern Baptists, *The Secret Place;* the Episcopalians, *Forward.*

17 It would seem that several different kinds of pamphlets on how to pray, adapted to different types of need, would be useful. George A. Buttrick's *A Way of Prayer* (Federal Council) is effective for some.

18 For example, see the pamphlet *The Protestant Heritage,* by Samuel McCrea Cavert (Association Press, 1947). Sheila could probably also profit from *A Primer for Protestants* (Association Press, 1947). Had Sheila been a Protestant considering marriage with a Roman Catholic, she could have profited from *If I Marry a Roman Catholic* (Federal Council, 1945).

19 See Herbert Yahraes, *Epilepsy: The Ghost is Out of the Closet,* Public Affairs Pamphlet No. 98, 1945.

20 See B. C. Gruenberg, *How Shall We Teach About Sex?* Public Affairs Pamphlet No. 122, 1946.

21 For other suggestions see note 11.

22 I have been unable to find references to discussions of the explicit use of Christian doctrine in pastoral work or counseling in terms of operational approach. Materials abound on the content of doctrine, but that is not the subject matter of this section.

23 See Reuel L. Howe's challenging article, "Personal and Social Implications of Baptism," *Anglican Theological Review*, October, 1945. See also "Anointing for Healing" by Warren D. Bowman (Church of the Brethren, Elgin, 1942), for a study of anointing in a church which practices it.

24 In addition to the background volumes mentioned in note 34, Chap. V, the following are useful as aids to the pastor in premarital counseling: L. Foster Wood, *Pre-Marital Counseling* (Federal Council, 1945); Roy A. Burkhart, *A Guide for a Man and Woman Looking Toward Marriage* (Hearthside Press, 1943). *The Bond of Honor*, by Howard Chandler Robbins and B. S. Easton (Macmillan, 1938), contains an excellent discussion of the meaning of the ceremony.

Chapter X: RESOURCES FOR LEARNING PASTORAL COUNSELING

1 The development of this process in my thinking has a history somewhat as follows. A college course in abnormal psychology included weekly visits to a mental hospital, with case demonstrations by the hospital staff. Although I considered this procedure then, and now, as unfair to patients, it opened my eyes to the possibility of learning through clinical observation. Following my first year in theological school I took a summer of clinical pastoral training in a mental hospital, dealing with patients and writing life histories after the fashion described in Chap. III. The importance and fundamental character of psychological dynamics was impressed upon me. Additional periods of clinical pastoral training extended my knowledge of the dynamics and led me in the direction of exploring approach and method in pastoral helping. When Russell L. Dicks began to use interview material in teaching, I was skeptical, not seeing how it could possibly include the references to dynamics which I was convinced were so important. My first teaching of clinical pastoral training was in the mental hospital, as assistant to Carroll A. Wise. There we had students write daily notes, but our emphasis was on writing systematic life histories, and we did not use actual interview reports. Donald C. Beatty and Anton T. Boisen had been my own teachers in clinical pastoral training, and the outline of the life history we used had been prepared by Boisen. I recall adding a section to the outline, dealing with history of the relationship between the student and the patient.

When I first taught or supervised clinical pastoral training in a general hospital, I made a little use of interview material. I still did not see the potential significance of it in contrast to indirect discourse reports. But with the students I insisted on a sharp distinction between factual reporting of what was definitely known about the patient or what occurred between the student and patient and what the student thought or concluded about it. This point had been made clear to me, especially by Beatty, Boisen, and Wise.

I left executive association with the clinical pastoral-training movement in 1938; and for around four years my ideas on the process of learning counseling remained about as they were, with one exception. The many conferences with ministers' groups on counseling and related subjects, and the number of the requests for help and suggestions on counseling, made me wonder whether the general answer I had previously given was as realistic as I had supposed. I had said, in effect, if a pastor or student asks *how* to counsel, that question cannot be answered at all until he knows more about what goes on inside the people he is trying to help. That meant his initial question must be parried and the discussion must center around understanding psychological dynamics before methods could be considered. But I began to wonder if this was really correct. Suppose that the student's motivation was lost before we ever got to the *how* question. Suppose, on the other hand, a way could be found to say: Here is the basic approach to *how*, and this illustrates *why*. But this clearly leads us next to what is behind the *how*, in the people we try to help and then in our relationship with them. Let's take up things in that order.

When the war came, and the Commission on Religion and Health joined first with the General Commission on Army and Navy Chaplains in conducting seminars on counseling for Army and Navy chaplains, and then with the Army and Navy Department of the Y.M.C.A. in conducting such seminars for chaplains, U.S.O. professional personnel, and pastors in communities adjacent to camps, I was compelled to think of ways to do the best possible job in a short time. My experience with the pastors who actually led these seminars—including Russell L. Dicks, Charles T. Holman, Donald C. Beatty, John Sutherland Bonnell, David D. Eitzen, and Rollin J. Fairbanks—led me further along the line of trying to find a quicker way of getting at the point than the use of life-history material, and a more concrete way than use of indirect-discourse interview material. It was not until 1943 that I came across Carl Rogers' *Counseling and Psychotherapy* and found it valuable. But Rogers, while making a significant case for teaching counseling through verbatim interview material, did not clarify my central question of how to relate the most concrete material to basic dynamics. From Rollin J. Fairbanks I picked up the teaching method of dramatic spontaneous interviews in 1943, and found this the most effective thing to date when speed was required— as in a week's conference or class or seminar.

Teaching a class on counseling at Union Theological Seminary in 1945, with Harry Bone, forced upon me the pedagogical-method question in a form which was midway between the requirements for short conferences and for clinical pastoral-training courses. I knew Russell L. Dicks had used students' reports of interviews in church contacts as well as hospital contacts, and I had begun to see that it might be possible to link these inductively with dynamics. I proposed this method of teaching to Harry Bone, and we decided to try it. The experiment was more successful than we had thought possible; and the learning by the students of approach and method, of dynamics, and of the relationship of one to the other went further than we had hoped in the brief time available. I repeated the teaching method at the Yale Divinity School in the same year and in 1947, and again at Union, with Bone, in 1946. The results in my thinking at this moment of writing may be found in the book as a whole as well as in this chapter.

2 Rollin J. Fairbanks is Director of the Institute of Pastoral Care. Massachusetts General Hospital, Boston, is the Institute's headquarters. He developed this method about 1942.

3 Naturally enough, Carl Rogers, working chiefly in a university setting, has given less attention to the differences in naturalness in the use of recordings than to studying them in his type of situation. Others, like pastors, who wish to use them, however, must consider whatever factors are essential in making their use natural in a particular setting, i.e., preventing the recording itself from putting the parishioner on the defensive.

4 J. Lennart Cedarleaf is experimenting with the use of a recording machine in connection with the study of religious ministry to older people, now being carried on by the Federal Council's Department of Pastoral Services. Roy W. Fairchild, John T. Shaffer, Kenneth R. Strom, and Jerry Zimmerman, theological students at the University of Chicago, have had courses on counseling and guided experience at the University Counseling Center and have had recordings made of some of their counseling contacts. A series of unpublished mimeographed reports by these men on the meaning of nondirective counseling for the pastor do not, unfortunately, present any material taken down on recording machines.

Shaffer presents some interview material, but it is taken from memory only and suffers from preoccupation with methodological details at the expense of dynamic understanding of the relationship. Fairchild's article, "The Reconstruction of the Minister's Attitudes in the Light of Client-Centered Therapy," is penetrating, but suffers from the absence of illustrative interview material and from clinging to the multiple-role concept of the pastor's task, despite his reaching toward a more integrated concept. Fairchild appears to be closer to my eductive approach than to Rogers' stated views on nondirective counseling.

5 See my *Clinical Pastoral Training* (Federal Council, 1945); "Clinical Pastoral Training Opportunities in 1948," *The Pastor,* March, 1948; *Religion and Health* (Macmillan, 1943); "What Clinical Training Does for Clergymen," *Information Service,* May 21, 1938; and various reports written during my term as executive secretary of the Council for Clinical Training from 1935 to 1938.

During the summers of 1932 and 1933, I was a student in clinical pastoral training; in 1934, an assistant supervisor; in 1934-35, assistant field secretary for the Council for Clinical Training while still a graduate student; and from 1935 to 1938, executive secretary.

6 While somewhat differing definitions of clinical pastoral training may be found, representing various views about what is most essential, a comparison of my definition with those expressed in the symposium *Clinical Pastoral Training* (Federal Council, 1945) will suggest that the similarities are greater than the differences.

Three doctoral dissertations with which I am familiar have dealt with clinical pastoral training. None of these has yet been published. That of John E. Bell, done at Teachers College of Columbia University, analyzed the work at one training center. That by Eugene L. Smith, at New York University, was based on a questionnaire study of pastors who had had clinical training, and attempted to see how the training had helped them in their counseling. The most recent, by Maria Brick, done at Teachers College of Columbia University, attempted to discover through intensive interviews the basic approach of pastors toward their task in church and community, with special reference to what contributions clinical pastoral training had made in formulating this approach. Dr. Brick's study is done with extraordinary skill, and was greatly aided by her previous training as a psychotherapist.

In 1936, the American Association of Theological Schools heard and approved an extensive report on clinical training made by a committee it had appointed. Brief reports were heard at subsequent biennial meetings and regional sessions; the Association has also expressed its interest in token grants to facilitate the training. In 1944, at the recommendation of the Pittsburgh National Conference on Clinical Pastoral Training—see the report *Clinical Pastoral Training* (Federal Council, 1945) —the Association adopted the statement of minimum standards then recommended by the clinical-training experts themselves.

7 See the article by Frank W. Herriott on clinical pastoral training and field work in *Clinical Pastoral Training.*

8 See Seward Hiltner, "The Psychological Understanding of Religion," *Crozer Quarterly,* January, 1947.

9 See the comprehensive volume *Sociology of Religion,* by Joachim Wach (University of Chicago, 1944). See also Anton T. Boisen's forthcoming book, *Religion in Crisis and Custom.* It attempts to link the sociological study of religion with the psychological study of religion.

10 For a brief review of the seminary situation see my article "Pastoral Theology in the Schools," in *Clinical Pastoral Training.*

11 For a sketch of currently available opportunities see my "Memorandum on Advanced Training and Career Service in Pastoral Counseling and Related Fields," *Bulletin of the Institute of Pastoral Care,* Autumn, 1947.

12 *Ibid.*

13 *The Pastor* is published monthly at 810 Broadway, Nashville, Tenn. The *Journal of Pastoral Care* is published by the Institute of Pastoral Care, Massachusetts General Hospital, Boston 14, Mass. The *Journal of Clinical Pastoral Work* is published by the Council for Clinical Training, 2 East 103 Street, New York 29, N. Y.

Index